THE ONE AND ONLY

KIRSTY MacCOLL

THE BIOGRAPHY

THE ONE AND ONLY
KIRSTY
MacCOLL
THE BIOGRAPHY

BY KAREN O'BRIEN
FOREWORD BY
BILLY BRAGG

ANDRE
DEUTSCH

This is an André Deutsch book

First published in Great Britain in 2004

This edition published in 2013 by André Deutsch
an imprint of the Carlton Publishing Group
20 Mortimer Street
London W1T 3JW

ISBN 978-0-233-00393-1

Grateful acknowledgement is made to the following for
permission to reprint extracts from copyright material:

Excerpt from "The Mower" by Philip Larkin (from *Collected Poems* ed. Anthony
Thwaite, Faber and Faber Ltd, 1990; Farrar, Straus and Giroux, 1993) used by
kind permission of Faber and Faber Ltd and Farrar, Straus and Giroux.
Kirsty MacColl lyrics used by kind permission of EMI
Ewan MacColl lyrics used by kind permission of Peggy Seeger
Billy Bragg lyrics used by kind permission of Billy Bragg

The publishers would like to thank the following sources for their
kind permission to reproduce the pictures in this book:

Pages 1, 2 & 4: Courtesy of Jean MacColl
Page 3: top: Kerstin Rodgers / Redferns; bottom left & right: Terry Hurley
Page 5: top & middle: Terry Hurley; bottom: Patrick Ford / Redferns
Page 6: top: Janina Struck / cuba-solidarity.org.uk; bottom: Carey Brandon / Redferns
Page 7: top left & right: Nicolas Asfouri / National Pictures / Topfoto;
bottom left & right: Judy Totton
Page 8: top: Phil Penman / Splash News; middle & bottom: Courtesy of Charles Dickens

Every effort has been made to acknowledge correctly and contact the source and /
or copyright holder of each picture, and Carlton Books Limited apologizes for any
unintentional errors or omissions which will be corrected in future editions of this book.

Printed and bound in Great Britain by CPI Group (UK) Ltd, Croydon CR0 4YY

10 9 8 7 6 5 4 3 2 1

"… we should be careful
of each other, we should be kind
While there is still time"

Philip Larkin, "The Mower", 1979

Contents

Acknowledgements

I am greatly indebted to Jean Newlove MacColl, Hamish MacColl, James Knight and Steve Lillywhite for their help and their memories.

Heartfelt thanks to the many others who also spoke with me, especially: Bono, Billy Bragg, Lu Edmonds, Pete Glenister, Phill Jupitus, Rob Miller, Frank Murray, Brian Nevill, Mark Nevin, Phillip Rambow, Dave Ruffy, Peggy Seeger, Fred Shortland, David Stark, Jon Webster, Matthew Westwood, Chris Winwood; to those who spoke off the record and to Kirsty's fans who responded to my invitation to share their thoughts and their favourite songs for the Electric Landlady section.

Special thanks to Rachel Calder and the Sayle Literary Agency, to my editor, Ian Gittins, for his skill, support and encouragement, and to Miranda West, Lydia Drukarz and Catherine Duncan at André Deutsch.

Also to Penny Ryder, for inspiration; the staff and students at the Cuban National School of Music, Havana; Cuba Solidarity Campaign; BBC World Service; Sean, Michael and Graham at Helter Skelter bookshop, London; Roger Quail; Andrew Craig; Sylvie Simmons; Chris Keable at the Ruskin College Library, Oxford, home of the Ewan MacColl/Peggy Seeger Archive; Candida Bottaci at Principle Management; Sarah Watson at Virgin Music; Toby Manning at the Billy Bragg office; Mushi Jenner at Sincere Management; Malcolm Taylor at the English Folk Dance and Song Society, Cecil Sharp House; Working Class Movement Library, Salford.

Love and gratitude to my family; to Margaret, the late Jim and all of the Bartles, Bairds and La Pines; Sean Body; Diana Quay and George Pensotti; Carol Brown and Ben Martin; Lorraine Gill; Sally and Pete Fincher; Alan Johnston; Pippa Gwilliam; Katharine Hodgson; Maeve Nolan; Mick Fish; Dave and Noreen Hallbery.

Author's Note: I have donated part of the proceeds of this book to the Justice for Kirsty campaign and the Music Fund for Cuba. My thanks to the publishers for also making a generous donation to the Justice for Kirsty campaign.

I have also donated reference material to the Ewan MacColl/Peggy Seeger Archive and the Working Class Movement Library.

Foreword

I never could understand how someone as outgoing and gregarious as Kirsty MacColl could be tormented by stage fright. After all, the Kirsty I knew was a person whose commanding presence could light up a room. Never afraid to speak her mind, she took no bullshit from anyone, deploying a dry, sardonic wit that shone through in her songs. On those few occasions that we performed together, she seemed to enjoy herself, revelling in the applause of the audience and cracking jokes.

Perhaps the demons that she was wrestling with were born of a sense of frustration at not being able to perform her songs as she heard them in her head. She was far happier in the studio, where she could realise the full potential of her musical vision. There she could layer her unique voice and marshal her musicians into a shimmering wall of sound. Her albums are a shining testimonial to her courage as an artist, willing to challenge preconceptions of what a woman should write about, daring to embrace musical styles from beyond the narrow horizons of pop.

She never had much time for the pretensions of stardom. What you saw was what you got. If she gave a fig about what others thought, she never let it show. What she cared passionately about was her family, Cuba and her songs. Karen O'Brien has drawn these strands together to paint a picture of a life lived to the full. Reading this book, it is hard not to feel a sense of anger at the fact that, during her lifetime, she was never acknowledged as a truly outstanding artist.

The irony is that even Kirsty herself, standing alone in the spotlight, the entire audience in her thrall, never really appreciated what a great talent she was.

Billy Bragg, 2004

INTRODUCTION

"Some lives read like a novel.
And some lives read like poetry..."

Introduction

Here are the treasures of Kirsty MacColl's childhood: a bright red ribbon, still tied in a pony-tail knot; school books with teachers' fulsome comments in the margin; a handmade birthday card, with "To Mum" scrawled in a child's best writing; drawings of her favourite bedtime story characters; a published poetry anthology, with an entry written by Kirsty. No more or less than many parents would keep, but held with a painful poignancy that most parents never have to experience. This is a childhood remembered, but no longer by the child herself; childhood mementos kept now for her own two sons, but no longer by the woman herself. Those we love live on in our memories and our senses – to touch what they touched brings them closer, and helps us to hold fast to them.

Kirsty MacColl died in a tragically senseless accident on December 18, 2000, at the age of 41. She had gone to the Mexican resort of Cozumel with her partner, James Knight, and her two teenage sons. While out diving off the coast in a zone reserved for swimmers and divers, Kirsty was hit by a powerboat that should never have been in the protected national park area. She died instantly.

Local police began an investigation immediately but from their inquiries, and others conducted by private investigators hired by Kirsty's mother, Jean, it soon became clear that there were inconsistencies in the account given by the driver of the powerboat, José Cen Yam. Cen Yam was an inexperienced deck-hand on the boat owned by an influential millionaire businessman, Guillermo Gonzalez Nova, who was also on board with members of his family.

Witnesses said the powerful boat was travelling at very high speeds in the restricted area. Cen Yam and Gonzalez Nova denied this, but port authority investigators dismissed their denial. Cen Yam's lawyers consistently argued that he did not bear any legal responsibility for the accident, saying the blame should be placed on the divemaster in charge of the family's trip. The dive team were found to bear some of the responsibility – they did not display a marker buoy, and the warning flag that their boat was flying did not conform to international standards.

While being critical of Gonzalez Nova, the Mexican judicial authorities pressed no charges against him but found José Cen Yam guilty of culpable homicide. On March 27, 2003, he was sentenced to two years and ten months in prison. However, under Mexican law the judge was entitled to offer the convicted man a one-peso fine for each day of his sentence. He did so: the total came to the equivalent of little more than £60. This merely led Jean MacColl and several of Kirsty's close friends to redouble their efforts for the Justice for Kirsty campaign, which they had launched in late 2002, believing that Cen Yam was simply being used to deflect blame from Gonzalez Nova, who they believe, as the boat's owner, is ultimately responsible.

Just months before her death, Kirsty MacColl told a journalist, "Whenever I go into the studio, I always operate on the principle that I might get hit by a bus tomorrow. I'd hate the obituaries to read, 'And her last album was her not-very-good album'." There was no danger of that. Her death came at a time when, after a gap of several years, her music – in the form of a new album, *Tropical Brainstorm* – was receiving both critical and commercial acclaim.

Kirsty's personal life was happier than it had been in a very long time. She was in love with James, and the deep unhappiness and depression that had accompanied the end of her marriage to producer Steve Lillywhite was consigned to the past. She had finally broken away from the strictures she wrote of in her song, "Bad". Kirsty had always resented being so often referred to only in relation to Lillywhite or her father, Ewan MacColl, the folk music legend, activist and playwright, and author of songs such as "The First Time Ever I Saw Your Face" and "Dirty Old Town":

> "I've been the token woman all my life:
> The token daughter, the token wife."
>
> —Kirsty MacColl, "Bad"

Kirsty MacColl left a relatively small body of work but it has provided a lasting legacy, sinking into the national musical psyche in a way that the chart hits of more commercially successful acts will never do. She was one of the great British pop talents – everything about her defied the conventional categorization of "pop", yet she embraced and defended the genre, redeeming it with sardonic and literate writing that had seldom been seen since the glory days of Ray Davies and the Kinks. Like Davies, Elvis Costello, Morrissey and Ian Dury, she created a kitchen-sink pop realism that was also funny, irreverent and endearingly catchy. Her five studio albums, in a career spanning nearly twenty years, became symbolic rescue missions to retrieve British pop music from all that was saccharine and shallow, manufactured and mainstream, and transform it into a defiant creature of intelligence and wit:

> Vitriol and misery have always been far easier to express in song. But a lot of people also think that humour implies you're not serious about the music. Which is stupid. I don't see the connection between being deadly serious and being good. There's a lot of serious crap around and there's a lot of people who want to be celebrities and take themselves far too seriously.

Kirsty MacColl was one of those rare talents who saw in pop music a vehicle for intelligent writing, a sardonic sensibility and a playful sexuality that had nothing to do with exploitation or manipulation. She believed that, "Perfect pop records are like four-minute orgasms":

> I like to make jangly, luscious melodic pop music but with lyrics that are more biting and down to earth than the average stuff you hear on the radio … I don't want to be presented as something I'm not. The pop world packages women. You're either a dolly-bird bimbo or soapbox sociologist. So many songs are written by men for women, and they obviously have a strange string of women around them: dopey cows in frilly dresses singing, 'Oh, baby, I can't live without you'. It's capitulation. It's shit. Who are all these wimpy women, anyway? All the women I know are strong and assertive. They're not wilting wallflowers who can't live without a man. I've never met anyone who couldn't live without a man.

MacColl's own refusal to pander to vain and vacuous sexualized "pop tart" images and her insistence on having a family life as well as a working life showed that women in pop could be multi-dimensional characters rather than one-dimensional clones. She was a pop craftswoman who had learned classical guitar and violin as a child, listened to the rock of Frank Zappa and Neil Young, the pop harmonies of the Beach Boys, and the punk of the Ramones. While still a teenager, she signed to the post-punk label Stiff, after dabbling with r&b-based pub rock with the Drug Addix. It was a far cry from her father's legacy:

> I was very aware of the fact that he disapproved completely of anything he regarded as commercial. It was a sin really, and there was nothing that his children could have done more to upset him than to want to become pop singers. As much as I loved him, I thought his outlook on what was valid and what was not was rather narrow-minded and slightly hypocritical. There are things about pop music that are good, you can have a message; ultimately a good pop single transcends all that ... it's not preaching, it's uplifting.

MacColl overcame agonising stage fright, depression and long periods of writer's block, and – refusing to compromise or follow the rules of Planet Pop – she created a career that gave her critical credibility and popular appeal. Her acutely autobiographical songs gave extraordinary insights into a woman who was much more complex than many could ever have imagined. For some, she was destined forever to be the woman behind "There's a Guy Works Down the Chip Shop Swears He's Elvis", or "Fairytale of New York", but those songs represent the tiniest fraction of what she really was.

For many, Kirsty MacColl will be seen as a some-time pop star in the eighties who had most of her hits written for, or by, other people. She worked with some of the biggest names in British and American pop and rock. Her duet with Shane MacGowan on the Pogues' "A Fairytale of New York" has made the song one of the most popular Christmas songs ever; she reinvented Billy Bragg's "A New England " and made it a hit; Ray Davies was so enamoured of her cover of his song "Days" that he invited her to duet with him at a Kinks concert. She even sang backing vocals on the Happy Mondays' "Hallelujah", the song that kicked off the "Madchester" music scene.

While Kirsty went through sustained periods of neglect by the industry, she would surely have taken solace from the words of Noël Coward – a writer she resembled in dry wit and acid-tongued observations – who, when asked how it felt to be treated dismissively by critics and written-off as unimportant and out of touch with the reality of life in post-war Britain, simply shrugged, "Well, in the first place, nobody of particular *importance* wrote me off. And in the second place, *I* didn't notice it."

Kirsty MacColl travelled frequently in Cuba and in recognition of her love for the country, its people and their music, the MacColl family and the Cuba Solidarity Campaign have established a memorial fund in her name to raise money to send musical equipment to Cuban schools and colleges, and provide materials for music and cultural projects throughout Cuba. It also works to develop closer cultural links and greater understanding between Britain and Cuba. The National School of Music in Havana has re-named the school's music library after Kirsty, as an enduring tribute to her life and work. Her portrait hangs in the library; beneath it, a single flower is replaced every day.

Treachery

F amily home movies from the sixties show a red-haired, pig-tailed little girl skipping along a footpath, hands clasped on either side by her smiling parents. For a moment they all look at each other then look at the camera, laughing, as the child is swung gently off the ground. It's a glimpse of happiness, a transient fragment of family life, savoured and then gone.

The child's parents, Ewan MacColl and Jean Newlove, did not subscribe to the literary critic Cyril Connolly's observation that there is no more sombre enemy of good art than the pram in the hall. Even before they'd married in the Manchester Register Office on April 13, 1949, they'd merged art, love, and passionate political commitment – in short, much that makes a creative life, well-lived – to form a partnership that had helped to shape one of the most influential of the great British drama companies, Theatre Workshop.

They were from very different worlds. Jean was the only daughter of an educated, artistic, middle-class couple from Lancashire. She'd taken dance classes from the age of two to try to stop her chronic stuttering; by concentrating on her dance steps, the young child successfully forgot to stammer. After leaving school, she had met the Hungarian-born pioneer of modern dance, Rudolph Laban, who chose her as his sole private pupil and teaching assistant. Laban's rigorous work on dance theory and notation had won him recognition in Europe as the "prophet of dance". He'd fled Germany after the Nazis came to power, settling in Manchester, where he continued his work. During the war years, Laban and Jean applied his system, the Theory of Efforts, to the movements of workers on the factory floor, helping them to achieve greater efficiency and a dramatic increase in output by improving both the way they used their bodies and their general health.

By contrast, Ewan MacColl – then Jimmie Miller – had educated and agitated himself out of the working-class suburbs of Salford, Manchester, where he was born on January 25, 1915. It was the place that would, decades later, inspire one of his best-known songs, "Dirty Old Town". His father, William (known as Will), a life-long socialist, had left Stirlingshire in Scotland to go south with his young wife, Betsy Hendry Miller. Betsy, also from sturdy Scottish stock, had been raised in Perthshire. After several miscarriages, three of her four children died in infancy; her tenacious Jimmie survived and his wants, whims, achievements and ambitions would place him at the very centre of her life until her death at the age of 96.

Ewan and Jean's son, Hamish, remembered his paternal grandmother, who lived with the family for many years, as being, "very good to me. She was good fun but mad as a hatter, like something out of Ivor Cutler's 'Life in a Scotch Sitting-Room'" - a reference to the Glaswegian humorist, songwriter and artist's surreally funny, outlandishly nostalgic, semi-autobiographical tale based on his Depression-era childhood in a large middle-class family in Glasgow:

"The piano candles lit, we cleared our throats and launched into 'Loch Lomond'. Several notes were missing. They had always been missing, except for two which I had levered out with a poker. 'Loch Lomond' was in E flat, so half the tune was missing."

—Ivor Cutler, "Life In A Scotch Sitting-Room"

Will Miller's life was dominated by the twin passions of singing and politics, just as his son's would be. The former helped to ease the demands and disappointments inextricably linked with the latter. The young Jimmie saw the price his father paid for involvement in the Communist Party and unionism, as he was often branded a troublemaker for defending workers' rights and taking part in strikes. He was also blacklisted, and struggled with long periods out of work. If anything, though, it only convinced the boy that if the bosses, the powerbrokers, their henchmen and lackeys are against you, you must be doing *something* right.

After leaving school and facing periods of joblessness, Jimmie spent his time in the local library, where the troubles and tribulations of the outside world fell away and his sole dilemma was simply, "Should I read for pleasure today, or should I pursue knowledge?" Nothing was boring or uninteresting to him, from Russian philosophers to the plays of Eugene O'Neill, and his own attempts to learn ten new words per day from *Webster's Dictionary*. He joined the Young Communist League and set up his own agit-prop theatre groups, Red Megaphones and Theatre of Action. With his first wife, Joan Littlewood, whom he married when they were both 19, he set up Theatre Union, an enterprise that foundered with the onset of the Second World War.

By the mid-forties, Littlewood and Jimmie Miller, who had by now changed his name to Ewan MacColl as a homage to the Lallans ("lowlands") school of Scottish poetry, had created a new drama company, which they named Theatre Workshop. They set themselves a single extraordinary task: to make theatre accessible to the masses, entertaining as well as politically enlightening and instructive. They would blend music, drama and dance into a politicized music-hall enterprise and take intelligent drama to the people, to church halls and miners' social clubs, to the grimy pit villages and leafy country towns.

It was to be the antithesis of the theatre of the day, the fey and winsome fare that typified middle-class England, the territory of the average theatre-goer, or the works of Shakespeare as defined by the heavyweights of the traditionalist Old Vic company in London. One of the worst insults Littlewood would level at an actor declaiming and emoting in an inauthentic way was a withering, "Oh God, you sound like the Old Vic!"

MacColl believed in "the necessity and the possibility of creating a popular theatre with a broad working-class base ... such a theatre would take all that was best from the theatres of the past and, at the same time, would create a new repertoire, incorporating all the new theatrical forms which were expected to evolve in the course of our work." The use of dance and movement would be essential to help the actors both explore their craft and improve the power of each characterization; they would acquire the same skills that enabled athletes and dancers to use their bodies with such precision.

Laban's work on the mastery of movement would prove invaluable. He invited the Theatre Workshop members to an open day, and they were so struck by his methods that they implored him to come to one of their performances. Laban, in turn, was impressed by what he'd seen,

3

and agreed to work as the company's movement teacher whenever they were in Manchester. During Theatre Workshop's summer break in 1946, the actors descended on Laban's Manchester headquarters where he and his personal assistant, Jean Newlove, began a training programme. When the summer break was over, it was agreed with Laban that Jean would continue to train the company in weekly sessions.

Ewan recalled: "She turned out to be a magnificent teacher, serious and good-natured, full of ideas and quick to recognize the unique character of Theatre Workshop. Under her tutelage the dormant capabilities of the actors in the group underwent a complete transformation and it wasn't long before our part-time tutor fell under the spell of the theatre and joined us. And it wasn't long before I fell under the spell of our dance teacher and married her."

It was some time before Jean even knew that Ewan and Joan Littlewood had been married years earlier. Neither of them had mentioned their brief union, which had lasted little more than twelve months. Both had been young at the time, and it had soon become clear that the relationship between Joan and Ewan was better suited to a working partnership than a romantic one. Joan and a young Theatre Workshop company member, Gerry Raffles, had fallen in love and been together for some years by the time Jean Newlove entered their world. By then, Ewan had already reinvented himself, shed his given name and his first early marriage, and taken the grimy streets and low expectations of Salford and made a springboard out of them.

Eight years Newlove's senior, Ewan MacColl was challenging, uncompromising and passionately committed to his work and his politics, which, it became clear, were for him indivisible. He had a huge appetite for life, as well as for Marx Brothers' films. For Jean Newlove, it was MacColl the artist who first enchanted her. "He was such a good writer," she says. "He was writing at that time, and he'd read what he'd written to me. It sounded marvellous. And he wrote me wonderful letters. But what I really loved was his singing. He sang so beautifully. He was also very supportive of my work. I remember the first time I took a class, he said to me, 'You're good! You're just like Joan.' That was high praise for me, that she could take people and move them, and I could too."

The co-operative spirit of Theatre Workshop was also immensely attractive to her: "I loved the whole set-up with Theatre Workshop. I had been with Laban for so many years, and I'd been the only student

4

studying directly with him. I'd loved that; no one else had that opportunity. Then when I went to Theatre Workshop, they were all my age except for Joan and Ewan, and that was nice too. They were so talented and in the evenings everyone would sing. Ewan would start singing, then one or two of them would join in."

Newlove had already formed her own dance company and toured eastern Europe while still being involved in Theatre Workshop productions. In Poland, she'd played the lead in MacColl's ballad opera, *See You in Warsaw, Johnny*. She remained with Theatre Workshop for fifteen years, working on dozens of plays including the West End productions of MacColl's *Uranium 235*, Brendan Behan's *The Hostage*, Shelagh Delaney's *A Taste of Honey* and two of the most successful stage musicals of the time, *Fings Ain't What They Used to Be* and *Oh, What a Lovely War*.

Joan Littlewood's colourful, idiosyncratic and in parts, fanciful memoir, *Joan's Book*, published in 1994 with the more accurate sub-title *Joan Littlewood's Peculiar History As She Tells It*, describes those times in great, if occasionally embellished, detail. The book was dedicated to Gerry Raffles: "May his long fight encourage all those young artists oppressed by our far-famed English Philistines." Jean Newlove, her closest friend and fellow traveller through most of the Theatre Workshop years, challenged Littlewood about some of her anecdotes, saying frankly that, "It just didn't happen that way!" Joan retorted, "I know, darling, but it's more interesting this way, isn't it?"

Littlewood, who never had children of her own, had been godmother to Ewan and Jean's son, Hamish, who was born in 1950. She was equally thrilled to carry out the same role for his sister, Kirsty Anna, who was born in Mayday Hospital in the south London suburb of Thornton Heath on October 10, 1959. Jean described her daughter as, "an extraordinary child, I realized that soon after she was born". But by the time of the baby girl's appearance in the world, the relationship between her parents had become strained beyond repair.

Far from being the basis of the good society, Sir Edmund Leach would say in the BBC Reith Lecture in 1967, the family, with its narrow privacy and tawdry secrets, is the source of all our discontents. Ewan and Jean's daughter had been conceived three years after he had fallen deeply in love with a young American folk-singer, Peggy Seeger, who was twenty years his junior. Initially unable to make an irrevocable choice, he'd wavered between the two women before setting up home with Seeger. What Jean MacColl didn't know at the beginning of her pregnancy was that Ewan's family commitments had already grown: "I found out Peggy had been pregnant when I was pregnant. I found out she'd had a baby in March; Kirsty was born in the October. Ewan had arranged to go on a tour of the States with Peggy, singing, so they went off with their baby. Ewan had said that when he came back, he'd come to stay with us permanently."

Ewan saw his daughter in hospital the day after she was born; he left 24 hours later for the tour of the United States, with Peggy Seeger and their seven-month-old son, Neill. Ewan's autobiography, *Journeyman*, published in 1990 a year after his death, does not mention Kirsty's birth. She was the only one of his five children whose birth went unremarked in his book, but it is not a sin of omission – Kirsty is mentioned in loving terms elsewhere, and the book has a photograph of a proud, beaming Ewan with his daughter on her wedding day. It is more an attempt to gloss over the excruciating emotional upheaval of the love that he felt at that time for his children and their mothers.

Ewan could articulate the lives of miners, mill-workers and fishing communities in Britain or of slain schoolchildren in South Africa, but could barely acknowledge the inarticulate speech of his own heart. Peggy Seeger sought to explain this, and the surprising omission of all but the most scant details of his inner emotional life and relationships with his three wives and five children in his autobiography, when she wrote in her introduction to the book:

> He could speak knowledgeably on a myriad of subjects – but not on his own emotions. He could conceive, write and produce a play – but found it difficult to communicate with his own children ... he was hurt and puzzled by his inability to communicate satisfactorily with his children, none of whom totally share his political convictions. He was very proud of their skills and of the fact that all of them are highly musical but found it hard to tell them so, for they are in a field of music with which he felt he had little in common ... to the day of his death a consistently good relationship with them was never established. As his relationship with them was on such an intense emotional plane, he simply did not know how to write about them in the book. So he left them out.

Ewan's emotional reticence and apparent disconnection with the deepest parts of his own inner life were sources of great pain, to himself and to those closest to him. They may well have had their roots in his own childhood; he speaks movingly in his autobiography of his feelings for his parents, the ever-present and unwavering devotion of his mother, and the painfully distant sense of his father's unexpressed love.

He had but one single memory of being embraced by his father in the whole of his childhood, which he recalled in *Journeyman*. During one summer school holiday, the young Jimmie had been sent to the foundry to take his father a cooked lunch. Amid the cacophony and over-whelming heat, his father emerged from the billowing clouds surrounding the molten metal:

> And gives me a quick hug … that hug makes me strangely jubilant. One small embrace. Not much to last a lifetime. There were no endearments either … I don't remember my father once uttering an endearment to me. Was it shyness or embarrassment that inhibited him, was it that appalling Scottish macho mentality that equates love with weakness? Perhaps. And yet I too, find diffi-culty in communicating my feelings to my children … I not only love them all but, for most of the time, I like them too. And yet, when we meet, a good deal of our conversation is about trivialities. Is it inevitable that children and parents grow further and further apart with the passage of time? Do we distance ourselves from our parents in order to become ourselves? Is such distancing part of the survival process?

If that is so, then Ewan resembled his father more than he may have thought. Both men, inhabiting the twin worlds of singing and politics, could articulate their feelings in those spheres in a way that they often found impossible in the realm of personal emotions.

Jean recalls the anxiety engendered by her husband's indecision: "The most painful thing of all was that he was lying throughout, because he couldn't face the truth and Peggy was pushing him to leave. He couldn't actually bring himself to do it. He was in love with two women, he said. I said to him, 'Why can't you work with Peggy, have a good working relationship but keep it separate?' He said, 'I can't. I wish I could.' So Peggy was pushing it, and I think she became pregnant to force the issue. Ewan had decided before Christmas 1958 that we would get back together. There was a reconciliation, and he said that he would come back. It was something which I looked forward to. I thought, 'Maybe it's really going to work now.'"

Ewan and Jean's son, Hamish, was eight at the time. He had spent the previous summer shuttling back and forth between his mother's and father's homes, and it had proved an expensive and unsatisfactory arrangement. Jean says that she and Ewan decided they'd get back together. "I was feeling much more optimistic about it. That summer, I had the most wonderful pregnancy. I thought, 'This is the last baby I'm going to have, I'm going to make the most of it.' Theatre Workshop had four shows running in the West End, and in my free time I'd go to the Palladium to see *Die Fledermaus*. I looked quite radiant and I felt absolutely marvellous. I was determined that I was going to be completely happy." She and Hamish left London for the south of France, to join Joan Littlewood and Gerry Raffles on their boat.

Ewan remained in London, and his resolve weakened dramatically. His commitment to Peggy had been strengthened by the birth of their son. They now had both a professional and a romantic partnership. Jean believes the music itself was a bond that connected them: "What she could do, which was great for Ewan, was transcribe music, and she could accompany him musically. Ewan *had* to have somebody to work with. Initially, he had Joan. Then he had Peggy." Jean's reconciliation with Ewan was thus short-lived, and they would never live together again. Despite this, they remained close and did not divorce until 1976 – and, even then, only on the grounds of having spent at least five years apart.

Ewan's relationship with Peggy, and the inspiration he gained from their musical collaboration, had reinforced his strongly-held view that he could achieve more in music than in drama. His gradual severing of ties with Theatre Workshop was all but complete. In 1956, the year he and Peggy became lovers, Ewan had written what would be his last work for Theatre Workshop. The play, *So Long at the Fair*, did not appear on the British stage but was performed extensively in Germany. Ewan wasn't concerned. Music had replaced the theatre at the core of his creative life.

In her autobiography, Joan Littlewood was dismissive of her former husband's decision:

One day, Ewan MacColl, James H. Miller, Jimmie, call him what you will, prime mover, inspiration, walked out, quit, buggered off – and, not to put too fine a point on it, resigned. Theatre Workshop had been his life, his pride and joy, the vehicle for all of his plays. ... Where was he going? To join the Hootenannys, one of the many groups of folk artists who'd become fashionable. Folk songs and singers were in demand at this time, and the Hootenannys offered real money. He'd never earned money with his plays in England and all the hopes and dreams of his youth had faded, but abandoning Theatre Workshop to sing in London pubs – what a waste!

Gerry Raffles told Ewan: "You have been with dedicated people, who will go on long after your Hootenannys are forgotten." However, Jean understood Ewan's decision and, for a time, shared his enthusiasm for traditional Scottish and English folk rhythms by including some of the folk dances in her own choreography. She also felt that Ewan's role in Theatre Workshop had never been fully acknowledged: "He really started Theatre Workshop, there's no doubt about that. It only became Joan's Theatre Workshop later because Ewan had left. But I sympathized with some of the things that he had to say about the parting of the ways with Theatre Workshop."

Ewan himself was sanguine, believing that it had been worth investing twenty years of his life in the pursuit of both an idea and an ideal: "All of us who worked in Theatre Workshop in those early days benefited from the experience in one way or another. We did not, however, make any lasting impression on the English theatre as a whole. For a short time, I believed that we had, but twenty years of theatre-going has since disabused me of any such notion. With a few exceptions, the acting is just as mediocre as ever it was, the productions just as puerile – gimmicky, pretentious and puerile. Other nations have produced a theatre of cruelty, a theatre of the absurd. We have produced a theatre of dullness. And what is more, we are proud of our dullness."

As a radical playwright and one of the greatest modern exponents of British folk music, Ewan MacColl had a revolutionary zeal about music and politics coupled with a passion for tradition, and pioneered the British folk revival, together with A.L. (Bert) Lloyd, in the fifties. His insistence that folk music could only be preserved as a living art if singers and musicians confined themselves to playing no other genre outraged less purist elements in the folk community. Many believed that trying to build sonic barricades to keep out the invading barbarian hordes bringing with them the American music of the fifties and sixties was perverse and pointless.

But Ewan's implacability did a great deal to retrieve and revive an irreplaceable art form that was at serious risk of being discarded. He loved songs that celebrated the lives of labourers and factory workers, but did not sentimentalize them: "There are no nightingales in these songs, no flowers – and the sun is rarely mentioned … They should be sung to the accompaniment of pneumatic drills and swinging hammers, they should be bawled above the hum of turbines and the chatter of looms, for they are the songs of toil."

CHAPTER TWO

See That Girl

F amily life had settled into a pattern for Jean, Hamish and Kirsty. Mondays to Saturdays would be theirs; Sundays would be Ewan's. He would come to visit and they would eat a huge family dinner, go for drives, explore the countryside and try to have a normal family life, if only for a few hours. Then he would return to his life, and they would return to theirs. But it was not an ideal situation for either family, and there was so much that remained unresolved in their emotional lives.

"He felt horribly guilty about leaving Jean," remembers Peggy Seeger. "He really loved her a lot. But there are certain other kinds of love that make you turn your back on everything. And that's what he did, and he felt very, very bad about it. He was, as they say, between a rock and a hard place. He did the best that he could."

But Ewan clearly often felt that he'd short-changed everyone, including himself, as his two families remained distant for many years. If he was with one set of children, he couldn't be with the others. He and Peggy eventually made their home in Cromwell Road, in Beckenham, on the outskirts of south-east London. By 1979, they'd had two more children, Calum and Kitty. Peggy Seeger recalls:

> I didn't see him with Kirsty until she was nine. She wasn't allowed to come over to our house until then. We shouldn't have put up with that but that's what the deal was. So, once a week, we didn't have Ewan. Every Sunday he went over to the other house, for years and years and years. He was a very responsible person for that; whether he was appreciated for it, I don't know, but he did it for years. Of course he probably thought he couldn't say too much when he came home on Sunday evenings. It didn't always go well because there was a lot of bitter feeling in there. It was a bitterness that

Kirsty was adult enough to get around in her later years, but in her earlier years, she would have felt very odd about coming over to the house of someone she'd heard so many awful things about. But when Hamish came over, when he was about seventeen, then Kirsty started coming over every now and then.

On one of her first visits, Kirsty sat on the sofa at Ewan and Peggy's home and enchanted her father with a faithful rendition of the English traditional folk song, "Lovely Joan", which had been a staple of the repertoire of hundreds of English folk singers since a number of versions of the song were collected by Ralph Vaughan-Williams in 1908. "She sang 'Lovely Joan' all the way through, and Ewan was just so proud of her," recalls Seeger. "It was wonderful."

But if the Sunday visits were often fraught for Ewan, they were equally so for Jean and Kirsty. "I wasn't a particularly happy child," Kirsty was to later confess, "and my Mum wasn't particularly happy either, because she'd been abandoned with two children. Everyone thinks I grew up in a family like 'The Waltons', sitting around playing acoustic guitar and singing folk songs. It sure as hell wasn't like that. There was a very miserable atmosphere. I wasn't a great part of my father's life and I felt detached from him. I can't say I looked forward to his Sunday visits. I was misunderstood and I couldn't express myself, which is why most people become artists. We've all been to the same concentration camp."

What is not in doubt is that Ewan loved his children, says Jean. "He would make an effort and he would come over, sometimes during the week and always for Sunday lunch, and he would be jolly. He always had something interesting to say about learning if he'd bought a book about something. But, just sometimes, it got a bit much for me. I'd be cooking a meal, with a job, looking after a sick child, sorting out a teenager. Just sometimes it would have been nice not to have to cook a family meal. Quite often when Kirsty was ill, it was a bit of a strain."

Kirsty MacColl's health had become a major concern. As a toddler, she frequently seemed to be poorly, listless and short of breath. Health crises came and went, as they do with youngsters. Then, when Kirsty was twenty months old, Jean decided to take her children on holiday to Poland. They boarded the train at London's Victoria station, with Ewan there to help them and see them off. Jean, Hamish and Kirsty were going to stay with friends: George Bidwell, an English writer, and his Polish wife, Anna.

Jean and Ewan had met Bidwell at the International Arts Festival in Warsaw a few years earlier. He'd urged them to come back for a holiday, but the idea only seemed feasible after one of Ewan's plays was produced in Poland and became a great success. Polish regulations prevented Ewan from taking the money earned from his work out of the country, so he encouraged Jean to take the children and spend the money in Poland while visiting their friends. "We decided to go when we found we couldn't get Ewan's money out of Poland," says Jean. "The authorities said it would undermine the economy of the country if we did!"

The family travelled by boat to Holland and then got a train to East Germany, where they were to change trains to go on to Poland. Communist bureaucracy struck when they reached East Berlin. "We had passports, but no transit visa or Polish visa," says Jean. "On the train, we were told we would need a transit visa. We paid for it but the guard didn't say we wouldn't be able to get another one coming back, and that we should have got a return visa. When we got to East Berlin, we had to wait hours to get the train to Poland."

Two friends from the world-famous Berliner Ensemble, a company that had forged links with Theatre Workshop during visits to Britain, picked them up and took them out for the day, sight-seeing and taking the children for a walk in the park. Kirsty saw an elderly man pushing a basket-weave pram with an older child walking by his side, and she went up to them. As a joke, the man put her in the pram and they began to walk away. "Kirsty was quite happy, quite unconcerned," says Jean. "So then he had to bring her back!"

Jean MacColl remembers Kirsty, even as a toddler, as remarkably self-possessed and confident. She was a pretty child with russet curls. When Jean later took her to the Theatre Royal in Stratford East, Lionel Bart remarked to her, "She looks like Rita Hayworth!" On their last night in Berlin, many of the Berliner Ensemble members came to the train station to say farewell. "I remember everyone shouting, 'Bye Kirsty, come again soon!'" Jean recalls. The children slept for the rest of the journey, waking to hear George Bidwell banging on the window as the train came to a stop in the Polish city of Poznan.

The Bidwells' home was in the heart of some of the most beautiful countryside in Poland: the Jelenia Gora region, bordering what was then Czechoslovakia. Famed for its forests, mountains, spas, river valleys, walking trails and national parks, the region's beauty and rich cultural heritage attracted writers, artists and poets, and was perfect for the children to explore. The Bidwell home even had a pond in the garden for them to swim in. The couple made the family feel at home, and showed them a part of the house they'd christened "Jean's Corner" and decorated with gifts she'd sent to them. Friends of the Bidwells were also staying in the house. When Kirsty first saw them at breakfast, she took one look at the husband, Jedec, and exclaimed, "Oh, boy!" For the rest of the trip, Jedec remained, "Oh, boy!"

The holiday was over too soon, and Bidwell drove the MacColls back to Poznan to catch the train that was en route from Moscow to the Hook of Holland. The family settled into their first-class compartment, laden with luggage and gifts of food from George and Anna. Hamish went to the restaurant car and bought chocolates with their few remaining Polish coins. The train lumbered towards the border with what was then East Germany, the German Democratic Republic. A ticket collector eventually appeared as the train neared Frankfurt, just across the border.

It was discovered that the family did not have a transit visa. The problem that had arisen on the journey to Poland was even worse now. Then, they should have been given a return visa; now, that was impossible. They were told they would be put off the train in Frankfurt. Political tensions were high at the time and security had been tightened as a result.

"The night before," says Jean, "the Cold War had suddenly heated up. I'd heard it on the radio, when George was listening to the cricket scores. The Prussian guard told us to get off the train at Frankfurt. He was very rude and arrogant. It was only about sixteen years after the end of the Second World War. First of all, I wanted Kirsty to look sad, but she was smiling and waving to everybody. And everybody was looking out of the windows of the train, to see what spies they'd caught. All they saw was a woman and two children. The guard said, 'Every minute the train is delayed, we are fined.' He ordered us off the train. As the train moved off, everyone was waving to Kirsty and she was waving back at them."

Jean asked to use a telephone, hoping to reach friends from the Berliner Ensemble, who might be able to make the drive from Berlin to Frankfurt. Her request was refused. As they stood on the platform, an official directed them to a hastily erected Red Cross tent that had been set up near the railway platform to help people in exactly their plight. The only other person waiting there was an elderly Polish man who spoke a little English. He told them he had been with friends, travelling to Holland but he hadn't had the necessary visa so he too had been evicted from the train. His situation was even more complicated; he had been travelling on a group passport and his group had had to continue without him.

Jean and her children were not allowed to leave the Red Cross area until the next train arrived, heading across Germany through Poland to the USSR. They and their new travelling companion were marched on to the train and told to disembark in Warsaw.

Jean opened the gifts of food they'd been given and shared it with the man. "I tried to jolly Hamish by saying, 'Isn't this exciting!'" she says, "and making a game of it, but the guard's nasty approach to me had upset him. Then the Polish ticket collector came along and tried to explain to me that I was going in the wrong direction. If you didn't have a ticket you were charged double. At seven in the morning, we finally arrived in Warsaw."

The MacColls had only one or two zlotys left. The rest had been spent hours earlier. As Jean surveyed the dismal scene and her two children, who were already tiring of their adventure, she sunk her hands deep into her pockets. In there was a scrap of paper with the phone number of the Bidwells' friend, Jedec, scrawled on it. Jedec had told her, "If you are ever in Warsaw, come and visit us." She had tucked the piece of paper into her pocket and forgotten about it.

Jean found a public phone and used the last of their Polish coins to dial the number, not even sure whether she was using the right area code, let alone whether anyone would be at home. The phone rang and rang and finally she heard a voice on the other end. She said simply, "Oh, boy!" aware that he would recognize Kirsty's nickname for him. "My God, Jean! Where are you?" he exclaimed. "Where are the children?"

Jedec immediately drove to the train station. It was an extraordinary stroke of luck that he had even answered the phone; he was just about to lock the door of his flat as he left for work. Jean spent the morning washing baby napkins while her friend sorted out their travel arrangements. He took them on a tour of Warsaw, a city then still recovering from the ravages of the Second World War. It had been scarred by the razing of the Jewish ghetto after an uprising there in 1943 and a city-wide rebellion the following year, as Poles tried and failed to oust the occupying German forces and were driven out in their tens of thousands, the city burning behind them.

With the MacColl family's spirits restored, having slept and eaten well, they resumed their journey the following day, with all of their paperwork now in order. The journey back across Poland, the two Germanys and the Netherlands proved uneventful until the train stopped at the Hook of Holland, and Kirsty celebrated their safe arrival by throwing her shoe out of the carriage window. Her chivalrous brother, then ten-and-a-half, stepped outside to pick it up from the platform and, just as he did so, the train started to move off. As Jean gasped, her son leapt back onto the train and reappeared, breathlessly, in the carriage seconds later.

For all of the adventures of the children's first trip to Poland, their second visit two years later would be even more eventful. The Bidwells' two cats had recently had kittens, and Kirsty was enchanted by them. "She loved them," Jean recalls. "She played with them all day. She was so happy. But in the middle of the night, she was fighting for breath and just couldn't breathe. She was so ill that George rang a specialist in Poznan, who, because George was so famous as a writer, said she'd like to meet him and that she would drive over."

Poznan was hours away, but when the doctor finally arrived, she gave Kirsty a massive shot of penicillin and they waited to see whether it would have any effect. The specialist told George and Anna that she felt that Kirsty could well suffer from severe asthma for years to come.

Jean sat with Kirsty for hours and, to help distract the child, made up stories for her daughter. "I started telling her a story about a white horse, Horatio. I introduced other animals. He was friends with a poodle, who was French. Kirsty loved these stories. Whenever she was ill, she'd always ask for a story. I hated it, because whenever she wanted to hear them, it meant that she was very ill."

The Polish specialist had given Kirsty enough medication to calm her condition, and she soon began to feel well enough to go outside to play with Hamish. Ten minutes later, Hamish returned, ashen-faced, carrying his sister. They were both smeared with blood. Kirsty had hit her head on a rusty iron gate and blood was pouring from the cut. But that crisis too passed, and she was left with only a tiny scar.

The rest of the MacColls' second holiday with the Bidwells was uneventful but happy. However, their return train journey again fell foul of Eastern bloc bureacracy when they were kept waiting for so long at a security check in East Berlin that they missed their train connection and spent the day in the west of the divided city, waiting for the night-train. It was a suffocatingly hot summer's day but they found a smart hotel and took a day room.

The children ordered ice-cold Cokes from room service, Kirsty luxuriated in a bubble bath, and they rested before taking a stroll around the shops. Jean bought the children a gift each. Hamish got a model kit while Kirsty chose a toy Bengal tiger that she immediately christened Benji. Browsing in a record shop, Jean was horrified to see a display of recordings of the Nazi Panzer divisions.

The family walked to one of the city's old churches that was being rebuilt after being severely damaged during the war. Visitor numbers were limited while reconstruction work was underway, but the four-year-old Kirsty slipped in behind a group of tourists just as the door was closing, leaving her mother and brother gaping on the other side. The next time the door opened, Kirsty appeared and pronounced herself unimpressed by the interior. They wandered back to the hotel to get organized for the onward journey home. Despite her precocious age, the memories of that trip would always stay with Kirsty MacColl:

A holiday in Poland might sound a bit grim to the uninitiated, but it was idyllic. There were fir trees and fields of the most beautiful wild flowers, not to mention wild strawberries. It probably wasn't so carefree for my mother, as I had an asthma attack and cut my head open while we were there. The only downside of that holiday, from my point of view, was that we had to go by train, as my mother was terrified of flying. It took a long time in those days to get to Poland by rail.

Back in London, Kirsty's illness returned. She was in bed for weeks at a time, and a firm diagnosis seemed to be elusive. Eventually, Kirsty was taken to an allergy clinic and given a barrage of tests. The results were conclusive. On a test scale of one-to-five, she had a perfect score for allergies to cat fur, and four out of five for an allergic reaction to dog hair. Hamish's pet cat, Solomon, one of a succession in the household to bear the name, was an unwitting culprit, as were the Bidwells' kittens.

A family friend, Brian Nevill, recalls visiting Jean's house when she lived near to his mother in Selsdon on the outskirts of Croydon: "Kirsty had this collection of strange things, like stick insects and lizards. She had the weirdest collection of frightening creatures in glass cases. She loved animals, but couldn't have cats or dogs because of her asthma."

The MacColl house became home to an assortment of reptiles and insects – anything that didn't have fur. Her parents would be despatched to local pet shops to get food for the creatures, such as pots of maggots and tasty, tiny fish. When one pet shop assistant remarked to Ewan that his daughter must have a wonderful collection of fish after his regular weekly purchases, he told her that the fish were simply a snack for one of the menagerie. The woman refused to sell him any more.

Jean MacColl's pioneering work with movement and dance brought her to the attention of an association of parents with gifted children. They asked her to work with the children and, because Kirsty was still too young to attend school, she would go along with her mother to the classes. "One day I was encouraging the children to act out 'creepy-crawlies'," says Jean. "Kirsty was standing upright and said she was an elephant. I assumed that was because she'd like to have stamped on the other 'creepy-crawlies'!"

However, it was Jean's work with gifted children that eventually led her to recognize similar potential in her own daughter: "At that time, I didn't know Kirsty was gifted. I knew she was bright, but then so was Hamish. I learnt that if you don't recognize a gifted child and help them, because they do need help, then you will have problems later. There were kids there of 14 and 15 who definitely had problems."

When Kirsty was six and had started at school, Jean took her to a specialist in Cheltenham to have her IQ tested. After a difficult and time-consuming journey, they arrived late for their appointment. They ran from the car park to the specialist's office and by the time Kirsty got there, she was very tired and very breathless. But she still tested at a highly impressive 168. The specialist believed that her true IQ was probably somewhat higher, given the stress she was under and her tiredness.

Kirsty had shown early on that she had a huge appetite for knowledge and a quick intelligence. Jean used to read to her, then stop at the most exciting part and leave the book with her. She learned to read so she could find out what happened next. "Mum came home one day," says Hamish MacColl, "and found Kirsty reading a Penguin science book. I think it was called *Men and Women*. It was about sexuality. She could read and we didn't know she could read. It was quite bizarre."

In 1966, Jean and Kirsty were featured on a BBC television documentary, "The Problem with Gifted Children". In it, Jean described how Kirsty's reading and her arithmetic were very advanced for her age, in spite of the fact that she had hardly had any schooling because of her asthma. A professorial-looking man questioned Kirsty: "What about your other school, I'm told you didn't like that very much?" A wide-eyed, softly spoken Kirsty replied simply, "No." "Why not?" she was asked. Kirsty replied with a voice that was barely above a whisper: "They were rather strict and just horrible."

Kirsty's asthma had worsened to become a chronic condition, and forced her to miss weeks and then months of school. During her first two years of school, she could not attend for more than a handful of days each year. By her third year, this had increased to about five weeks. Jean made up for it by teaching her at home:

It was very sad, because she was a child who loved school and wanted to go. But the headmistress had a policy of sending the children outdoors, no matter what the weather. The head of the asthma clinic at Great Ormond Street Children's Hospital sent a letter saying Kirsty should not go out in all weathers, but they did send her out and she got pneumonia. I went to a parents' day and her teacher said, "Kirsty is always asking questions!" I said I thought that was a good thing, that she was showing an interest. Kirsty said to me later, "If the teacher would tell me exactly what she wants me to do I'd do it – but she just waffles."

Jean enrolled Kirsty in a school for sick and disabled children, feeling that the staff would be more understanding. The school had its own nurse, and there was a more sensitive environment, given the medical problems of many of the children. "The headmaster told me that he wished he could run the school the way that Kirsty had suggested – just when they get down to maths the bell goes and they have to stop, and if they could only do maths all day, they could really get things done! He said she was quite a character."

Kirsty's strength of character could not, however, make up for her physical frailty. Her appetite was poor, she began to lose weight and severe asthma attacks were becoming more frequent. During a school outing, the children were taken to see some horses and were allowed to pat them. Kirsty's exposure to the horse-hair triggered another bout of asthma, and hours later at home, as the child gasped for breath and vomited repeatedly, Jean called a doctor for an emergency house-call. He gave Kirsty an injection, and reassured her that she'd be feeling fine in the morning. But her condition worsened and Jean called an ambulance to take her daughter to Croydon Hospital. The waiting seemed interminable and finally it became clear that the ambulance was not on its way – it had been sent to the wrong address. Another ambulance was despatched and, safely in hospital, Kirsty weathered yet another health crisis.

This was one of countless stays in hospital. Ewan would often join Jean at Kirsty's bedside; his youngest child, Kitty, would also suffer from asthma throughout her childhood. Hamish, Jean and Ewan would try to keep Kirsty's spirits buoyant. Jean would create more chapters of their Horatio horse stories, and his adventures became especially enthralling when Kirsty most needed to be distracted – when she was feeling at her worst, or when, as once happened, they realized that she had overheard the family of the child in the hospital bed next to her being warned by the doctors to prepare themselves for the worst. Kirsty had heard every word, and couldn't escape wondering whether death would also be her fate.

Given Kirsty's later affinity for Cuba, it might have cheered her back then to know that Cuba's adopted son and revolutionary hero, Che Guevara, struggled with asthma throughout his life. Che's father, Ernesto, after whom he was named, wrote movingly of the perpetual anxiety of a parent listening to their child's painfully laboured breathing, fearing that with each severe asthma attack, the next gasp could be the last. "I never got used to hearing him breathe with that particular sound," he said. Che's asthma, too, had disrupted his own and his family's life. After being diagnosed at the age of two, the family tried to ease his suffering by moving from his birth-place near the Argentine capital of Buenos Aires to Alta Gracia, a spa town with a dry climate in the central highlands of Cordoba province.

Chronic asthma overshadowed Kirsty's childhood, dominating entirely the years that should have been her most carefree and energetic. But like so many children with severe health problems, she cultivated the life of the mind when her body let her down. Other artists have done likewise. Joni Mitchell, who survived polio as a child and spent a year recovering at home and learning to walk again, has said, "Polio probably did me good. Otherwise I would have been an athlete. I lost my running skills, but translated them into something less fast and more graceful; I became a dancer. I believe convalescence in bed develops a strong inner life in a young child. I think it solidified me as an independent thinker."

For the teenage Hamish, it was particularly painful to watch his sister battle illness and endure setbacks for years on end, and feel powerless to help her: "She had been in and out of oxygen tents and ill for a lot of the time … one of the effects that had on me was that I wanted her to be strong, I wanted her to survive. I loved my sister … but I would always be tough with her, not rude or nasty or anything like that but I wouldn't be terribly affectionate or give her the love that I felt like giving her, because I wanted her to be tough. I should have just been myself."

If Hamish's brusqueness hurt Kirsty, she didn't show it, and on some level may even have understood her brother's "tough love" approach. She soon found ways of responding in kind. "My sister used to tell me off for the way I treated my girlfriends," Hamish recalls. "She thought I was appalling in the way I treated some of them, which I probably was."

By the time Kirsty was nine, she was dividing her schooling between being part-time at the local primary school and part-time at the school for sick children. For an entire year she had weekly injections to try to control her asthma and the extreme allergic reactions that could be brought on by touching animals or being stung by a wasp or bee. When she did go back to full-time school, she excelled. In her first major report, she was marked "Excellent" for science. Jean recalls, "I said, 'That's very good, Kirsty.' She just said, 'You know and I know, it doesn't mean a thing.' We'd gone out and bought O-level science books, and even though she wasn't at that level, she could read and she could follow things and get what she wanted out of them."

Kirsty loved schoolwork and threw herself into her studies, but was often frustrated at the lack of scope: "I wanted to be inventive and experimental. At school, I asked to study subjects like science, metalwork and chemistry as well as the arts, but the powers that be channeled you into one area and it was all very limiting." Unusually, she had parental approval for an attitude that many teachers might have found challenging. "The teachers wanted her to specialize," says Jean MacColl. "I realized that she might be being channeled one way or the other at school and I said, 'Keep your options open; if you have a real interest in something, keep it alive.' I knew I had a very talented young daughter."

To encourage Kirsty, Jean would often cite the example of Albert Schweitzer. The German theologian, musician, doctor, missionary and Nobel Peace Prize winner had decided at an early age that he would devote the first thirty years of his life to learning and music, and the rest to the service of others. "I would tell her that Schweitzer had two talents," says Jean, "and he used them both. He was in Africa looking after people and then, when he ran out of money, he would go on tour around the world playing concerts to raise money, and then he'd go back to Africa. I said, 'That's a wonderful life. You can do anything you want to do in life. If you want to do it, you'll go for it.'"

Jean's mother, Norrie, by then widowed, had moved to London when Kirsty was four. Her arrival, and Jean's enduring friendship with Joan Littlewood, had helped to create a sense of an extended family for Kirsty and Hamish. Littlewood, their godmother, and her partner, Gerry Raffles, doted on Hamish and Kirsty. They saw them every week for years, and thought nothing of taking them everywhere, from walks in the park to boating holidays, posh London restaurants to West End members' clubs. "We used to go out on her boat with Gerry," says Hamish MacColl, "or I'd go to the theatre and hang out with Joan. And in the evening, we'd go out and have a meal, or we'd go to a club. She was very, very important in our lives."

Littlewood was such a natural with the children that she showed that particular gift to embarrass them that youngsters usually associate only with their parents. "I went to the Tate Gallery with her once," says Hamish, "to an exhibition of mobiles by an artist that she knew. There were signs everywhere saying 'Do Not Touch'." Littlewood, of course, ignored them all and encouraged Hamish to enjoy the tactile experience of the tantalizing installations.

"I spent a lot of the time, when I was with Joan, feeling very embarrassed," he says. "It was the same with my dad. He'd take me to Croydon to buy shoes, and he'd sing at the top of his voice walking down the street. I was ten years old and I would be so embarrassed." Ewan, for his part, found this highly amusing: "I think part of it was the fact that he could wind me up so much," Hamish concludes.

In her autobiography, Joan Littlewood recalled one of many visits by Hamish and Kirsty to the home she shared with Gerry in Blackheath, south-east London. With the couple's friend, John Bury (known as Camel), they'd taken the children out to play in the snow in nearby Greenwich Park: "When we arrived at the hilltop where Greenwich Observatory stands, we found Gerry and Hamish taking turns to toboggan down the steep slope which leads to the Queen's House. I don't know which of them was enjoying it most. Camel asked Kirsty if she'd like to look in at the banqueting hall. Kirsty replied, 'Yes, it's too cold to be standing about'."

While Gerry and her brother careered down the snow-covered slopes, Kirsty, Joan and Camel wandered into the magnificent Painted Hall of the Royal Naval College. The grand hall was decorated with lighted candles in branched candlesticks. Camel told Kirsty: "I used to eat here every day when I was in the Navy." Kirsty exclaimed, "I can still smell the onion soup!" The child gazed up in awe at the far less prosaic baroque ceiling, decorated with James Thornhill's allegorical paintings and *trompe l'oeil* fluted pilasters. Littlewood mused later, "Walking home quietly, across the snow-covered park, I felt at peace with the world …"

Years later, while in his early twenties, Hamish was living with Joan and Gerry and helping Joan with a charity project she'd launched – a children's theatre group. Gerry had gone to the south of France, where his boat was moored and, in his absence, Joan was doing last-minute preparations for his forthcoming birthday celebrations. Hamish was studying martial arts and Chinese philosophy and had been learning about the I Ching, the ancient system of divination. "Joan was worried about Gerry's birthday," says Hamish, "and what she was going to do for his birthday. She was renting a marquee. We looked up the I Ching and it said 'danger' or 'death'. I'd never seen that in the I Ching before. Gerry went into a diabetic coma and died on his boat."

Ewan had long since broken with Theatre Workshop, and Jean was devoting her time to teaching and to her daughter. Kirsty became the focus of her energies. A treasured and indulged child, she had the benefit of her mother's full attention. When Hamish was a young child, his parents had often been away for long periods – his father with Theatre Workshop and his mother either with the theatre company or her own dance troupe. But on Kirsty's birth, Jean was happy to relegate the demands of the theatre and the dance world. The mother's hopes and fears, ambitions and anxieties were visited upon the child whose conception and birth had failed to save her marriage. Mother and daughter formed a tight little family unit, with just the two of them at home together for much of Kirsty's childhood and teenage years.

Given the nine-year age difference with Hamish, Kirsty was like an only child at home with her mother in Selsdon. "They lived in a very open-plan house," says Steve Lillywhite, who married Kirsty in 1984, "and I remember Kirsty not liking that. When we moved into our house in Ealing, she loved having closing doors. Her childhood had been very open-plan and when she got the chance to be private, she loved that."

Kirsty absorbed much of her mother's unhappiness and disappointment over the split from Ewan. The child also struggled with being loyal to her mother, and mindful of the constant presence of the pain Ewan had caused, while simultaneously loving her father and wanting him to be a part of her life. Kirsty would come to feel acutely the weight of her mother's expectations on her, and as a teenager, with a strong personality the equal of her mother's, wrestled intermittently with their loving but occasionally claustrophobic relationship. Her childhood was in some ways very lonely, says Steve Lillywhite:

There was this overbearing power of her mother, and this father who was promising everything and never delivering anything. I remember Kirsty saying he was always sending postcards from wonderful exotic places, and writing, "I'm doing this, I'm doing that". It was never, "What are you doing?" He was never really that interested. He just imparted his great wisdom on to her. For the great man of the people that he was, he was only comfortable in the company of people who knew who he was.

Childhood, Kirsty MacColl, would later say, "was just something I had to get over in order to get on with my life."

Ewan remained a regular visitor and a part of family life but his growing success, his tours and the media attention seemed a world away from the struggles that Jean felt she and the children had with money, with Kirsty's asthma, and with the logistics of day-to-day life in a single-parent family. Family holidays had normally been spent at the British seaside, or with Joan Littlewood and Gerry Raffles on their boat. When Kirsty was seven, she went to Ireland for the first time, travelling with her mother and grandmother, Norrie, who was then 70. Within two years, Norrie died, so the memories of those times shared by the three generations became very precious. However, memories of Kirsty's second trip, at the age of nine, were less rosy.

While in County Kerry, Kirsty became seriously ill with pleurisy. They were a long way from a hospital so a local country doctor was called. He gave Jean a vial of white powder, telling her to mix it with water and give it to Kirsty. He added bluntly, "Then she's in the hands of the angels." Whatever it was, it worked. The symptoms eased, and while still confined to bed, Kirsty became well enough to feel bored with her books and comics. Jean set off for the nearest village to find a diversion and came back with an alto melodeon. It was an instant hit, including with the other guests in the country inn where they were staying, who soon came to know the shy, musically gifted English child.

When she was around 16, Kirsty went on holiday to France with Ewan, Peggy and their children. "I didn't really get to know her until

23

Ewan and I took Neill and Calum and Kirsty to France," says Seeger. "That was very interesting, because that was the first time that I'd spent any time with her. She had a wonderful wit, very, very quick, and she was very kind to me. We weren't close, we didn't have any heart-to-hearts, but there was no sniping or anything like that that one might expect from a stepchild. She always got on very well with the boys."

Soon it was Kirsty's love of music that provided a balm, a means of both escape and self-expression, and a distraction from the severe asthma attacks: "Music was a kind of release that you could get lost in and it saved me from the outside world. It was the only thing that lifted my spirits." She adopted Hamish's musical tastes: at nine years her elder, he encouraged her to think beyond children's nursery rhymes and nonsense songs. She heard the Beach Boys sing "Good Vibrations" and listened to the Beatles and Phil Spector's iconic Wall of Sound productions. At the age of five, she played those songs over and over again, and was thrilled to be given a fifteen-shilling record token for Christmas. When she was too ill to go to the record store to spend it, Hamish went for her and came back with "Keep on Running" by the Spencer Davis Group, and the Beatles' "Day Tripper".

Kirsty's musical tastes extended from the Beach Boys to Frank Zappa (whom she would eventually meet, at a punk gig in London in the late seventies), to West End and Broadway musicals. They also included playing the lead role in her school's production of *Oh, What a Lovely War!* which had first been produced by the theatre company formed by Ewan and Joan Littlewood. Kirsty further fell in love with the Bernstein and Sondheim musical *West Side Story*, the stylized reworking of *Romeo and Juliet* as a tale of the young street gangs of New York, using contemporary music, dance and narrative in a way that had seldom been done in film musicals before its release in 1961. Kirsty dreamed of being like Rita Moreno's character, Anita – street-smart, brave and unutterably cool – rather than Natalie Wood's doomed Maria. The music that accompanies this story of late fifties Capulets and Montagues – the Jets and the Sharks gangs – had a heavy Latin influence, reflecting the Puerto Rican background of the Sharks and this too appealed to Kirsty.

A Mexican mariachi record she heard at home and played relentlessly also sowed the seeds of what would – three decades later – become an abiding passion for Latin music: "I just thought, 'Wow, isn't it fantastic?' It sounds like they're about to gallop off on their horses every three minutes. That's when I realized that people who speak Spanish have a better time than we do!"

Having fallen in love with the music, Kirsty longed to duplicate those sounds herself – and discovered a natural talent. At primary school, she played violin in the school orchestra and, at home, would perfect her skills by standing in front of the television, watching "The Andy Williams Show" and playing along with each song. Ewan paid for Kirsty and his son Neill to have guitar lessons with a professional teacher named Mr High. Over ten years of lessons, Kirsty and her tutor entered several competitions as a duo, and frequently won. She took up the oboe at high school, and loved that too. "It didn't seem, when she was young, that music was any more of a gift than her other gifts," says Jean. "She was always very good at drawing, she was very good at reading and writing, and she could do art. I helped her pursue everything."

Kirsty's relationship with her father's brand of music, however, was more ambivalent.

"I wasn't really into folk music," she was to say. "'It wasn't particularly because I had anything to prove against my dad. I was a different generation; I grew up listening to Radio One. My dad hated pop music with a vengeance. He just couldn't tolerate it, he was very intolerant of anything that wasn't his thing."

Indeed, Ewan MacColl derided the pop and rock marketplace, believing it was the antithesis of the authenticity and originality to be found in folk. In his autobiography, he raged against the mainstream music machine: "There were new prophets now like Mick Jagger and Jimi Hendrix, young Turks in revolt against ... what? Melody, perhaps? Audibility ? Coherence ? Shirts with buttons?" He was equally scathing about the political apathy of the musicians creating much of this music: "As for the much-publicized road to revolt, it led directly to the multinational, multi-billion-dollar music industry, while that other mystical revolutionary highway petered out in the desert of the CIA and army-sponsored drug culture."

Peggy Seeger explains that Ewan "assumed that most people who went into pop music were not interested in politics, which was daffy, because he knew perfectly well that some of them were. But the big problem was that he just could not understand the words of many pop songs. People of our generation couldn't. So that made him not listen to pop music as a rule."

Ewan's lack of interest in "modern" music was such that he very visibly fell asleep at Elvis Costello's debut public performance. Costello, who later went on to produce the Pogues' second album, *Rum, Sodomy and the Lash*, as well as carve out his own stellar path, recalled in an interview in 1989, shortly before Ewan died, "The ironic thing about ending up producing the Pogues is that for a long time I hated traditional music because I had to suffer the narrow-minded attitudes in the folk clubs, the woolly-jumper folk ... And Ewan MacColl fell asleep in the front row ... I imagine he's not the kind of guy who would be appreciative of the Pogues' rendition of 'Dirty Old Town'. But I'm sure he'd like the money."

Hamish MacColl recalls once answering the phone at home and being stunned to hear a voice he'd only ever heard singing some of the best-known songs of the sixties.

It was Bob Dylan, wanting to speak to my dad. But my dad hated Bob Dylan, he hated the Beatles, so he answered the phone and spoke to him in this snotty voice and basically told him to fuck off – although not in those exact words! He had a big chip on his shoulder. My dad would have been the best capitalist in the world; he would have out-Rupert Murdoch-ed Rupert Murdoch, because he was very competitive. He didn't like the fact that the Beatles were instantly famous when he'd worked at it all his life.

In Ewan's mind, says Hamish, there were only three kinds of authentic music that were worthy of his approval: "Classical music, traditional folk music and jazz. That was it. Everything else was rubbish as far as he was concerned. That didn't sit too well with either me or Kirsty, because we were both quite into the charts and pop music."

Kirsty's frustration with her father's intolerance of the music that she and her brother loved was considerable: "We were completely different generations. My dad was quite old when I was born, and I just thought his outlook on what was valid and what was not was rather narrow-minded. It just seemed to be dated and slightly hypocritical. There were other things about pop music, and you can have a message, but ultimately a good pop single transcends all that and that's why it's popular among millions of people, because it's not preaching; it's uplifting."

Hamish had been his father's young engineering assistant when friends and folk cohorts like Bert Lloyd, Isla Cameron, John Cole and Ralph Rinzler would cram into the kitchen of their flat for recording sessions around a single microphone. Ewan had hated his experience of recording in the huge, impersonal studios of HMV in 1950, so later determined to record at home whenever possible. He writes touchingly in his autobiography of one such home recording session with Bert Lloyd, when Hamish was just five or six and already highly competent at the controls: "He also recorded our next project, a five-album set of Professor Francis James Child's *Popular Ballads of England and Scotland*. I can still hear that small, commanding voice shouting, 'Three, two, one, go!' and can still picture the lovely, curly head poised intently, as he turns the cumbersome dials on the elephantine old Ferrograph."

What Ewan never knew about one of those sessions with the old Ferrograph was that his beloved first-born almost didn't make it to the end of the recording. "There was one thing Dad didn't notice," says Hamish, "because he was crap at DIY and things like that. Typically, he had joined the flex of the Ferrograph to the flex of something else with some insulation tape, and I remember putting my hand on it during a recording and going rigid because I was getting an electric shock. I couldn't move and I couldn't tell anyone and I had to wait until the recording stopped and they switched it off."

Hamish's emotional relationship with his father had been grounded in nine years as a family by the time Kirsty was born. His early exposure to Ewan's music and the closeness that sharing those early recording sessions helped to cement between them engendered a different view of the music the two siblings would later create themselves. "It was impossibly difficult," says Hamish:

I must have been 35 before I wrote a song that I was actually happy with, because every time I heard it, I was listening to it through his ears. Kirsty had already written Dad out of the picture by saying, "Well, he's a man, he's messed my mum around," so she did her own thing, she was quite happy making her own decisions on what she liked and what she didn't like. One of the reasons that Kirsty got away with it, and I didn't, was that I remember going to a concert once and Dad was singing and I cried my eyes out, and I remember thinking that this isn't right because you can make all of these people cry in the audience, even if they disagree with you, even if they think what you're saying is crap, you can manipulate and push people's buttons so well, that you can make them all cry.

I became highly suspicious of words and people's ability to manipulate them, and as a consequence I never wanted to write any songs with words. I was just interested in writing music. Kirsty didn't have that kind of close

27

relationship with Dad at an early stage, so she never had that problem. She
was able to write words very well without any hang-ups.

Kirsty's relationship with her father inevitably coloured her view of his
music and it provoked a powerful reaction in her. In her mind, his music
became inextricably associated with his "other" life, and his betrayal of
her mother. "My dad would bring his records over and leave them," said
Kirsty, 'but I found it very hard to listen to his work. It was too painful."

Given time, however, she developed a quiet pride in Ewan's achievements. This surfaced in an unlikely way on a school day-trip to France.
The sight of a gold-coloured Rolls Royce at the ferry terminal enthralled
Kirsty and her friends, who rushed up to the man behind the wheel and
demanded to know who he was. He told them his name was Jimmy
Webb and that he was an American songwriter. Kirsty was thrilled
because she'd heard many of the songs that had made Webb one of the
most successful songwriters of the sixties and seventies.

By 1970, Glen Campbell alone had had five Webb compositions in the
US Top 30 charts: "By the Time I Get to Phoenix", "Wichita Lineman",
"Galveston", "Where's the Playground, Susie?" and "Honey, Come
Back". Emboldened by her knowledge of his music and her father's own
not-inconsiderable reputation, a normally shy Kirsty approached Webb
and said, "My dad's a songwriter too. He wrote 'The First Time Ever I
Saw Your Face.' " "And Jimmy Webb looked at me," Kirsty was to relate,
"as if to say, 'You sad child, what a terrible lie!' "

Bright at school and passionate about music at home, Kirsty was
offered a scholarship to attend the prestigious Millfield public school in
Somerset. However, her mother refused to let her accept it, feeling that
the recurring asthma ruled out a move so far from home. Instead, she
attended the local high school, Monks Hill Comprehensive, which was
later re-named Selsdon High School.

It was there that Kirsty honed her acoustic and electric guitar skills in
after-school lessons, first picking up a guitar at the age of 13 to play
along with Neil Young's classic album, *Harvest*: "I always wanted to be
a guitar hero when I was a kid: I wanted to be *that man on stage*. I never
thought of myself as a girl." For years, Kirsty was to prefer music and
guitars to boys. The other girls were dismissive: "They thought I was a
little crazy, but it didn't bother me that I was always out on a limb."

One teacher, Chris Couchman, who gave her guitar lessons, recalls
Kirsty as "a lovely person, and it was clear that she would be successful.

She was involved in all kinds of drama and had an incredible sparkle."
Another teacher, Brenda Kidd, described Kirsty as "bubbly and quite
cheeky. I remember her sneaking off PE one afternoon to go and see the
rock band Emerson, Lake and Palmer. I said to her, 'How will that help
with your future career?' I had to eat my words later."

Kirsty MacColl's hometown was hardly the pulsating rock and roll
heart of London, but it did have an historic past. In Saxon times,
Croydon had been a market town, and became an influential medieval
trading post and a home for various Archbishops of Canterbury. It had
been a London borough since 1883, the site of London's first airport in
1915 and, in the sixties, the concrete-clad centre of south-east England's
financial and insurance services. Hundreds of thousands of non-Brits
know nothing more of Croydon than the often chaotic scenes and inex-
orable waiting-times they will have experienced at the high-rise
building known as Lunar House, the central base of the Immigration
and Nationality Directorate of the Home Office.

But Croydon does have a grudging rock and pop heritage. Local
musical luminaries include Status Quo's Francis Rossi, folkie Ralph
McTell, Procul Harum's Matthew Fisher and Peter Sarstedt. Captain
Sensible and Rat Scabies of the Damned had as teenagers worked as
cleaners in the suburb's entertainment centre, Fairfield Halls, longing
each week for that perfect band audition advertisement to appear in
Melody Maker. When it did, the Damned were born.

As Sensible and Scabies auditioned prospective band members, they
demanded answers to a series of questions: "Are you the greatest
guitarist in the world?" If the answer was a humble "No", the person
was dismissed immediately. If someone answered in the affirmative,
they'd then be asked, "Do you like Eric Clapton?" The rock answer,
which would have been greeted with contempt, was "Yes". The required
punk answer was a thundering "No!"

The auditions descended into gladiatorial-style psychology tests,
with prospective band members enduring the sight of various Damned
musicians stripping naked and hurling gobs of spittle over those audi-
tioning. But one guitarist stood out, as Captain Sensible recalls: "This
one guy was really grooving to it. He was shrieking with laughter while
he was playing, doing this tricky routine while we were naked and
gobbing at him. We said, 'That was marvellous. We'll definitely put you
on the short-list.' Then we said, 'We've gotta get that lunatic back'."

Thus a nascent guitarist and songwriter by the name of Robert

Edmonds came to be known as Lu (short for lunatic). When Lu later met Kirsty, he saw how her Croydon background had emphasized a kind of Englishness that was beyond him. Growing up in Venezuela, where his father was stationed as a British military officer, there was a huge gap in his knowledge of the kind of cultural references in which MacColl was steeped:

> I'd always thought I was British but, meeting Kirsty, I realized I wasn't. *She* was British, but I wasn't. I suddenly realized what I had missed, and how culturally hip she was. She always said, "I've got a degree from the University of Croydon." I'd say, "But Kirsty, there *is* no university there." "Yeah," she'd say, "that's what I mean." She totally had her shit together. She knew all that stuff, all the cultural references, all of the films, the cartoons and the jokes. She'd listened to loads of records. If you're going to write a song you have to be tuned into that: what's next, and what is going to work, and what's going to resonate with people. She knew what was what, and that came down to music and being young in London. I was just clueless; I knew nothing. Kirsty never suffered from that; she was really part of that south London scene.

Kirsty MacColl may have grown up in Croydon, but after she left, she felt no pang of homesickness or nostalgic longing for the place. When a magazine once asked her to list things and places she loved and hated, she placed Croydon on the second list: " ... because I was born there. I never go back."

CHAPTER THREE

You Just Haven't Earned it Yet, Baby

Kirsty left high school in 1976 and as a concession to her parents – both of whom wanted her to go to university – she enrolled at Croydon School of Art. It was to prove a short-lived foray into the visual arts. Six months later she dropped out, disillusioned that the freedom of art school had not dispelled the frustrations of feeling institutionalized, frustrations that had dogged her through her school years. She also believed the course was a waste of time: "Most other people at art college were only there because their parents expected them to do something, and art college is an easy way out – easier than finding a job or applying yourself to a project. When I realized I was there for the same reason, it seemed dishonest and I left."

During a time that she was later to describe as "waiting for my life to happen", MacColl interspersed periods on unemployment benefit with a series of temporary jobs. But cleaning, working in the mail order department of Bonaparte Records and washing dishes for the recipe-tasters on a women's magazine proved hardly more challenging than art school lectures. The latter task, though, had one compensation: "You got to eat everything they'd made and they were all cordon bleu cooks, so it was really good ... unless they were doing One Thousand Things To Do With Peas". She also played a lot of snooker, deciding that "pool halls are the unemployed's equivalent of a men's club."

But it was MacColl's musical frustrations that drew her away from art classes, dead-end jobs and the pool hall, and she soon found the outlet for all that fizzing creative energy. It was her brother Hamish's friend, musician Brian Nevill, who got her interested in working with a band when they first met in 1976. "I got her to come up to a rehearsal of my band, the Tooting Frootis, who were quite well-known around London on the live circuit," he says:

> Two years later that band morphed into the Drug Addix, her first band. The first incarnation, the Tooting Frootis, was a kind of rock 'n' roll, rockabilly, and country good-time sort of band. We used to rehearse in the basement of a record shop in Camden. There were three other guys in the band, they were all new to her but two of them came from the general Croydon area. Kirsty had brought her guitar and she really had a lot of spunk, she wasn't overly shy; her attitude was, "Okay, I'm here, let's do something". She did a version of "You Send Me", the Sam Cooke song, but I think she got her version from Steve Miller. We didn't do it as a band but the band knew it; we went from the beginning to the end of that song with her playing electric guitar and singing that one arrangement while everyone else played the other one. We couldn't budge her from it!

The Tooting Frootis broke up later that year. Kirsty had realized that the classical guitar style she'd learned at school wasn't going to be much use in a rock band, so she started taking lessons from the group's guitarists, Noel Brown and later, George Lloyd. Brown, Lloyd and a local singer, Rick Smith, decided to revive the band, whose name had been derived from the south London suburb of Tooting and an excruciating pun on the Little Richard classic, but within nine months that line-up too had been abandoned. It made way for a new incarnation of the group around a nucleus of George Lloyd, Rick Smith and Kirsty MacColl, who adopted the *nom de punk* of Mandy Doubt. They took the comedic element of what the Tooting Frootis had been doing and called themselves the Drug Addix.

This name was arguably the most punk rock thing about the band; their influences were more rhythm 'n' blues and pub rock than two-chord thrash. The Addix would rehearse for free in a room in the Swan and Sugarloaf pub in Croydon, alongside Brian Nevill's new band. "Kirsty's humour was a big part of the Drug Addix," he says. "We'd go and see the band around London when they were gigging in pubs. Considering Kirsty's later well-known stage fright, at the beginning you'd never have known it was there. She just didn't have it then."

U2 frontman Bono saw the Drug Addix at a rare appearance out of London when they played a tiny Dublin club, McGonagle's. He was 16, and not unimpressed by the punky demeanour of the band's striking backing singer. "I didn't know Kirsty was that person until years later," he says. "We just used to go to every gig at McGonagle's. There might have been some alcohol involved. I think we might also have tried to chat her up."

Kirsty and Rick Smith had by now begun a relationship and were living together in a flat in the south London suburb of Thornton Heath. The Drug Addix's musical career was launched on the same day as that of Billy Bragg. Bragg was a working-class, east London lad who would later become the Renaissance Man of contemporary British singer-song-writers, lauded as the Ewan MacColl/Woody Guthrie of his generation, who combined a social conscience, political activism and a refreshingly kick-ass philosophical take on British cultural life.

In June 1978, a small London-based record label, Chiswick Records, simultaneously released three EPs as part of a set called *Suburban Rock 'n' Roll*. The Drug Addix, who Bragg would later describe as Croydon's answer to the Velvet Underground, released "The Drug Addix Make a Record". It featured Rick Smith's self-consciously provocative parody of Lou Reed-style seedy urban reportage, "Gay Boys in Bondage", along with "Addington Shuffle" (named after New Addington, a suburb just a tram-ride away from Croydon), "Special Clinic" (the euphemism for hospital clinics treating sexually-transmitted diseases) and "Glutton for Punishment". Bragg's band, Riff Raff, had recorded "Cosmonaut" and the third band, the short-lived the Jook, released their eponymous EP. Each single was issued in a limited edition of 4,000.

The Drug Addix EP captured the attention of Stiff Records, the visionary indie label that grew out of the mid-seventies British pub rock scene to become pioneers of punk, new wave and anarchic pop. Stiff paid for the band to record some demos. However, the label founders, Dave Robinson (who had managed Ian Dury, Graham Parker and Brinsley Schwarz) and Jake Riviera (the former tour manager for Dr Feelgood) were unimpressed with everything but the girl. "There was a great irony there," says Brian Nevill. "The guys in Drug Addix were real lads, and she was just seen as the 'chick' in the band and the girlfriend of one of the guys." At 18, Kirsty had the perfect mix of street attitude and personal style, with smudged-black raccoon eyes, short skirts and leather jackets covered in agit-prop badges.

"She fitted perfectly," says Dave Robinson. "We didn't have any girls who wrote and had her kind of attitude, which was fairly in-your-face.

She wasn't sweet. She wanted to interview the record company. She'd obviously come with an attitude. She wasn't just sitting there, saying, 'How wonderful to get a record contract'." Instead, Kirsty MacColl signed to Stiff Records, having bluffed them into thinking that she had a huge back catalogue of her own songs to offer them:

> I left the band just because it wasn't any good. It was pretty awful! And I was the token girl. After I left, Stiff Records called and said, "We'd like you to come and play us anything you've got." I said, "I thought you didn't like the demos," and they said, "We hate the band but we quite like you!" When they asked if I had any songs, I said, "Oh yeah, loads!" even though I hadn't at all. Then I thought, "Oh God, I'd better write something before I go in to see them."

MacColl hastily finished her tale of teen love-angst, "They Don't Know", which she recorded in Stiff's mobile studio. Lu Edmonds, by then a member of fellow Stiff signings the Damned, played on the record. He recalls: "She turned up, very nervous and pulled out a guitar. With her very, very long nails on her left hand, she played, 'They Don't Know' very accurately, trying to stop her fingernails from breaking. We'd gone through the second take, and we got to a point where I got completely confused, I didn't know what was going to happen next so I just launched into this solo which stuck. We did the take and everyone went, 'That's great!' but the song wasn't quite finished so Kirsty had to whistle the end. That's another skill that Kirsty had that many people don't know about."

On its release in June 1979, "They Don't Know" became Kirsty MacColl's debut single on Stiff. The edgier, self-penned B-side was "Turn My Motor On", which had been a staple of the Addix's live sets. Billy Bragg was among the first fans of the new discovery: "I admired her ability to sound like the Shangri-Las. As a singer, she was a one-woman girl group, with one of the most distinctive voices I had ever heard, and in a previous era would have made a tidy living writing songs for Phil Spector's Motown artists."

Philip Chevron, the guitarist with the Pogues, was equally impressed: "The exact moment I fell in love with Kirsty MacColl was just 113 seconds into first hearing that record on the radio, when she sang, 'BAAY-BEEEY!!' It was a moment so perfect that when Tracey Ullman covered the song, four years later, she didn't try to compete with it. She simply had Kirsty do it again." Only Kirsty's older brother, Hamish, was left cold by the song: "When 'They Don't Know' came out, I didn't like it at all. I was horrible to Kirsty because I thought it sounded like Twinkle – and she thought that was a compliment!"

The song arrived at the start of a summer that many had longed for. The UK's winter of discontent of 1978–79 had been marked by industrial disputes, food shortages and power cuts, with unemployment rising to levels not seen since the thirties. There was a growing disenchantment with the policies of the Labour government; among these policies were the much-derided Youth Opportunities Programmes, designed as short courses for teaching rudimentary skills to the burgeoning numbers of unemployed young people. The programmes were eventually abandoned after persistent criticism that they were no more than ineffective stopgap devices, primarily aimed at appearing to reduce the unemployment statistics. The winter of discontent brought the minority Labour government of James Callaghan crashing to its knees and on May 4, 1979, Margaret Thatcher swept into the prime ministerial residence in Downing Street. Her Conservative Party had a majority of 43 seats.

This was the social and political climate that fueled the early punk sensibility of Stiff and now, in Kirsty MacColl, the label had an offshoot that raged not at the machine or the forces of global capitalism, but at grown-ups who didn't understand the intensity of teen love. The reviews of "They Don't Know" were excellent: on British pop radio, only the stalwarts of the mainstream, Abba with "Does Your Mother Know?" and Paul McCartney and Wings with "Old Siam Sir" were receiving more airplay.

However, the curse of bad timing that was to dog MacColl's musical career took effect from the outset. A strike by independent distributors meant that, despite all of this attention, it was impossible to get copies of the single out of the warehouse and into the shops. "They couldn't sell any records, so it never got into the charts," says Lu Edmonds. "Imagine what would have happened if it had got out. It would have been a hit, and Kirsty would have got there three or four years earlier with her own song, on very much her own basis."

Interviewed by a music journalist on the single's release, MacColl was remarkably self-possessed: "I've had pretty good publicity so far, but the papers tend to play cat-and-mouse. The old build 'em up, knock 'em down routine, of which I hope I'm not a part. If this one's a hit, they'll probably slag off the next one. They might like it for different reasons, I don't know." During the interview, conducted in her lunch break from a short-lived job at the Croydon office of *Exchange & Mart* magazine, she shrugged off suggestions that one so young could easily be manipulated: "I'd like to reserve the right of some artistic say. It's important to be commercial, but it's more important at the business end. This sounds a bit of a cliché, but I think integrity is important."

MacColl was determined not to be typecast by either her father's musical legacy, which was already being mentioned in interviews, or the sound of her single. She ringingly declared: "I like lots of different styles. As time goes on I might establish one particular style, but at the moment I just want to try everything. I like Steely Dan, the Beach Boys, the Ramones, the Band, the Kinks and I'm mad on Linton Kwesi Johnson. And I like a lot of sixties music and fifties doowop."

It wasn't surprising that Ewan's considerable shadow was already falling over his daughter's fledgling musical career. Years later, Kirsty was to muse:

> I was very naïve when I started. When I had my first single out in 1979, the record company wrote a press release without telling me. The first time I did an interview somebody asked me about my dad, and I said, "How do you know who my father is?" They said, "It's in your press release". The record company had obviously thought, "Let's angle it as, 'It's in the genes, it's genetic music'", which is just a real insult. I wrote a teen ballad: I was a teenager at the time, so that's what I did. What did *that* have to do with my parents?

MacColl also felt a measure of discomfort at the expectations that seemed to surround her as the musician offspring of a famous musical parent. "My father was very well-known to the older generation," she would later say, "and there was a presumption among people that I would be singing folk and doing his songs. I was very much determined to do my own songs, the way I wanted to do them."

Lu Edmonds remembers Kirsty's idiosyncratic mix of confidence and reserve. "She was very determined," he says. "She knew what she wanted and she had ideas about how to get it. She was very good at motivating people and getting them involved. She did this incredible bit of networking, where she'd go and see people and convince them to come down and play for her. It wasn't like she found this band and that was *her* band. She was always trying to find new people to work with. But she was shy, not arrogant. It wasn't that sort of confidence."

Stiff appeared the perfect home for Kirsty. Robinson and Riviera had started the label despising the corporate politics, entrenched old-school attitudes and vacuous vanity projects that they saw in much of the established music scene of the time, which was dominated by giant labels throwing vast amounts of money at Californian soft-rock bands like the Eagles, or the cash cows of British and European pop such as Rod Stewart and Abba. Robinson and Riviera had a mission to revolutionize the industry, or at least the small part of its territory that they could colonize and claim as their own independent homeland.

Robinson recalls, "I thought the record companies were very amateurish, and there seemed to be a cartel that said, 'This is the music you'll have because this is the music we've invested in.' Jake and I had the same kind of attitude: we had something good here, and we needed to tell the world. We also thought if you had a good songwriter and he or she could sing their songs, you were ahead of the game."

Stiff shunned the conventional industry philosophy and subverted the accepted orthodoxy of finding a formula and recycling it ruthlessly. They favoured eclecticism over relentless repetition. The only rule was that there were no rules; their promotional t-shirts famously bore the legend "If it ain't Stiff, it ain't worth a fuck". There again, their other tongue-in-cheek motto was "If they're dead, we'll sign 'em".

The label had originally been launched in punk's long hot summer of 1976, financed by a £400 loan from Dr Feelgood's singer, Lee Brilleaux. The recording budget for the label's first single, Nick Lowe's "So It Goes" b/w "Heart of the City", was a paltry £45. Yet that absurdly modest investment in music history had paid dividends beyond all expectations. While the mainstream industry scoffed at the presumption of the upstarts, Robinson, Riviera and their friends were trying to keep up with the demand for Lowe's single.

The artwork and packaging of that first single set Stiff apart from much of the staid output of the huge art departments in the major labels, and made the Stiff visuals an integral part of the experience. The black carrier bag bore the slogans "If it means everything to everyone … it must be a Stiff" and "Today's Sound Today". Etched into the vinyl itself were not-so-hidden messages: "Mono-enhanced STEREO, play loud", "The world's most flexible record label", "Three Chord Trick, Yeh" and "Earthlings Awake".

Robinson and Riviera soon had their choice of any pub rock band, r&b outfit or pop wannabe that had ever been laughed out of a major label's office. Demos that had been thrown away unheard or played to derisive laughter flooded into Stiff's chaotic ground-floor premises. Nick Lowe was to describe the hordes passing through Stiff's doorway: "Almost any nutcase who had a bit of front would get a try-out at one time from Stiff, until it got completely out of hand. But for a while they were the best people around, those people that none of the other record labels would touch. They had genuine front, which used to scare proper sensible record companies."

One man with unimpeachable "genuine front" was the self-styled Cockney with the bravado of a music-hall maestro and the mind of a funked-up punk, Ian Dury. His own experience with major labels – they had simply ignored him – informed his tribute to the company that released his *New Boots and Panties* album in 1977: "Stiff was aimed at people whose arses were hanging out in the industry and couldn't get a look in," he said. "We were the unemployables really. We didn't fit into any of their stupid categories, since the record industry is run by shoe salesmen and drug dealers. We took *New Boots and Panties* to every single label, but they were just fucking stupid."

Robinson and Riviera had signed some of the most singular talents on the emerging music scene, among them Dury, Elvis Costello, Wreckless Eric and the Damned, who were the first British punk band to tour the United States. In 1979, the year that Stiff released Kirsty MacColl's first single, they also signed the north London-based ska band, Madness, who were to become one of the top-selling groups of the eighties. Nick Lowe had become Stiff's resident producer, along with Liam Sternberg, and they promoted the label mantra that the record company and the artists were partners, rather than parties in a conventional power-based employer/worker relationship.

"When Stiff Records was going," says Lowe, "I was a little bit older than most of the punk groups, and I became a producer because I was slightly more experienced and could help some of these groups make credible records. Punk was not a musical thing necessarily. It was more of an attitude thing, but I liked the attitude. I got to work with some really good people – and some terrible ones as well – and it all seemed totally natural, as if our time had come. Practically everything I did, or I was producing, or that my friends did, was a hit. We took it almost for granted. We actually thought something was a flop if it didn't get into the Top 20."

Stiff seemed unstoppable, even after the departure of Lowe, Riviera, and Costello in 1977 to the Radar label. Sex and drugs and rock 'n' roll, or at least Ian Dury's anthemic single of the same name, had revitalised Stiff and started a run of chart acts that would also include Madness, Lena Lovich and Jona Lewie. It proved impossible to categorize Stiff acts beyond their variety; Celtic iconoclasts the Pogues, the punk credentials of the Damned and Television's Richard Hell, the veteran music-hall comedian Max Wall (with a cover of Ian Dury's "England's Glory"), the conventional pop of Dave Stewart and Barbara Gaskin ("It's My Party") and the Belle Stars ("Sign of the Times") all rubbed shoulders with the quirky Lene Lovich ("Lucky Number"), Lewie ("You'll always find me in the Kitchen at Parties") and Tenpole Tudor ("Swords of a Thousand Men"). Then there were reggae figureheads Desmond Dekker and Eddy Grant, and even the metal of Motorhead.

However, despite its successes, Stiff didn't have the depths of resources to sustain loss-making artists or indulge in long-term career development. Kirsty recorded a second single, "You Caught Me Out"/"Boys"; the A-side written with Pete Briquette and Simon Crowe of the Boomtown Rats, and "Boys" written with George Lloyd, the guitarist with Drug Addix. The single was originally scheduled for release in October 1979, but after repeated delays and seemingly endless takes on a final mix, it was shelved. The single now makes rare appearances as a collector's white label.

Soon afterwards, MacColl left Stiff with few regrets and little acrimony. She was to recall: "We didn't come to blows at all. Most of my best friends work at Stiff, but I wanted too much control really, or more control than I was getting. There were any number of little things, but I think it was really because they didn't have my publishing." MacColl had, instead, signed a publishing deal with Chrysalis, and it is the publishing end of the industry, Lu Edmonds observes, "that is the no-brainer. They just sit back and collect the money."

Dave Robinson was not entirely surprised at MacColl's decision to quit Stiff: "After we'd released a couple of her records she felt that we weren't doing as good a job as she thought we could have done." One of Kirsty's closest friends was Robinson's personal assistant, Annie Pitts, who decided that a holiday in the sun would help to erase Kirsty's disappointment at the failure of "They Don't Know" and Stiff's inability to capitalize on it in the face of the distributor's strike. Kirsty's relationship with Rick Smith had also foundered by this time and she'd moved out of their flat in Chiswick. "She was in a bad way," recalls Lu

Edmonds. "Annie paid for her to go on holiday to Formentera. She went off and had a really, really good time."

MacColl's enjoyment of Formentera was partly down to hearing Spanish music in every bar. It reinforced the view that she'd formed as a child, listening to the Mexican mariachi record at home, that somehow, anything that sounded that exuberant and that much fun had to be good for you. While away, she had also met an half-Argentine half-Irish fellow holidaymaker who had given her an album by the Fania All Stars, New York-based Latin musicians who'd mixed elements of Cuban, Puerto Rican, Afro-Caribbean and Brazilian music to make their own brand of salsa. MacColl fell in love with the music.

"I'd never heard anything like that before," she was to recall. "I was completely transfixed, just because it was so outside my own upbringing and different to everything else you heard." Her memories of the music, the much-needed holiday and the kindness of Annie Pitts would later inspire a song named after the woman who became a life-long friend, god-mother to Kirsty's son and provided a haven of calm in troubled times. The song,"Annie", would finally be released years later on a MacColl compilation album.

Kirsty had dallied briefly with the idea of forming a just-for-fun covers band with her Stiff label-mate Jane Aire. Jane's brother, Dave Ashley, recruited some musicians for the band (including Mark Nevin, with whom Kirsty would later work), but after just one rehearsal of Gina And The Tonics, MacColl decided it wasn't for her. Lu Edmonds had also played in Aire's band the Belvederes, in a loose configuration of his own former band, the Edge, which had folded in 1978. Of the Edge, he fondly recalls: "We were a very weird band. We never had a hope as ourselves but we did this record with Jane Aire, which Liam Sternberg produced, and we nearly became Peter Gabriel's band. He was interested in us for a while."

MacColl threw herself into writing new material. Her earliest songs had not been been especially complex, but they had inspired her to continue writing, knowing that if she was competent enough to construct a clever sixties pastiche like "They Don't Know", she was certainly capable of extending her thematic and musical range. She was also gaining the valuable insight that she was not destined to write alone; she could often achieve far more with a collaborator, and she trusted her instincts about potential co-writers. Lu Edmonds was one of them:

When Kirsty was pretty much in-between labels, she had her publishing with Chrysalis. In those days publishers had little studios for their poor writers who didn't have their own set-up. They wouldn't charge you; it was part of the service. Kirsty and I used to go up there a lot. Chrysalis had one of the first portastudios and they had this weird little seventies drum machine that would have bossa nova rhythms or whatever, and a very good echo machine in a little box. There was a really nice guy who ran it; he really helped us with engineering. Kirsty wrote a very Beach Boys song called "Under the Night" with a guy named Pete Johnson. If she ended up with four or five songs finished, Chrsyalis would say, "All right, go and do some demos" and they'd basically pay for the demos. They paid for two or three sessions down at RMS Studios in Thornton Heath in 1979 and 1980. RMS was quite a cheap studio but a really nice one.

Edmonds used his contacts to enlist other musician friends to play on these tracks. Among them were drummer Jon Moss, briefly his Damned bandmate and soon to be in Culture Club, Dave Burke from Johnny and the Mopeds, Charlie Morgan, Glyn Havard and Dean Klevatt, who played keyboards and was later in pop singer Betty Boo's band. "The way it worked," says Edmonds, "was that I might have some basic ideas and I'd get into the studio and lay them all down and give her a cassette, and she would take it away and figure out the lyrics and melodies. Then we'd go into the studio and work it out there."

MacColl had already found a new collaborator in Phil Rambow, whose closest friend was her new boyfriend, Glenn Colson. Colson was a music publicist whom she had met while still with Stiff, where he handled Elvis Costello's publicity. The romance took their friends by surprise, not least because of the age difference; Colson was then 30, Kirsty barely 18. Colson, says Rambow, was always so consumed by his work that he had little time or energy for relationships:

But one night, at a friend's birthday party, he turned up with this absolutely gorgeous, red-haired, incredibly witty girl. He introduced us, telling her that I was a singer-songwriter who was signed to EMI and he said to me, "This is Kirsty, she's signed to Stiff." We got talking and she said, "So you're a songwriter, let's get together and write". We swapped phone numbers and Kirsty called me soon after. She said, "I've got a good idea for a song: 'There's a guy works down the chip shop, swears he's Elvis ... ' "

Rambow put the phone down and immediately began working on the song. He had put together a chord structure for the chorus and other parts of the song by the time he called her back twenty minutes later. Kirsty went straight over to his flat, and together they wrote what would become one of her best-known songs. However, Rambow is sanguine about Kirsty's reasons for wanting to work with him, and jokes that they may not have entirely been music-oriented: "Kirsty was madly in love with Glen for a very long time. I'm convinced one of the reasons she wanted to write with me was because I was staying at his flat. If I hadn't been living there, she would probably never have rung."

The novelty Nashville-style "There's a Guy Works down the Chip Shop (Swears He's Elvis)" would establish her trademark as quirky themes and unlikely characters, and would be forever fixed in the music-buying public's consciousness as the quintessential Kirsty MacColl song. She said of it: "It was about 'Elvis' being a state of mind. I still see a bit of Elvis in self-deluding men the world over." Thankfully, her trademark humour retrieved it from any knees-up pub sing-a-long ditty associations.

It also captured the attention of the man who would become her manager. Frank Murray, a jocular Irishman, had first met MacColl when he was running one of London's most popular gig venues, the Electric Ballroom in Camden Town. The Drug Addix had played there in 1978 as support for the Greedy Bastards, a short-lived and unlikely band comprising two Sex Pistols (Steve Jones and Paul Cook), Thin Lizzy (Phil Lynott, Scott Gorham, Brian Downey and Gary Moore), Jimmy Bain (Rainbow/Dio) and Chris Spedding. Their set included Thin Lizzy and Sex Pistols songs. That evening, Kirsty, as the Addix's Mandy Doubt, had gone to collect her band's fee from Murray. They chatted briefly then Kirsty went off to join her boyfriend and Addix band-mate, Rick Smith. It would be a year before Murray heard her name again – on the radio, when "They Don't Know" was played.

In the meantime, Kirsty had decided that, if her career was going to advance, she needed a manager. By now, Murray was becoming increasingly well-known in the business as a gig and tour manager and MacColl asked mutual friends to put her in touch. They spoke on the phone but made no definite arrangement at that stage. It was a chance conversation between Murray's wife Ferga and Kirsty, at a New Year's Eve party above another famous Camden landmark, Rock On Records, which eventually united manager and client. Kirsty retrieved a tape of new songs and demos from her bag and asked Ferga to take it home to her husband who couldn't be at the party. "My wife came home with the tape," says Murray, "and it included 'There's a Guy Works down the Chip Shop … ' I thought, 'Now *there's* a hit if ever there was one.' We took it from there."

Frank Murray's instincts were flawless. By the time they joined forces, MacColl had just signed to a new label, Polydor. They released "Chip Shop" as her second single on the label, as a follow-up to her cover of the Carole King/Gerry Goffin number, "Keep Your Hands Off My Baby". "Chip Shop" became so popular in 1981 that it earned Kirsty a guest spot on the Christmas week edition of Britain's most popular TV music programme, "Top of the Pops". This was highly unusual in that it wasn't a seasonal song, it wasn't a Number One, and it wasn't even in the Top Ten.

"The way the Christmas 'Top of the Pops' was done," explains Phil Rambow, "was that the DJs would just pick their favourite songs. And 'Chip Shop' was one of them." The single was to reach a respectable Number 14 in the UK chart. A Polydor executive of the time, who later left to become one of British pop's most successful star-makers, Pete Waterman, says: "Kirsty wrote this little song which I think is one of *the* classic records. I put the money up for that and we produced it. It was a lot of great fun and it got Kirsty started, really brought her out."

With a Top Twenty hit, the omens were good for Polydor's new young signing, but Frank Murray began to have misgivings about the lack of effort that the label was putting into building Kirsty's profile: "We didn't think Polydor were working the record in the right way. "Chip Shop" was getting played on the radio; it had the record for the most number of plays in a single day on Radio One. But it only got to Number 14 in the charts. It should have been a Number 1 record. I don't know what it was with Polydor, but they definitely messed up on that one."

With a collection of songs, including some written with Lu Edmonds, Phil Rambow and other musicians who'd played on the demos, Kirsty MacColl began work on her first album. Her nucleus of studio musicians included Edmonds, Glyn Havard and Gavin Povey, all from the Edge, as well as Rambow and drummer Lee Partiss, who was later with the Oyster Band. Squeeze keyboard player Jools Holland, guitarist Billy Bremner, and horn-players including Rico Rodriguez and John "Irish" Earle from Graham Parker's band the Rumour, also contributed. Barry

'Bazza' Farmer, who had previously engineered "They Don't Know", produced the sessions.

The album, *Desperate Character*, was released in June 1981. Tellingly, it included two versions of "Chip Shop", both the mainstream pop one and a less successful country jaunt. MacColl and Rambow had re-worked the original to try to capitalize on a potentially strong American market. They dropped the reference to "chip shop", which would have mystified an American audience and substituted "truck stop", which would have immediately conjured up the same associations of white-trash male bravado as the original version of the song. But Phil Rambow recalls that their efforts were in vain:

> We worked for about two weeks on that, trying to think what would be right. I came up with "truck stop" so we went back into the studio and we did a regular-speed version with "truck stop" and a speeded up country-style version. Of course, no one was even remotely interested in America anyway. Nothing happened: "truck stop, chip shop", it didn't matter! Yet the song itself was transatlantic, that's part of its whole appeal.

After a stint of sleeping on Frank Murray's couch, MacColl had moved back to west London, to Ladbroke Grove where her friend, Brian Nevill, had offered her his spare room. It was while staying with Nevill that they met a musician they'd both revered since childhood: Don Everly.

Brian had given Kirsty an album and a vintage publicity shot of the Everly Brothers, who by then had broken up acrimoniously. When Kirsty heard from a friend at Chrysalis that Don was going to be in London for discussions about his music publishing, she begged her friend to let her meet him. "We had this little joke," says Nevill, "about how funny it would be if she let slip that she liked his brother a lot, and what a *faux pas* that would be." Many a true word is spoken in jest. Soon afterwards, MacColl returned to the flat and told Nevill that she had met Don Everly, and within a few seconds, had nervously blurted out, "I always liked your brother better!"

"This was at a time when people used to say, 'Don't mention his brother'," says Nevill. "It says a lot about Kirsty's powers of conversation and connectedness with people that he was still talking to her for quite a long time afterwards." However, there was more to come. Kirsty told him she'd invited Don Everly to drop into the flat some time before he left London. A few days later, her friend called to say she was bringing him over. There was a knock on the door, and her friend asked, "Is it okay if Don comes in?"

A very shy Don Everly entered their flat. "He came in for a couple of hours," marvels Nevill. "We just sat talking. I had the best part of a bottle of whisky, which he helped us get rid of. We got lots of stuff out for him to sign, including the hits album that I had given Kirsty. He went into great detail, telling us he'd been a speed freak and had almost died, which has news to us. He was saying, 'I was really sick then, you can see it in the cover photo'. But we couldn't."

When MacColl moved out of her friend's spare room, it was to a flat in Willesden Lane, north-west London, and later, to buy her own flat in nearby Shepherds Bush in 1982. Brian Nevill visited her there, and Kirsty gave him a lift home. The pair called in en route to visit her friend George "Ras Levi" Oban, who was in the reggae group Aswad. While parking her car, MacColl bumped the vehicle in front. While she was distracted, a passer-by snatched her handbag through the open back window. MacColl went into George's house. Waiting for her outside, Brian Nevill suddenly became aware that the small matter of the bump, which had not even caused a dent, had not been dealt with, as the other car's driver and his friends surrounded him:

> Just then, Kirsty came out of the house and was standing on the pavement, shouting at the top of her voice, "Right, I want my fucking handbag back and I want it now!" People started running around, and within a minute they came back with her handbag. Somebody had found it in a garden. Everybody, including me, was going "Wow!" She just wouldn't take any shit from anybody. That happened a lot with Kirsty.

MacColl's self-confidence had received a huge boost when "Chip Shop" charted. The hit gave her enough money to buy her new flat, and she became the focus of media attention, says Brian Nevill:

> What was unusual about her having that hit was that, instead of just doing interviews with the music press, she was talking to papers like the *Daily Mirror* because there was an angle. It wasn't so much because of her father; that did seem to sneak in, though she always played it down. It was more like, "Here's a novelty record about a guy who works down the chip shop, it's tabloid-worthy, and she's a young girl!" Today, you can open a tabloid and it's all about gossip and celebrity. But this was twenty years ago. She was a pioneer of that in a way.

Yet the observational, novelty hit "Chip Shop" was not characteristic of the rest of the album. By now 21, Kirsty was clearly able to look critically at her own life as well as those of the semi-fictional characters she had created. Her relationship with Glen Colson had already inspired one song, co-written with Philip Rambow: "She came over to the flat one day," Rambow recalls, "She was talking about Glen and said, 'I'm just a lonely alcoholic teenager in love.'" That lament formed the heart of a track on *Desperate Character* called "Teenager in Love". Rambow, though, had misgivings:

> I didn't like the version on that first album. She didn't sing the melody; she sang the fifth harmony instead of the lead and it didn't have the same impact. I remember telling her about it after I heard the album, and Kirsty said, "Oh, it doesn't really matter!" I thought that, had it been properly recorded, it would have been a fantastic follow-up to "Chip Shop" because it was so jocular.
>
> People told Kirsty, "The BBC will never play a song with the word 'alcoholic' in it." But it was also about Kirsty's attitude to herself at that time. "They Don't Know" had come out, and it was a pop song. My attitude was, if you're lucky enough to be accepted into the heart of the great British public, you're very lucky and you shouldn't rock the boat, you shouldn't go outside of the box as it were. And "Chip Shop" was a song that had made people smile. When I suggested to Kirsty that she should maybe re-do "Teenager in Love", she was very against the idea. She got really upset, and said, "No, I'm just not interested in being a novelty artist." She wanted credibility.

Kirsty also wanted the approval, support and encouragement of her label. This wasn't always easy to find. While she accepted their judgment on the choice of singles, for instance, Polydor's marketing strategy left her feeling uncomfortable. Frank Murray believed their attempts to foist a particular image upon Kirsty were doomed: "When the record company saw the single happening, they then came down like a pack of wolves and immediately started trying to change her image. Everybody thought, 'Let's make her into some kind of teen queen,' and Kirsty wasn't into that. She fought it tooth and nail."

The album artwork, which had a mildly surreal cover photograph of MacColl lost in mountains of blow-dried hair, was an example of this clumsy image making. "We all hated the album sleeve," says

Rambow, "but we couldn't just tell Kirsty, 'that sucks!' Nowadays, people like Kirsty would be encouraged to be themselves and do exactly what they want to do. But in those days, it was very different."

A hurried tour of Ireland to promote *Desperate Character* was arranged in October, with an itinerary that took in Cashel, Loughrea, Monaghan, Strandhill, Limerick, Dublin and Letterkenny. Frank Murray believed a brief visit to his homeland would give MacColl a more relaxed introduction to touring than a similar trek around Britain, where the audiences would be bigger and there would be more travelling and more pressure on her. Ireland, he felt, would be gentler, friendlier and much more fun. He turned out to be both right and wrong.

Even before leaving London, MacColl was apprehensive about the trip. However, she took solace, albeit indirect, from an unlikely source: "I will be going out on the road, but I'm terrified at the thought," she said. "However, after seeing Bruce Springsteen, I've either got to get on with it or slit my throat. Apart from anything else, the on-the-road life doesn't appeal to me at all. It's not my idea of heaven." In fact, it was to become more like her idea of hell.

MacColl headed for Ireland with her backing band, culled largely from the musicians who'd played with her on recent demos and the *Desperate Character* sessions: Lu Edmonds (who had by then quit the Damned), Phil Johnstone, keyboardist Gavin Povey and drummer Jon Moss. She christened them, somewhat unceremoniously, the Horn. The advertisements for the shows wisely confined the title to a more sedate "Kirsty MacColl", although the posters naturally touted "Chip Shop" as her hit single.

Gigging around the London pub circuit in the Drug Addix had not prepared MacColl for cavernous ballrooms in Irish towns and rural villages, full of farmers, their wives and local teenagers who'd come along expecting a grand show. Alcohol was not sold in the ballrooms, so the audience would have their fill at the pub beforehand and be up for a night of music and dancing, recalls Lu Edmonds:

We would arrive at five in the afternoon, and set the gear up. Then we'd drive 25 miles into the next town to check into the hotel, and then at about 11, after we'd had a meal, we'd get in the van and drive back to this godforsaken place. And it would be packed. They'd have just come out of the pubs. And it would be a Wednesday. At about one o'clock we'd start playing, and we were expected to play until three or four in the morning.

Kirsty's inexperience meant that, instead of telling the band – or the sound engineer – that they were too loud, and asking them to adjust accordingly, she tried to match them for volume to be heard above the instruments. It didn't work; she simply shouted herself hoarse on stage each night. The band shared her anxiety, as they raced through the set and finished too early to send the punters home happy. Frank Murray had to insist they go back out on stage after finishing their hour-long set in thirty minutes flat: "The first gig we did in County Cork, I never saw a set done so fast in all my life! I even took Kirsty off the stage and let Gavin Povey sing a rock 'n' roll medley. We were pulling every kind of song out of the hat for people to sing, just to fill out the set."

Lu Edmonds recalls that, "We were all expected to get up and do one or two songs. The music didn't figure. We had quite a lot of country & western and rock 'n' roll songs that the audience knew. Basically, the band was irrelevant. We were there to facilitate the meeting of boys and girls. There were certain set ways of doing things, which we eventually worked out: don't rattle through the set, give them a couple of minutes between songs, and tell jokes. We were meant to actually shut up for three or four minutes between each song to give the boys and the girls a chance to talk. Theoretically, the tour was a great idea – if only Kirsty had relaxed."

At one gig the band almost fell foul of the prevailing political tensions in Ireland at the time. The months of hunger strikes launched by Republican prisoners at the Maze prison in Northern Ireland had come to an end on October 3, 1981, a week before Kirsty began her tour. The protest had claimed the lives of ten prisoners. The first and most famous of them, Bobby Sands, had died almost exactly five months earlier. Lu Edmonds recalls that the atmosphere was tense as one of the first gigs of the tour got underway in Monaghan: "It was a really weird atmosphere. While we were playing no one really hassled us too much but when it came to the end and we said, 'Thanks a lot for the gig', people started shouting, 'You fucking Brits!' They didn't attack us, but they really let rip. We all just fled to one room and stayed there for the rest of the night, smoking and drinking."

Elsewhere, tales of life on the road lightened the mood. "We had some interesting times," says Edmonds. "We even got booked into a brothel in Dublin. Kirsty and Frank had to go back to London to do a television interview and we were booked into this really horrible hotel. We thought we'd just stick with it for a night but at 5am we were woken by shouts of, 'Get out of bed! You're out of here!'" The band quickly discovered that they were expected to vacate their rooms to make way for an influx of local prostitutes and their clients. It was also, quite literally, a fleapit hotel. "I had flea bites all over me in the morning," says Edmonds. "So we checked into a new hotel, rather rebelliously."

Such misadventures aside, the mood on the road was a very happy one. Everyone was in high spirits, usually quite literally. After a gig in Strandhill, four miles west of Sligo, MacColl and the Horn drank black velvets until dawn broke and then careered across the sand dunes at the town's beautiful beach, with the Atlantic breakers crashing in front of them and the magnificent Knocknarea Mountain behind them. They even somehow managed to make their gig the next night in Cashel.

Cashel is the County Tipperary town dominated by the spectacular Rock of Cashel, the limestone freak of geology on which is built the most complete Romanesque church in Ireland, and an extraordinary sprawl of medieval buildings. Legend has it that it was on the Rock that Saint Patrick picked a shamrock to illustrate the notion of the Holy Trinity – the Father, Son and Holy Ghost – and thereby gave Ireland its most beloved emblem. The luck of the Irish was evident in the hotel bar, as MacColl and her band settled in, recalls Lu: "We were in the hotel, and someone had just won something at the races. In came the jockey and the trainers and the champagne flowed. There was a lot of drinking going on. On that tour, we would come down for breakfast and then get in the van at ten, but not before you'd had a Paddy's [Irish whisky] so everyone was well-oiled for the journey. Frank did a wonderful job as tour manager. He was totally relaxed, he never shouted at anyone. We made all the gigs, we got paid, we got fed well, and we stopped in lots of nice pubs. Everyone had a lot of fun."

Keyboard player Gavin Povey found the Horn's brief Irish tour especially memorable. At one of the dates, he met his future wife. For his part, Frank Murray would in later years describe the Irish jaunt as "one of the funniest times of our lives":

The tour was hilarious. But Kirsty had bad stage fright. It's a paradox: somebody wants to be a singer and wants to go on stage, yet they're scared to do it. You'd think it would be the most normal thing for them to want to do: "Hey, I can sing, I'm a songwriter, I want to sing my songs on a stage". But there is this X-factor there that is really hard. Coming close to the gig, you'd see it starting to have an effect on Kirsty. She'd start biting her nails, and things like that. The nerves would start to kick in.

Kirsty was only nervous and ill at ease on stage where, ironically, she most needed to be relaxed and confident. In fact, despite all of the adventures and larking about with her band, the tour proved counter-productive for MacColl. It only served to highlight her total inexperience in such venues, and induced a decade-long dread of live performance. The Irish tour left Kirsty MacColl with a trepidation that she would struggle to shake off for years:

It was disastrous. I was so terrified every single night that it was just absolutely overwhelming. I couldn't cope with it at all and that put me off for ten years. "Performing" is a word that is over-used. My vocals are fairly deadpan; I tend to be more expressive with words than I am with delivery. It's that English attitude of "Don't make a fuss, it's embarrassing!" I couldn't do all that screaming and bleeding on the carpet. I'm just too reserved and shy.

Reflecting on her daughter's dread of performing, Jean MacColl simply says: "She always thought that the audience wanted more than she was able to give. They expected her to dress and behave in a certain way, and she wasn't prepared to do that."

Kirsty wasn't the first female singer to dread live shows. Kate Bush had a legendary aversion to live performance, but found that she could make it tolerable by divorcing herself from concerns about how *she* looked, and think of her on-stage persona as simply a character, one remove divorced from her. "I don't want to be up there on stage being me," she explained. "I don't think I'm that interesting. What I want to do is to be the person that's in the song. If I can be the character in the song, then suddenly there's all this strength and energy in me, which I wouldn't normally have. Were it just me, I don't think I could walk on stage with confidence."

However, Bush's character-laden songs, often dominated by role-play and fantasy, gave her plenty of scope for this escape route. Kirsty MacColl's lyrical characters were clearly more autobiographical, less dramatic and more prosaic, making them so much harder to hide behind. Lu Edmonds believes that, at that time, Kirsty's strengths lay more in the studio than on the stage:

She was good in the studio. She had all of the talent for careful preparation and putting things together. Performing was a real shock to her and she hadn't done much. She had been the sort of "be-bop" girl in the Drug Addix. She wasn't actually that confident of her singing, she didn't have a very loud voice. In a way you could say that she was a much better vocal musician than a vocalist. She had this incredible gift for harmony and really had something very special. She had this ability to think about writing and what should go where; it wasn't done all in the moment. She could really calculate and think and lead people to a point, which is not what performance is about, in a way. It's only part of that.

There was no sign of nerves, however, when MacColl had to perform on television or deal with journalists in interviews. She appeared relaxed and confident during the former and, while occasionally affecting a thinly disguised disdain during the latter, she approached neither with any trepidation. It was somehow a little easier to step outside her insecurities in those situations, in a way that she could not do in front of a live audience.

She appeared on all of the British TV music programmes, to promote *Desperate Character*, including "Top of the Pops", "Razzamatazz" and "6-5 Special". Her friend Brian Nevill was in her band for several of the shows and saw in her "a consummate show-person. I noticed immediately that she had this fantastic camera sense," he says. "She learned really well and really quickly as she was going along. And she dealt with interviews very well."

However, there were things that Kirsty MacColl couldn't deal with as easily and, on these occasions, her insecurities would rush to the surface. Criticism of her looks, her weight, her fashion sense would often prove disproportionately wounding, says Nevill: "If you're a girl in this business, someone's going to come along and be really bitchy about you, for no other reason than the colour of your dress or something like that. These things came up quite a lot, and they'd devastate her. I saw her in tears over it. It was heartbreaking to see that people in the press could do that to someone. Those were the things that made her think, 'Okay, I don't want to do that. I just want to write songs or be a producer.' But the same industry is just going to come up and say, 'Oh, *really*?' "

The next single to be taken from *Desperate Character* was "See that Girl". This was an unlikely, low-key choice for a follow-up to "Chip Shop", and could not have been more different to its predecessor. "You just thought, they've had one great single already," says Brian Nevill, "and 'See that Girl' is just a throwaway. What was that all about? It was so weird. Why didn't they try to capitalize on her success?"

In November, Kirsty's cover of a song by her beloved Beach Boys, "You Still Believe in Me", was also released as a single, backed with her own "Queen Of The High Teas". Together with Gavin Povey, she used vocals and synthesisers to recreate the Brian Wilson composition as a faithful homage to its *Pet Sounds* source. Frank Murray would later describe Kirsty's version as "just incredible, a lost masterpiece". However, to Brian Nevill, that was another spectacular lost opportunity for a chart-storming hit: "It could have been one of the best Christmas singles ever," he says. "They just needed to promote it on the radio and sell it as a Christmas record. It had a Christmas vibe, there were bells on it, they were doing the Brian Wilson/Phil Spector homage, it was such a great version and it disappeared without trace. It was so sad."

The dominance of synth-pop and post-glam new romanticism in the mainstream of British music at the time meant that, without imaginative and energetic marketing from Polydor, MacColl's melodic lyricism simply got lost in an already overcrowded pop marketplace. As W.C. Fields once said: "Those were the good old days. I hope they never come back."

CHAPTER FOUR

All I Ever Wanted

When Kirsty MacColl left Stiff, she thought she was signing to a company that was the antithesis of the shambolic but passionate anarchic eclecticism at Stiff. Mainstream, moneyed Polydor Records seemed to offer her market access, career development, top-of-the-range recording facilities and an army of publicity and marketing people to help shift what in industry parlance are "units" and "product" and to the rest of us is music. However, her new employers brought their own preconceptions into the equation.

MacColl's post-"Chip Shop" singles had not lived up to their predecessor's success and *Desperate Character* failed to make a dent in the album charts. Nevertheless, Polydor still hoped to capitalize on MacColl's now obvious gift for creating two of the most successful sub-genres within the world of pop – the novelty song and the sweet love song, both of which had irresistibly sing-a-long choruses.

Polydor quickly sent Kirsty back into the studio to record a follow-up to *Desperate Character*. Frank Murray assembled a broad range of musicians including his friend Jools Holland and other stalwarts from the first album such as Lu Edmonds and Rico Rodriguez. Bass-player Pino Palladino, ex-Marmalade mainstay Junior Campbell and Hans Zimmer, who would later become one of the most successful sound-track composers in Hollywood, completed the numbers. In just a week, they'd recorded five songs for the album, which had the working title of *Real*.

Kirsty invited Brian Nevill to her new flat in Shepherd's Bush to listen to the tapes. He was impressed by what he heard: "It was so different from the first album, and it was a new direction and very mature," he says. "The songs were good. She'd made her first visit to Berlin and she wrote a song about it, called 'Berlin'. There was no girl-group influence, no rockabilly, no guitar-group stuff; it was very funky."

MacColl delivered *Real* to Polydor, but it so contradicted the company's vision of her as a "teen queen" that they simply didn't know what to do with it. Polydor wanted infinite variations on the winning formula of "Chip Shop" or covers of great rock and pop classics. However, nobody from the label had even visited the studio during recording sessions; it was hardly surprising that the finished product defied their expectations.

"The first album material was pub rock, rockabillyish," MacColl was to reflect, years later. "The second was much more techno. There was a lot of programming on it." She had wanted to expand the themes she wrote about, and experiment with the music she used to frame those themes, and expected Polydor to encourage and praise her for doing it. But neither got what they wanted; both ended up feeling disappointed. Polydor saw no commercial merit in *Real* and refused to release it. This was a bitter blow, remembers Frank Murray:

> Kirsty had started to get very experimental, but nobody at Polydor showed the slightest interest. They listened to it for a while and they just decided they weren't going to release it. It was a really hard blow for Kirsty. She was writing stuff with her brother Hamish, some very clever songs. There were a lot of quality musicians on the record, and the record was really good. But Polydor wanted the three-minute pop song every time, and that wasn't on Kirsty's mind by then. Kirsty was very headstrong and the one thing she'd react to was somebody trying to force her to do something. That was like a red rag to a bull. If Kirsty didn't want to do something, she wouldn't do it. And if you did get her to do it begrudgingly, she'd only do it half-heartedly, and you were never going to get the result you wanted.

For Kirsty MacColl, her major label opportunity had promised a lot, but Polydor's refusal to release the follow-up to *Desperate Character* was near to soul-destroying:

> They just wanted twelve versions of "Chip Shop". It was all very frustrating. You spend three months working on something, pouring out your heart and soul, writing songs and getting the best musicians. You get it all done in the studio, and then the record company refuses to release it. If you don't like it yourself when it does come out, you may think it could have been done

better but if it isn't released then you start to think, "Why bother?" I can't see why Polydor signed me up really, except I may have been a tax loss.

Her former collaborator Jools Holland maintains that *Real* was an album that Kirsty could have been proud of: "The lyrics were very sharp. There was nothing wrong with it, but there wasn't a simple pop song of 'Ooby-doo, I love you, you super-duper person you'." Kirsty MacColl's relationship with Polydor Records thus came to a swift and inevitable end.

The album was shelved and forgotten for almost 25 years, until Steve Lillywhite discovered it in Polydor's archives while collecting material for inclusion in a MacColl box set in 2004. "Kirsty described it as her unborn child," he says of *Real*. "It was the opposite of 'Chip Shop' and she wanted to make a statement and say, 'I'm a serious artist.' It came across as being a bit dour and flat; it was a very soporific record. But now, listening to it, you'd probably get the same feeling from a Dido record, so in that sense it may have been well ahead of its time."

MacColl's former Chiswick Records label-mates, Matchbox, whom she had come to know well when their paths crossed during promotional tours of Europe, asked her to sing vocals on their single, "I Want Out". She agreed to appear with them at one of their London gigs. At the Venue in Victoria, MacColl sang "Chip Shop" and joined the band for "I Want Out", but found even being on stage for such a short time a nerve-wracking ordeal. Her stage fright problem was clearly getting no better.

Kirsty made another tentative foray into the studio in August 1983, when she revived a track from *Real* and re-recorded it. "Berlin" was released as a single (backed with "Rhythm of the Real Thing") by a tiny independent label, North Of Watford. It only sold a few copies, but Frank Murray was determined to find his charge another deal. Murray began negotiations with Dick O'Dell, who had started his own independent label, Y Records. Y would eventually boast an impressively eclectic and leftfield roster, including the Slits (whom O'Dell managed), The Pop Group, Pigbag, Sun Ra, Diamanda Galas and Shriekback.

However, the day before Kirsty was due to sign a contract with Y Records, Frank Murray took a gamble. He got back in touch with Stiff Records. Concerned that Y were too small to give Kirsty the marketing and distribution she craved, Murray phoned Dave Robinson to inform him that she might be available to re-enter the Stiff fold if the conditions were right. His gamble paid off when Robinson agreed. "Prior to that," says Murray, "Kirsty didn't want to go back to Stiff, but we saw them as the lesser of two evils. I said to her, 'This is the best deal on the table.'"

Disillusioned with her major-label experience and warily encouraged by Stiff's new courtship, MacColl returned to the label that had given her her first radio play success. The timing was good for Stiff, too. Having recently signed the television comedian Tracey Ullman, they were planning to follow up Ullman's March 1983 Number 4 hit, a cover of the pop classic "Breakaway", with her version of MacColl's "They Don't Know".

Producer Pete Waterman says of the Ullman cover: "Kirsty MacColl and I were great friends. I took the song to Tracey. Tracey, my friend the producer Pete Collins and Kirsty all worked on that, so it was very personal to me. That was the first time I'd ever really made a record that I wanted to make for me. It was a sixties pastiche record, very much what I wanted to do, and was one of the first records that I can actually say worked exactly how I wanted it to."

For all the hype about Ullman, the re-recorded song still had the MacColl trademark, albeit unwittingly. "Those penny-pinchers at Stiff had Tracey sing over Kirsty's original backing track," recalls Billy Bragg. "When Ms Ullman couldn't quite reach the high notes, they kept Kirsty's vocal."

Despite these restrictions, Ullman's cover was a rapid success, reaching Number 2 in the British charts in September 1983. This brought inevitable comparisons with its writer's original version of the song, which had languished unsold four years earlier because of the distribution strike. MacColl was to reflect:

I don't think it failed because it wasn't good enough. It wasn't any better or worse than Tracey's version: it was practically the same. If there hadn't been any obvious reason for its failure, I would have been disappointed, but at least there was. As it was, it got plenty of airplay, started my career, got my name known and got me a record deal. I am glad it was finally a hit, because it's a nice song.

With Ullman in mind, Kirsty and her co-writer and pianist Gavin Povey wrote another power-pop song that underscored MacColl's girl-group influences. "Terry" was the tale of a young woman warning off a trouble-some Lothario with the threat of her Brando-esque boyfriend, the eponymous Terry. "Terry seems to be a really good name for a lovable rogue," said MacColl at the time. "He's similar to the Marlon Brando character in *On The Waterfront*, and she thinks he's the greatest thing since Elvis." When the idea of recording an album of teen ballads was mooted by Stiff, MacColl decided to keep the song for herself. But when Stiff quickly lost interest in the ballads album concept, MacColl offered it to Ullman and also recorded it herself as a single, which was released in October 1983.

Stiff invited Kirsty to produce Tracey's version of another of her songs, "You Broke my Heart in 17 Places", which was to be the title track of Ullman's debut album, released in late 1983. It included two MacColl compositions – the title track and "They Don't Know". Ullman's short-lived but energetic career at Stiff ended with the release of a follow-up album, *You Caught Me Out*, in 1984, which also boasted two MacColl songs, the title track and "Terry".

MacColl's vocals may have been used to enhance Tracey Ullman's inferior singing skills, but Ullman proved to be a good friend when Kirsty's career at Stiff started to look shaky and her confidence and song-writing energies needed reviving. Ullman took Kirsty out for a drink, bought her dinner and encouraged her to continue writing. "I was a bit lost at the time," said MacColl, "so it all gave me the incentive to write again." However, she later admitted that being around Tracey Ullman's expansively gregarious personality could occasionally prove exhausting. "We hung out a bit," said MacColl, "because I wrote quite a lot of stuff for Tracey after that. She's a nice girl and very talented, but she is always acting. It's hard to relax."

With "They Don't Know", MacColl created a template for the retro girl-pop that was to emerge in the early to mid-eighties. The genre served Tracey Ullman extremely well until TV stardom and the US beckoned, and it laid down a lush red carpet for the teetering stiletto heels and the sixties homage package that was the beehive-coiffured Mari Wilson, with her Supremes-inspired backing singers, the Wilsations (including Julia Fordham, who would later eschew choreo-graphed sixties cutie-pie kitsch for new generation Joni singer-songwriterdom). Kirsty also prefigured the smiley, almost-brainy Valley Girl pop of the Bangles. They were similarly dogged by the "novelty" tag, largely due to one of their biggest hits, the absurdly irresistible "Walk Like an Egyptian", which was written by Liam Sternberg, whose pop-harmony production values had been much in evidence on "They Don't Know".

Kirsty's own gift for pop writing was to inspire one young woman who would go on to reign as one of the pop princesses of the eighties: Kim Wilde. "Kirsty was only a year older than me, and I remember them playing 'They Don't Know' on the radio," Wilde admitted. "I thought, 'If Kirsty can do it, *I* can do it'. I met her when we were both dating blokes in the same band (Tenpole Tudor). She was an angel. I thought she was a really gutsy girl to tackle such a male-dominated industry, then the eighties became filled with female singer-songwriters." Wilde was to abandon the music business in the nineties for a career as a professional gardener.

As a side-project, in a rare collaborative project with her brother, Hamish, Kirsty had written the soundtrack for a travelogue on the Spanish island of Lanzarote. *Lanzarote: Land of Parched Earth* was distributed in British cinemas in 1983 as a short film to precede the spy thriller *Gorky Park*. Hamish recalls: "We got the job through my manager. We didn't get any money, but they paid for the instruments and we got our names in huge letters on the screen. We made the instrumental music together. Kirsty went for the Beach Boys' layers and layers of strings and I went for wackiness. The synthesizer had just come out and made it possible for anyone to write music without having professional musicians in tow. That was great."

The travelogue explored the stunning volcanic landscape of Lanzarote, the once fertile farmland devastated by a series of eruptions and transformed into arid basalt plains, caves and columns, as well as the more well-known touristy beaches and photogenic villages of white-washed houses.

One of Kirsty's favourite bands at the time was Simple Minds, and she had talked Frank Murray into going to one of their London gigs with her. When Simple Minds were back in town a couple of months later for recording, Murray got a call from a friend who was working with the band, Frankie Gallagher, who invited him to come down to the studio. Kirsty needed no persuading to join him at Shepherds Bush's Townhouse studios to meet Jim Kerr and the other band members. "She was blown away by that," recalls Murray. Simple Minds seemed similarly impressed with her, and the next time they were in London they met up again, socialized and talked about music. Kirsty gave the band a tape of several of her songs, including some she'd written with Hamish.

The friendship continued and when Simple Minds wanted some stylish background vocals on their 1984 album, *Sparkle in the Rain*, they called her. Kirsty was to later describe it as "like being asked to join the

Beatles, or something!" Turning up at the studio, she was introduced to the band's producer, Steve Lillywhite, who was already becoming one of the most successful of his generation.

Lillywhite had left school in 1972. A 17-year-old bass player in a school band, his sole ambition in life was to make a career in music. He found a job in a recording studio, and spent the next five years working as a general assistant and tape operator: "Basically I would sit in a room and press buttons on a tape recorder and record bands. People would tell me when to press play and when to stop. It was the music business, but not very sexy at all. It was also a time when studio technicians still wore white coats, so it was very much 'certain jobs for certain people'. Engineers back then were like laboratory technicians."

Tiring rapidly of the unchallenging life of a tape operator, Lillywhite spent weekends in the empty studio, teaching himself how to engineer. Needing some real musicians to practise on, he invited an unknown band called Ultravox to come and record some tracks. The demos were sent to Island Records, where the label founder, Chris Blackwell, and his team were sufficiently impressed to sign Ultravox to their first deal in 1976 and send the band straight back into the studio.

Lillywhite was asked to co-produce Ultravox's debut album with Brian Eno, who had left Roxy Music three years earlier to pursue solo projects. Lillywhite's production work on the self-titled *Ultravox* album had been carried out during two weeks' holiday from his full-time studio job, but Island hired him as one of their in-house producers and he quickly began work with Steel Pulse and Eddie and the Hot Rods.

After negotiating a freelance contract with Island that enabled him to work with bands signed to other labels, Lillywhite took on the glam-punk of the former New York Doll Johnny Thunders and his 1978 solo album, *So Alone*. He also produced Siouxsie & The Banshees' first hit single, "Hong Kong Garden" in the same year. An avalanche of work followed, from the punk/new wave of XTC, the Psychedelic Furs and the Members (whose drummer was Lillywhite's brother, Adrian) to the anarchic but catchy post-Genesis pop/rock of Peter Gabriel's third solo album (self-titled, as were all of Gabriel's first four solo releases). This album spawned Gabriel's first solo Top Ten hit in the UK, "Games Without Frontiers" in March 1980; Steve Lillywhite's whistling (along with that of his co-producer Hugh Padgham and Gabriel himself) and Kate Bush's vocals helped the track along.

However, it was to be his working relationship with a feisty group of passionate young Irishmen and their English bass-player that cemented Steve Lillywhite's reputation. And that only came about because of the death of Joy Division's singer, Ian Curtis. Joy Division's producer Martin Hannett had produced U2's third single, "11 O'Clock Tick Tock", but within days of its May 1980 release, Curtis committed suicide. Hannett was too distraught to complete U2's debut album.

U2 asked Lillywhite to fly to Dublin to work with them. For the next three years, he was to spend long periods of time with the band in their Windmill Lane studios, and produced their first three albums: *Boy* (1980), *October* (1981) and their breakthrough, *War*, which entered the UK charts at Number 1 in March 1983.

Lillywhite had two further major album commitments in 1983. One was with the Scottish rock band Big Country, whose Lillywhite-produced debut *The Crossing*, released in 1983, boasted rousing anthems "In a Big Country", "Inwards" and "Fields of Fire" as well as romantic ballads. His second was with the other great Scottish band of the eighties, Simple Minds.

While it would be many years before Lillywhite would work again with U2, his friendship with Bono had led to an introduction to Simple Minds' frontman Jim Kerr. Kerr had invited Steve to produce their *Sparkle In The Rain* album, which proved to be one of their most successful. The anthemic single "Waterfront" reached Number 13 in the UK chart in late November 1983, and "Speed Your Love To Me", featuring backing vocals by Kirsty MacColl, hit Number 20 the following January. Three weeks later, *Sparkle in the Rain* topped the album charts.

While Kirsty was only in the studio for a short time, her brief initial meeting with the producer would shape the next decade of her life – and his. "Kirsty was one of the biggest Simple Minds fans in the world," says Steve Lillywhite. "There was a lot of talk about Kirsty coming down to the studio to do some backing vocals; she was bugging them to come and do it." The band phoned Kirsty from the studio, inviting her to join them at the recording session, and with a second request – could she please pick up some cocaine for them on her way over? MacColl happily complied and the session went extremely well, recalls Steve:

> She came round and she did fantastic backing vocals. I remember looking through the door in the studio and seeing her dancing while she was

> singing and she was absolutely gorgeous. I got her phone number. She
> thought it was to do with production. The last thing on her mind was some
> randy producer.

The pair discovered a common musical language, not to mention the fact that the first single either had ever bought had been "Keep on Running" by the Spencer Davis Group. Kirsty would later say that Steve fell in love at first sight; she maintained that she was so nervous singing with her favourite group that she barely noticed him:

> I'd heard of his reputation as a producer and I was surprised how young he
> looked – rather like a jolly sixth former. I assumed he'd be going out with a
> Page Three girl or something. He was very nice but I didn't really pay any
> attention to him. It was work.

But for Steve Lillywhite it was love even before first sight. "For some reason," he says, "I knew I was going to get married to her, before I even met her. It was an absolute fact of life. I don't know why. I was thirty years old, I was successful, she'd just had 'They Don't Know' as a big hit in America for Tracey Ullman. It was the last thing on her mind. To start with, I was the one completely pushing the relationship."

Lillywhite was – and is – acclaimed, with some justification, as one of the greatest music producers of his generation. But despite the career successes, he was single and unhappy:

> I was on a pretty good run. I went straight from that Simple Minds session
> into a Big Country session and I had lots of energy. But I was also lonely
> and I was on my own, and I was looking for a mate. Falling in love or finding
> a partner is much more to do with the timing than the person; you just
> happen to be open in your mind to that at that time. I was insecure and I
> was lonely, and I was fascinated by her as well.

MacColl had been enjoying a short relationship with one of Stiff's press officers, Andy MacDonald, but this was at an end. On October 1, 1983, he had met the woman he would soon marry, Juliet de Valero Wills, while accompanying Kirsty to the studios of BBC Radio One, where she was a guest on the *Pop Quiz* programme. Wills, as co-manager of the ska revival group the Selecter, was at the studio with a fellow guest, Selecter vocalist Pauline Black.

So when Steve Lillywhite called Kirsty, and then carried on calling, she agreed to go out with him. Their first proper date was at a Bonfire Night party held by Virgin boss, Richard Branson. By then she, too, was smitten: "I couldn't believe he was so nice," she marvelled. "I kept waiting for the truth to come out, some deep, dark secret, but he was wonderful." A day later, Kirsty was quoted in London's *Evening Standard* as saying of the party, "It all started with a big bang under a starlit sky!" The pun was intentional.

Less than two months later, MacColl accompanied Lillywhite to a Big Country show at Barrowlands in Glasgow on New Year's Eve. As the last stroke of midnight rang out and the venue echoed to traditional Highland bagpipes and a mass rendition of "Auld Lang Syne", the producer proposed. This had been one of the most memorable years of his life. He'd found his Midas touch in the studio with U2, Simple Minds and Big Country, and now he'd found love. In the less than romantic surroundings of the mixing truck at the Barrowlands, Kirsty's first words of 1984 were to accept his marriage proposal. After the show, they went back to Jim Kerr's house for a joint Hogmanay/engagement celebration with the Simple Minds singer and several other friends.

Back in London, Steve moved into her flat in Shepherds Bush. The next few months were dominated by his production work, including stints in Paris producing a solo album for ex-Abba vocalist, Frida, for whom Kirsty co-wrote four songs and provided backing vocals. It was while in Paris working on the album, *Shine*, that MacColl met a man who was to become a close friend and musical collaborator: Pete Glenister, the former guitarist with an early eighties pop band, Hitmen, which had recorded two albums for Columbia in 1980 and 1981.

After his band broke up, Glenister had worked with Terence Trent D'Arby and Bruce Foxton, the Jam's former bass player, for whom Lillywhite was producing several tracks. On hearing that Lillywhite was going to Paris to record with Frida, Glenister outed himself as a passionate Abba fan. "This was a very unfashionable thing to be at the time," says Pete Glenister. "I remember having a discussion with Steve at the time because he wasn't into Abba at all. I was really excited about it."

A week or so later, Steve called to invite Glenister to join him in Paris on the Frida sessions. Once there, Pete and Kirsty got to know each other: "Kirsty was basically vetting all of the songs for Steve and doing a bit of co-writing. I had some songs and ended up writing something with her for that album. We ended up just hanging out for five or six weeks, and had a great time. We got on really well and used to go shopping together: I spent a lot of time with her."

Lillywhite was by then spending long periods working abroad, having been advised to take up tax-exile status to avoid punitive British taxation levels. Visits to France for the Frida sessions, then to Sweden where he was producing Big Country's *Steeltown* album at Abba's Polar Studios in Stockholm, were part of this new regime. But in the throes of an all-consuming romantic relationship, the work and his tax status lost the importance they'd once had. It's probably no coincidence that neither the Frida nor Big Country albums were among Lillywhite's most successful in a glittering, awards-laden career. He decided, not unreasonably, that if he was earning enough to become a tax exile, then he was earning enough to pay the taxes in the first place. "I lost a lot of money," he says, "but it's all to do with how happy you are."

Steve moved back to London, where his soon-to-be mother-in-law was overseeing frenetic wedding preparations. In an interview with a teenage magazine, *19*, Kirsty talked about her plans for a lavish traditional wedding:

> I was always anti-marriage, but that was before I met Steve. Before he came along, I was always attracted to lame ducks and homeless, unemployed men who needed constant looking after. A lot of the time I preferred to live alone, rather than chance another fleeting relationship. It just seemed so pointless. I think Steve and I are compatible and we want the same things. We're both looking for a straight, enduring relationship.

MacColl was then 24 and semi-famous for her chart singles, her hits for Tracey Ullman and her TV theme tune for the Channel 4 series "Dream Stuffing". The *19* writer, Jan Kaluza, described Kirsty as being, "sufficiently alluring to become This Year's Pin-up should she so wish it: pouting provocatively on 'Top of the Pops' and from the covers of magazines and posters." The published article, headlined "The Real MacColl" was illustrated with a photo of Kirsty crawling on all fours in a short, skin-tight black dress, black fish-net tights and high-heeled shoes. It was yet another pouty early image that smacked of pandering but in the article Kirsty protested (somewhat lamely, given the photo shoot) that:

> I don't particularly like being on stage, all dolled up, as I find it a bit soul-destroying, and in many respects I can't do myself justice that way. I prefer

writing songs and making records. I love being in the studio. I don't enjoy performing very much; I get scared. I find it less than glamorous having to tour the motorways of Britain and Europe and America, getting changed in draughty toilets and eating awful motorway food.

The privations of basic on-the-road life would not be much in evidence as the wife of the man who had just been named Producer of the Year by *Rolling Stone* magazine. Steve Lillywhite and Kirsty MacColl married on August 18, 1984, in the Anglican Church of St Leonards, Church Lane, Chelsham, very near to where Kirsty had grown up. Kirsty arrived at the church in a pink Cadillac, driven by a pink-suited chauffeur, 45 minutes late for the ceremony. She explained later: "My friend, who was doing my hair, got stuck into the champagne early in the morning and she was pretty slow." Despite the calming presence of her father, Ewan, as she got out of the car the bride admitted to being "practically hysterical with nervousness: I kept wanting to giggle."

Ewan MacColl's own working life and music was a universe away from the glitz and glamour of the celebrity pop world, but he could see his daughter's new status within that milieu. "Kirsty lived in a different world, and he recognized that," says Peggy Seeger. The song that Ewan had written for Peggy years ago, "The First Time Ever I Saw Your Face" had become a modern classic and would bring Ewan his greatest financial success, with dozens of cover versions recorded by different artists. Kirsty's father famously described Elvis Presley's take on the number as sounding like Romeo at the bottom of the Post Office tower, singing up to Juliet.

Nevertheless, Ewan had to explain that he couldn't afford to pay for his daughter's lavish and elaborate wedding. Peggy Seeger remembers Kirsty reassuring them: "Don't worry, Steve's a millionaire!" Lillywhite says the fact that Ewan took the traditional role of proud father and gave Kirsty away was enough for her: "It was a big thing for him to walk down the aisle with her, but he didn't really get involved. Kirsty was just amazed that he even did that."

In the congregation at the church, surrounded by countryside on the outskirts of Croydon, were members of U2, Simple Minds, Big Country and Frankie Goes to Hollywood. The most moving part of the ceremony was when Bono read the lesson, from Corinthians 1:13: "When I was a child, I spake as a child, I understood as a child, I thought as a child: but when I became a man, I put away childish things ..." Later, at the reception at the Selsdon Park Hotel, guests danced and drank the night away. "The reception was great," said Kirsty. "I've never had so many friends together in one place at one time. My mum kept Holly Johnson [of Frankie Goes to Hollywood] on the dance-floor for ages until he complained of exhaustion."

Even a glass of red wine accidentally spilt across MacColl's cream silk wedding dress by her new husband was laughed off. The couple spent their wedding night in the Ritz Hotel in central London, although their honeymoon was spent in Barbados. They had toyed with the idea of going to China instead, but the sun-drenched, beach-lounging weeks they'd imagined in the Caribbean didn't quite live up to expectations: they arrived during the rainy season, and the worst floods for more than eighty years.

MacColl would later joke in interviews that she got the most sought-after producer in Britain to work with her by sleeping with him. However, the constant references to her husband's – and father's – musical backgrounds eventually began to rankle. She had been making records for five years before she met Lillywhite, and was bitterly frustrated that she couldn't escape the implied criticisms that it was only thanks to the efforts and influence of the two most important men in her life that she had achieved any success:

> People are always asking, "What's it like being the wife of Steve Lillywhite and the daughter of Ewan MacColl?" They say, "Her dad's a famous song-writer; no wonder she's in the business." And now they say, "She's married to someone who's a successful music producer, so no wonder she makes records." The implication is that I only went into music because certain men guided me that way. I'm constantly asked, "How do you combine a career and family life?" They never ask my husband, or Sting, that question. It's plain old sexism, really.

This resentment was something that Kirsty MacColl, arguably, never quite escaped. "She was really tired of it," says Pete Glenister. "She'd say, 'Look, my father left and I hardly knew him!' Kirsty was her own woman. I think she knew she was a good songwriter. She always had strong opinions about what she liked and what she didn't like, what was good and what was bad."

Kirsty had been three months pregnant on her wedding day, and as Steve Lillywhite consolidated his position as the favourite producer of some of the biggest bands in rock and pop, her own career appeared set to lose its importance as she awaited the birth of their first child. Jamie Patrick MacColl Lillywhite was born on February 20, 1985. His maternal grandfather came to see him: "We went around when Jamie was born," remembers Peggy Seeger. "It didn't happen a lot. Ewan held his grandchild and was absolutely over the moon, but hardly showed it. He had this kind of bashfulness when he felt very emotional about something. I don't know where that came from."

Ewan's inability to show his emotions was so often seen in that reserved distance or an analytical, almost clinical approach. When Jamie was three months old, Kirsty and Steve were invited to Ewan and Peggy's home for a birthday party for their youngest child, Kitty. Just as they were all about to sing "Happy Birthday" and watch Kitty cut her cake, Jamie – who had been asleep in his cot in another room – started to cry, and Kirsty went out to console him. In her absence, everyone started singing "Happy Birthday"; within seconds, it became clear that Steve Lillywhite's own spontaneous and energetic rendition could not match the MacColl/Seeger family's carefully structured harmonies. As the final verse ended, they all applauded and Ewan remarked to one relative, "I really liked that fifth you sang." The MacColl family then proceeded to analyze the techniques in the constituent harmonies in a family sing-a-long of "Happy Birthday".

"All of them are spectacular technicians," says Steve Lillywhite. "Neill, Calum *and* Peggy Seeger, who is a brilliant guitar player. But none of them have that creative spark. With Kirsty, because she wasn't brought up with her father's overpowering influence, her creative talent was allowed to develop more because she wasn't a part of that."

Ironically, however, motherhood was to be accompanied by an unexpected resurgence in Kirsty's popularity. Her new husband had always felt that Kirsty's vocals deserved a less one-dimensional approach than had been used on them in the studio in the past. MacColl had challenged him to help her transform a song by Billy Bragg, called "A New England". Lillywhite recalls: "Kirsty said, 'I've got this song that Billy Bragg wrote. It's a great song but it sounds like a demo. I know I can make it a pop song.'"

Kirsty had recognized the potential in the song after seeing Bragg perform it at a gig she'd been to with Andy MacDonald. MacDonald was about to leave Stiff to set up his own record label, Go! Discs, to which Bragg would soon sign. The following day, she phoned Frank

Murray. "She was really excited," says Murray. "She said, 'You've got to hear this guy, Billy Bragg. He's just made this record.' She played me his album and it was brilliant, just so refreshing at that time. And Kirsty fell in love with 'A New England'."

In 1983, Bragg's voracious appetite for touring had helped immensely in promoting his debut album, *Life's a Riot with Spy vs Spy*. The album had originally been a collection of demos funded by Bragg's music publisher, Warner Chappell, but it was picked up by one of Charisma's senior A&R people, Peter Jenner, for the label's Utility imprint. He had made a written promise to Bragg: "We expect to release, unless it is indescribably ghastly, a record of some sort ..." Soon afterwards, Virgin Records took over the near-bankrupt Charisma and Jenner was among a number of employees who lost their jobs. He became Billy Bragg's manager. After setting up Go! Discs, Andy MacDonald had negotiated with Virgin to buy the rights to *Life's a Riot* and re-released it on his new label in November 1983.

MacColl had been impressed by Bragg's pared-down, no-bullshit style on the album and in his live shows: "He just got up on stage with his guitar and sang," she said. "I thought, 'This bloke's brilliant!'" When the pair finally met, at a Bragg gig at the Fulham Greyhound in London, they liked each other instantly and admitted to being mutual fans.

"She came up and spoke to me, and I was a bit in awe of her," says Bragg, who, despite his band Riff Raff being signed to Chiswick at the same time as the Drug Addix, had only become aware of MacColl's music when he worked in a second-hand record shop in London's East End. "The interesting thing about Kirsty for me, as a songwriter, was that she was writing songs and she was Ewan's daughter ... I really liked her whole vibe, her sensibility." Ewan MacColl had not been a major influence on Bragg's own music, unlike Dylan, Tim Hardin or Simon & Garfunkel, but he was familiar with his songs, and one or two would later creep into his repertoire.

Bragg and MacColl discovered they shared the same sense of humour. Kirsty was to later tell Lu Edmonds: "That Billy Bragg came around and he was really funny. I asked him, 'Do you want a drink, or something?' and he said, 'No, thanks, I'm a Muslim!'" At their first meeting, MacColl had also said that she would love to do a version of a song that was already a staple of Bragg's live set, "A New England". Bragg was happy for her to do it.

MacColl had decided that, at two minutes and thirteen seconds,

Bragg's original version was too short for a single. The lyrics, written from a male narrator's point of view, also needed a gender overhaul. She invited Bragg to her flat and cooked him a large breakfast while he added an extra verse to the song and changed the narrator's gender. So Bragg's original lyric, "People ask me when will I grow up to be a man/But all the girls I loved at school are already pushing prams", became "People ask me when will I grow up to understand/Why all the girls I knew at school are already pushing prams". Likewise, "I put you on a pedestal, they put you on the Pill" was changed to "I put you on a pedestal, you put me on the Pill", and "I'm just looking for another girl" became "Are you looking for another girl?"

Bragg's entire new verse read as follows:

> "My dreams were full of strange ideas
> My mind was set despite my fears
> Whenever things got in the way
> I never asked that boy to stay
> Once upon a time at home
> I sat beside the telephone
> Waiting for someone to pull me through
> When at last it didn't ring
> I knew it wasn't you ..."

—Billy Bragg, "A New England"

While Kirsty had loved the song when she first heard Bragg sing it, she felt a different arrangement would transform it: "I always thought 'A New England' would be great with loads of harmonies; it's such a good melody. Billy does it in a very rough way, and it's like a busker doing a really good Beatles song." MacColl reverted to her favourite sixties Beach Boys-inspired layered vocals that still made the song sound utterly contemporary.

With her husband as producer and a full band backing her, including Pete Glenister on programming and guitar, and Simon Climie on keyboards, MacColl recorded her version of a song that melts love and longing into politics and realism. Bragg had originally written the number after watching two satellites cross the sky far above the countryside in Northamptonshire. At first the narrator mistakes the satellites for two shooting stars, crossing in perfect parallel, then muses: "Is it wrong to wish on space hardware? I wish, I wish, I wish you'd care."

MacColl's cover version went into the UK chart on January 19, 1985, a month before Jamie was born. It peaked at Number 7, which earned MacColl another appearance on "Top of the Pops" but the thought of a hugely pregnant woman appearing in front of the cameras was almost too much for one faint-hearted producer to bear, as Frank Murray remembers: "The guy at 'Top of the Pops' didn't like Kirsty turning up pregnant. He didn't think it right that a pregnant woman should be singing on the show. He was a cranky bastard! By the nineties, everyone was singing on 'Top of the Pops' pregnant and showing off their bare bellies. But at that time, this guy was not happy. I couldn't begin to understand why this was a problem for him."

The video was filmed on a housing estate at the end of Abbey Road, the north-west London address made famous by the Beatles. It was a bitterly cold winter day, with Kirsty in the final weeks of her pregnancy. Filming was intermittent, with frequent breaks so that she could rest, as Billy Bragg explains:

Kirsty was hugely pregnant with Jamie, which was difficult. She had to work really hard. But she couldn't do anything about it, it was just one of those timing things. The music business is a lot more difficult for women. It's still a racist, sexist industry, despite all of its pretensions, particularly if you were like Kirsty and didn't look like a teenager. When Kirsty first appeared, when she was in her early twenties, it all fitted in fine and she looked much of a muchness with people like Rachel Sweet. But as she got older and better, as she matured and her voice improved, so the sexism that's endemic in our industry started to work against her.

Bragg loved MacColl's new version of his song. His devoted fans, however, were not as easily convinced: "We were on the road, and I got my sound man to play it as part of the music before the gig to see how the punters reacted. They were really freaked out by it, I'm sorry to say. Some of them thought it was a sacrilege. When it was released, a few people complained about it, that something had been done to the purity of Billy Bragg's work. I was thinking, 'Leave it out, this is great! This proves that I can write great pop songs without *having* to write a great pop song. This is really, really brilliant.' So I was very happy with it and very happy for Kirsty when it took off."

One disgruntled Bragg fan wrote to the *NME* complaining: "Ironic, isn't it? That to get played on Radio Uno you have to write a brilliant song and get it absolutely ruined by some pregnant, middle-aged, middle-of-the-road pop singer." The editor of the letters page proved unsympathetic: "Go away, cloth ears, we rate it, as Billy does, a great version."

The *NME* letters' editor and Billy Bragg were not alone in their admiration. Shane MacGowan opined, "Her version of 'A New England' turned a good song into a great song." By the time MacColl's single came out, Bragg's album *Life's a Riot* had sold about 80,000 copies. Within a month, the success of her version of "A New England" sent his album sales soaring to 120,000, earning Bragg his first gold record. And thanks to Bragg's insistence that all of his records had the lowest possible price, the album sticker stated, "Pay no more than £2.99" – the same price as Kirsty's 12" single.

Steve Lillywhite describes the success of "A New England" as "a whirlwind … a real breakthrough. It turned out really well, and it still sounds like a great record today." Stiff urged Kirsty to follow the single with another one immediately, before the momentum was lost. She recorded "He's on the Beach" about a close friend who'd abandoned Britain for a much happier life in Australia. "We went straight back into the studio," says Lillywhite, "to do 'He's on the Beach' because there was pressure. But Kirsty never followed up a hit with a hit; there would always be a flop after a hit. And she was not physically recovered from giving birth; she should have been relaxing and having a chilled-out time with her baby. But she was stuck in the studio and I was still living the lifestyle of a crazy eighties partying boy. 'He's on the Beach' was good, but it wasn't a hit."

Pete Glenister recalls, "Kirsty was up and running after 'A New England' but it was very hard to get any momentum with a baby." The new single had failed to make any impact, and the disappointment was compounded for MacColl when Polydor attempted to cash in on the success of "A New England" by repackaging highlights from her *Desperate Character*, along with some tracks from the *Real* sessions, and releasing them on an album to be titled *Kirsty MacColl's Greatest Hits*. After vociferous protests from MacColl, the company agreed to drop "Greatest Hits" from the title but insisted on packaging the album, somewhat confusingly, in the same sleeve as *Desperate Character*, and without any reference to the musicians featured on the tracks.

By late 1985, it was clear that Stiff Records was in deep financial trouble. Early the following year, the label declared itself bankrupt, and MacColl found herself being considered along with the goods, chattels and assets, with a contract to be sold on to clear the company's debts. ZTT Records, the record label co-owned and run by record producer Trevor Horn, later absorbed the company.

The hiatus in Kirsty's recording career coincided with the arrival of a sustained period of a creative ailment that was, on and off, to trouble her for much of her artistic career: writer's block. "If she was feeling depressed," says Dave Ruffy, a musician who was to become one of Kirsty's closest collaborators, "she might have writer's block because she couldn't find that 'place' again. But she did find it – regularly." It would have been little consolation to the stricken songwriter that she was, at least, in very good company.

Fame, acclaim and talent offer no protection against writer's block. Noël Coward confided in his journal in 1945: "Made a little progress musically today, but my mind and hands feel heavy. It will pass soon, I hope. I know nothing so dreary as feeling that you can't make the sounds or write the words that your whole creative being is yearning for." For some, such as Joni Mitchell, a form of crop rotation works: when the field of writing is barren, she turns to painting.

Faced with this problem, Tom Waits believes that, "it's important to light a fire under yourself. It's hard to feel familiar and comfortable with the uncomfortable and unfamiliar, but I think it's important, so that you feel that you're carving new wood and throwing a rock through the window now and then." Waits' one-time paramour, Rickie Lee Jones, once described writer's block as, "No ideas at all, no focus, no interest. Not the cup that runneth over." She found a singular cure: "I studied Cat Stevens, Paul McCartney, and Curtis Mayfield: the coolest. I wanted that sexual energy. I'd felt it; I just needed to write it." For his part, Steve Earle owns several different guitars and believes each is capable of producing different songs; if one fails him, he does the rounds of the others until something good emerges.

One of MacColl's favourite song-writers, Ray Davies, has described a highly personal form of "sensory plotting" to get himself writing again: "It's all jumbled-up thoughts that come out, and you put yourself on that emotional plane, in that corridor, and it leads to an idea. You just get yourself into the role, the moment. It's all based on the truth; otherwise it would be purely cosmic and have no substance. There's nothing wrong with writing cosmic thoughts, but it has got to tie up mathematically. I hate math, but I love symmetry."

For Kirsty, the solution lay in collaborating with others on their projects. She threw herself into a series of musical partnerships that were to occupy her greatly over the coming years. This arrangement held many advantages for her. She got a creative buzz and could have fun and work hard, but without the responsibility of carrying an entire album. In no time, MacColl became a one-woman small-world effect on eighties music.

In a variation of American psychologist Stanley Milgram's "six degrees of separation" social experiments in the seventies, it became possible to follow the links between a significant number of eighties bands, songs and albums through Kirsty. Milgram set out to uncover the connections within our social networks of friends, acquaintances and colleagues. He demonstrated that a chain of only five or six intermediaries connects us all to each other. And so it became with Kirsty MacColl's musical adventures through much of the eighties, as she waited to be disposed of along with the rest of Stiff's assets:

I was left sitting around the house waiting for the receiver to sell my contract before I could record again. The only thing I could do legally was session work so every time the phone rang, I'd say, "Yes!" just to get out of the house. I never imagined having babies, I never imagined getting married. I always thought I'd be a full-time miserable sod. I wasn't writing my own stuff when I was pregnant and I felt like all my brain cells had turned to jelly, so if I got a call from someone who I respected as an artist, saying, "We're making a record and we'd like you to come and sing on a track," then I'd be glad to do it because it felt like I was still alive!

The painter Maro Gorky Spender had similarly remarked that she had tried to return to painting after giving birth to two children in two years, "but my brain didn't work". (She too had been prey to the daughter-of/wife-of template that so irked Kirsty, as the daughter of the Armenian artist, Arshile Gorky and wife of Matthew Spender, son of the poet Sir Stephen Spender.)

But the popular notion of Kirsty as a songwriter-turned-housewife, chained to the babies for years on end, is far from the truth. "Like ninety-nine per cent of mums, she had absolute, wonderful love for her children; she was a great mum," says Steve Lillywhite. But she also tried to remain focused on her career, however intermittent it might have been:

> She was always working. She would be doing demos or singing on my productions, helping me out. She never just descended into domestic life and gave up music. There was always music, always, all the time. She never gave up music for family life. We were lucky enough to have a full-time nanny. If the kids ever saw us first thing in the morning, it would have freaked them out!

Kirsty MacColl became one of the most in-demand session vocalists in Britain in the mid-to-late eighties, guesting for artists as diverse as the Rolling Stones, Talking Heads, Van Morrison, Robert Plant, Simple Minds, the Smiths and the Wonder Stuff. MacColl was later to work with both Johnny Marr and Morrissey when the Smiths broke up, co-writing with Marr and guesting for Morrissey on several songs including "Interesting Drug", of which she remarked: "It's a very funny song, he's a very humorous writer, very articulate. Wit is essential because if it ceases to have any fun value – and you *can* be fun and intelligent at the same time – then people think, 'Oh, sod it, give me Kylie instead!'"

Philip Rambow believes that the music industry itself was partly to blame for Kirsty's decision to opt for cameo spots at this point in her career:

> She'd say, "Okay, no one wants to sign me to a record deal, I'll be a backing singer." She became everybody's favourite backing singer. She'd walk into the studio and she'd say, "This is the way I work, if that's okay with you. Just leave me alone and I'll do my stuff and if you like it, that's fine and if you don't, we can change it." She'd just go for it. She'd do layered vocals and three-part harmonies. But one of the reasons she went that route is because no one would sign her up.

Although the mainstream pop milieu of the eighties was far removed from Peggy Seeger's own folk world, she was impressed with Kirsty's chameleon approach. "She sang with so many people, she traversed the scene," says Seeger. "Kirsty was incredible. She sang in bands with almost everyone who was anyone back then, and was very well respected for her ability to make harmonies and to correct other people's texts; to make comments on their words. She had a very, very good word sense."

Steve Lillywhite was producing several of the acts Kirsty worked with at the time, and his wife was an obvious choice whenever he was searching for the perfect setting for immaculately assembled vocal arrangements: "In terms of my career, she had the fantastic knack of doing backing vocals on something I was producing, to make it better but not imposing 'Kirsty MacColl' on it. She would be completely chameleon-esque." And so she was able to tailor her own very distinctive style to artists as diverse as David Byrne and Climie Fisher.

"I got asked to work with a lot of interesting people around that time," she was to reflect, "a lot of people that I really admired, like the Smiths and Talking Heads. Those became very productive relationships; they weren't just like doing a backing vocal gig. They asked me because they wanted my vocal arrangements. I do a kind of one-woman Beach Boys thing." Johnny Marr confirms this statement: "That technique could only have been done with one person. She knew how to stack her voice; it was a very clever thing that she'd worked out. It was very deliberate, the way her voice sounded. If you got a bunch of people singing those harmonies as she'd mapped them out, it wouldn't be nearly as cool."

With her own work, MacColl was even more relentless in her search for the perfect harmony, layering track after track, says Steve Lillywhite:

I would be recording the harmonies. She would get halfway through and I'd say, " No, that's the wrong note", and she'd say, " Just let me do what I'm doing, I've got this plan". So I'd just carry on and then she'd do one other piece of the jigsaw that connected the whole thing. A lot of people, when they sing a harmony to a lead vocal, will just do a third above or a third below, and keep it very modular. What she would do is dance around the melody with her harmonies. It was an amazing talent. A lot of the times, she would want to put too many harmonies on. She hated the sound of her voice when it was just one voice. She loved it when it was Brian Wilson-esque.

While working on the Rolling Stones' *Dirty Work* album, Kirsty was given guitar lessons by Keith Richards. She was remarkably unfazed by his guitar-legend status. Johnny Marr, who also worked on the album, recalls a late-night jam session:

I remember about half-three in the morning, me and Kirsty and Keith Richards playing Everly Brothers songs. She would say, "The key's too low, change the key," so we'd change the key, and she'd say, "No, down a little bit," and we'd go down a little bit, and then she'd say, "Do it like you were doing it before, but just up one". We would say, "That's what we're doing," and Kirsty would say, "No, it *isn't* what you're doing!" Keith Richards was looking over at me with this hangdog expression. I just thought, "This is brilliant, she's berating Keith Richards. She's kicking his arse!"

Steve Lillywhite affectionately describes Richards as having "that old English 'a woman's place is in the home – a man's work is real work' attitude" that would seemingly be at total odds with Kirsty's own strong personality and forcefully expressed views about where her place should be in the world – and the recording studio: "When we were in the studio once, Kirsty went up to Keith and started talking to him. One of the roadies came up to me and said, 'Steve, Keith won't like this, the producer's missus talking to him when he's trying to work. This has happened before and this could be a flashpoint here. She's asking him about playing guitar!' But, of course, Keith took to Kirsty like crazy. He just loved her, and there was never any problem. They were kindred spirits in a certain way. She was one of the guys; she loved their company."

MacColl was equally underwhelmed by the fame of Irish rock gods, U2. Steve Lillywhite had returned to work with the band on what would become their career-defining album, 1987's *The Joshua Tree*. Kirsty joined Steve in Dublin while the album was being recorded, and would often visit the studio. When it came time to order the tracks, to sequence the album, Bono remembers that Kirsty intervened:

She said, "I know what to do, you're all too close to it. You should listen to me; I'm very good at this. My idea is, pick the best song first, and have the second-best song second, and the third-best song third. If it all works out, when you play side two, it will be your favourite in six months." It was amazing. I think there was a little more artfulness than that, but she took it very seriously and Steve was very encouraging and said, "Actually, she's oddly good at this." It's innate DJ skills. The contour of an album can decide whether the whole is greater than the sum of the parts; that's really what is going on. It was an exciting time, Steve and Kirsty were in love and they were losing themselves in music and a little bit of alcohol. At the time it was revelry and it was a fiesta.

Released in March 1987, *The Joshua Tree* entered the UK chart at Number 1. Its first week sales of 235,000 copies made it the fastest-selling album in British chart history at that point. One month later it also topped the US album chart, and U2 were on the cover of *Time* magazine. "Both Kirsty and I always thought of ourselves as outsiders," reflects Billy Bragg, "even despite the fact that she hung around with people like U2 and so on. I always thought that she felt a bit like me, that we weren't part of that highly polished eighties pop thing; we were outside of that. But Kirsty was bound to end up mixing with those people because she was so talented at what she did, not just as a songwriter but also as a voice, once she got into the studio. She was exceptional. She could do things that other people could only do with machines."

Around this time, MacColl renewed her friendship with Mark Nevin, whose latest band, Fairground Attraction, had just had a massive pop hit with the single "Perfect" from their debut album, *First of a Million Kisses*. By then, Kirsty and Steve were a *bona fide* celebrity couple, recalls Nevin:

> It was all, "Oh, we were out with Bono last night," and "David Byrne's on the phone." It was kind of overwhelming. Now that I was in this sort of world, now I had made this money and I was successful, I didn't know where to go to hang out because you still have your old friends but they kind of become weird after a while. You'd always end up buying them dinner or something because they couldn't afford to. So it was nice to be hanging out with other people who could afford to buy dinner as well.

Steve Lillywhite's next high-profile project was with the Pogues, the glorious, inspiringly ramshackle Anglo-Celt band who were by now also managed by Frank Murray. Their guitarist Phil Chevron had proudly defined their ethos by saying, "We represent the people who don't get the breaks. People can look at us and say, 'My God, if that bunch of tumbledown wrecks can do it, so can I'."

The band's singer, Irish-born Shane MacGowan, had been in punk outfits the Nipple Erectors and the Millwall Chainsaws. He had then formed Pogue Mahone – Gaelic for "kiss my arse" – with musicians and drinking pals, Spider (Peter) Stacy, Jem (Jeremy) Finer, Andrew Ranken and James Fearnley in north London in 1983. They formed their own eponymous label to release their first single, "The Dark Streets of London", which was promptly banned from daytime radio programmes by the BBC when it learned of the English translation of "pogue mahone".

One month later Stiff signed the band, reputedly for half a crate of Guinness, and released their debut album, *Red Roses for Me,* late in 1984. Elvis Costello produced the next year's follow-up, *Rum, Sodomy and the Lash;* the title was taken from Winston Churchill's description of life in the Royal Navy. This album included the Pogues' thrashy homage to Ewan MacColl, with their cover of his Salford saga, "Dirty Old Town", a version that helped to bring Ewan's work to a new audience and a young generation, even though MacColl failed to appreciate this.

Yet it was Ewan's son-in-law Steve Lillywhite who was to produce what would be the Pogues' landmark album *If I Should Fall From Grace With God* in 1988. This was their masterpiece, even though Jeff Gordinier of *Entertainment Weekly* reflected that: "The album that blasted their tunnel vision to smithereens wound up doing the same thing to them that *London Calling* did to the Clash: it ruined them. Pretty soon the fun went out of their live performances and the experimental dabbling got ridiculous." In fact, the Pogues/Clash synchronicity went even further: the Pogues had supported the Clash on tour, and Clash frontman Joe Strummer would later join the band to replace the increasingly wayward and wasted MacGowan, who quit the Pogues in 1991.

But in 1988, *If I Should Fall From Grace With God* was acknowledged as the Pogues' finest moment. "I thought, 'Wow, this is something different for me,'" says Steve Lillywhite. "Being in Ireland with U2, I'd become quite interested in Irish music. The Pogues took traditional Irish music and expanded it and they were fantastic musicians. I was lucky to get a great band at a great time. In all the madness, I managed to keep it together and I'm very proud of that record."

Just as their original name had caused controversy until Stiff persuaded them to abridge it, pressure over their unashamed politics had forced them to re-edit the video for an early single, "A Pair of Brown Eyes", as it showed them spitting on a poster of the then British Prime Minister, Margaret Thatcher.

If I Should Fall From Grace With God was to trail controversy in its wake when one song was banned for its political content. "Birmingham Six" highlighted the flawed convictions of six Irishmen found guilty in 1975 of bomb attacks on two pubs in the English city of Birmingham, which had killed 21 people and injured more than 160 on November 21, 1974. The Court of Appeal in London was to quash their convictions in March 1991, freeing the Birmingham Six after they had spent sixteen years in British prisons. The IRA later described the bombings as "regrettable"; those responsible have never been brought to justice.

The Pogues also had to change the lyrics of the song that would become their best known, "Fairytale of New York". American audiences balked at some of the language, including the word "faggot", which was changed to "haggard" when the Pogues appeared on US television shows. Once again, Kirsty MacColl found that renewed musical fame arrived with a child. On September 3, 1987, she gave birth to Louis Stephen MacColl Lillywhite, her second son; three months later, she was being feted for one of the most unlikely Christmas hits of all time.

MacColl's duet with Shane MacGowan – himself a Christmas baby, born on December 25, 1957 – cast them as a quarrelsome Irish immigrant couple down on their luck in New York City one Christmas Eve. He is drunk on ale, nostalgia and false hope; she is bitter with realism and recriminations. The song was to cement MacColl in the public consciousness. It has become a seasonal staple, a post-modern Christmas fable, despite Kirsty's initial reservations: "When I was asked to sing it, I was a bit dubious, as I had a fear of folk music that only someone with a folk-singing parent could have. But I said I'd give it a go and if they didn't like it, they could get someone else. They liked it."

MacGowan and the Pogues banjo-player, Jem Finer, wrote the song in 1985: "I had written two songs," says Finer. "One had a good tune and crap lyrics; the other had the idea for 'Fairytale' but the tune was poxy. I gave them to Shane, he gave it a Broadway melody, and there it was. It's not the usual sort of festive record, but it's true to life. After all, more people argue, get divorced and commit suicide at Christmas than any other time of the year."

The song had originally been intended as a duet between MacGowan and the band's bass-player, Cait (pronounced 'Cot') O'Riordan. The two had already recorded a demo, a pre-Christmas release date was fixed, and a cover photograph was taken. But the band struggled to get exactly the right arrangement, and as a deadline became imminent for releasing the single and distributing and promoting it in time for the Christmas market, Frank Murray reluctantly shelved plans to put it out. They had simply run out of time. It would be another two years before the Pogues would record again, by which time O'Riordan had left, a few months after marrying Elvis Costello in 1986.

Frank Murray still believed that "Fairytale" could be a hit – if they could find the right woman to play counterpoint to Shane MacGowan: "I said to the band at various intervals, 'We need to get someone like Kirsty MacColl.' As it happened, I got Steve to produce *If I Should Fall From Grace With God*. He was married to Kirsty and everything fell into place. It worked out perfectly."

Shane MacGowan saw the merit in the idea immediately: "I just thought … *bang*! What a brilliant idea! 'You scumbag, you maggot, you cheap lousy faggot …': what a brilliant person to do those lines." Billy Bragg concurs: "The real defining moment is when he sings, "I could have been someone", and the fact that she runs rings around Shane. You need to be a pretty forceful personality to take on the Pogues and come off better. And I think she does. It's her song as much as their song."

The song is constructed seamlessly, with perfect inflections in the call-and-response between MacGowan and MacColl – all the more surprising given that they never recorded it together. While recording in Ireland, Shane had sung the track himself then written out the lyrics, indicating the lines for MacColl to sing later. Lillywhite took MacGowan's recording and the lyric sheet back to London with him:

> In the studio at home, I basically made "holes" where Kirsty's vocals were supposed to be. She heard his voice but they never sang together. It took a long time to do Kirsty's vocals, to get them absolutely right. It's much more difficult than you might think to sing that song, and she did a great job to put the harmonies just where they were. Because it wasn't her song, she couldn't fill it with harmonies. We really had to make sure that the lead vocal was just great and we did that.

Lillywhite returned to Ireland. When he played the tape to the Pogues' singer, it was clear from the expression on MacGowan's face that Shane knew he had more work to do. "His vocals were shit, to be honest," says Steve. "So I said, 'Shane you've got to sing this again,' so he went in and had to give a performance to match Kirsty's. It took us a whole day to do those vocals." The extra effort paid rich dividends.

In Christmas week of 1987, "Fairytale of New York" reached Number 2 in the UK charts. It was only kept at bay by the Pet Shop Boys' electro-pop ditty, "Always on my Mind". Frank Murray broke the news to the band when they were all in the bar at the Holiday Inn in Glasgow, the day after a sell-out gig at Barrowlands. They were sanguine about it, ordered up another round, and gave an impromptu rendition of the song with Jem Finer at the bar's piano.

Their Number 2 slot did guarantee an appearance on "Top of the Pops". In 2003, when the programme's presenters were asked to name their enduring memory of the 40-year-old show, ex-Radio One DJ Mike Read named the Pogues/MacColl appearance as his personal highlight, describing it as "absolutely magical". From the outset, the song was clearly exceptional, its bittersweet lyrics forming a much-needed counterpoint to the saccharine, commercialized hype and forced jollity of the season, the overly sentimentalized nonsense of the Yuletide novelty hits and the quick cash-ins for the Christmas market.

Few other songs can match the anarchy of its lyrics when set against the prevailing tide of cheery seasonal sentiment. In the pantheon of great Christmas hits, "Fairytale of New York" is arguably joined only by John and Yoko's "Happy Christmas (War is Over)" (1972), Jona Lewie's "Stop the Cavalry" (1980) and Band Aid's "Do they Know it's Christmas?" (1984). Furthermore, the Pogues' song is now as ubiquitous at Christmas as Slade's "Merry Xmas Everybody" – and, for most people, far more welcome.

The video for "Fairytale" was shot in New York, in grainy black and white, without a single gaudy concession to the colours of the festive season. As MacColl and MacGowan spar and then reconcile, walking the mean streets together, the mournful band play in a smoky downtown dive, and the real "boys from the NYPD choir" sing "Galway Bay". The actor Matt Dillon has a walk-on role, tumbling MacGowan into the "drunk tank" of an authentic New York Police Department cell. "It was great *craic*," recalls MacGowan. "We were in the city for ages. It took three or four days to shoot."

There was talk of the band's heavy-drinking life imitating the video art of the drunk-tank. However, MacColl loyally defended the Pogues against suggestions that they were little more than a riotous bunch of drunkards who just happened to make music, snapping at a *Record Mirror* journalist: "A couple of them drink, but that's not unusual out of a bunch of eight guys. You shouldn't generalize. That's a load of boring old nonsense anyway. They're great musicians; anything else is superfluous."

Kirsty was invited to join the Pogues for one gig during their tour of

France and Germany in 1988, as they set off to promote the single and their new album. She agreed, and the night was a triumph. She phoned Steve Lillywhite immediately afterwards and he could hear the jubilant Pogues partying in the background:

> She said, "Ah, Steve, you know how I said I would only come out to do one gig? Well, they've asked me to do the rest of the ten days. That's okay, isn't it?!" It was a great way for her to start back into it again. She sang two songs. She sang the big hit, so she would be given so much love; the moment she walked out on stage, people would go, "Oh, it's that song!" It was a win-win situation for her. It was a great way of getting confidence. It was like having training wheels on a bike; she couldn't fall off.

MacColl thus became accepted as another member of the Pogues family, just as would happen with Joe Strummer in years to come. "Unmistakably, the tour bus was a classier joint with her on board," says Phil Chevron. "She genuinely brought out the best in everyone. Hotel bars at four in the morning were good, too: a solicitous Kirsty holding forth – to whichever Pogue she had not yet managed to drink under the table – about the dangers of the lifestyle."

Onstage too, she stole the show. "The audiences saw one of their own in Kirsty," says Frank Murray. "She wasn't in the papers daily talking about what new handbag she bought yesterday, or whether she had an energy bracelet, or whatever you're supposed to do. People knew that Kirsty was the genuine article." Spider Stacy recalls, "One thing that really sticks in my mind is the response that she used to get when she walked out on stage to do 'Fairytale'. The audiences absolutely loved her."

While MacColl would also join the band on stage for their rendition of her father's song "Dirty Old Town", "Fairytale" quickly became the highlight of every single performance, recalls Philip Chevron:

> When Shane MacGowan ruefully laments, "I could have been someone", this was the moment when, every night without fail, the tear ducts would do battle with the heartstrings. Two thousand, sometimes ten thousand voices raised in reproach, united with our flame-haired cheerleader, our big sister, the Maureen O'Hara of our brighter dreams: "Well, so could anyone!" I would try to catch her eye in the midst of the moment and would sometimes be rewarded with a conspiratorial wink. It was an open secret

that chronic stage fright had long since separated Kirsty from her audience. Now, kidding herself that she was somehow camouflaged by this octet of ramshackle guys she became, well, Kirsty Galore.

Chevron was right. It was exactly that welcoming, enveloping "camouflage" that held the key to Kirsty being able to go out on stage without being paralysed by anxiety, agrees Frank Murray:

When she came onto the stage, the crowd went crazy for her. Kirsty got all of this love from the audience. The Pogues' fans saw her as a Pogue. And she was singing what has now become an iconic song; it's not just a Pogues' song, it's become a crossover. Kirsty would come on and sing two or three songs, and she had no worries. The show was not depending on Kirsty, so when she went on stage, everything was ready for her, the crowd were going crazy. She came on stage and she was their sweetheart. Then Shane would take her hand and try to waltz with her around the stage. I think the crowd had sympathy for her because Shane was not always in the best condition to waltz! But she could go on stage and totally relax.

MacColl loved her touring experience with the Pogues. Her decision to go on stage with them each night had one major side-effect: it cured her of that crippling stage fright that had made her own tour, many years earlier, such an ordeal. She was to later marvel at her newfound freedom:

Gigging with The Pogues made me realize that you could actually enjoy being on the stage. I'd never quite experienced that before, so I could never work out why people did it. But I realized that there was a lot of fun involved as well, and it gives you a completely new approach to singing.

Steve Lillywhite also realized that his wife's involvement with the Pogues was her stepping-stone back to being able to play live. "There's a big difference between coming on as a guest and being *the* person," he says. "I always think of Bono as being the ultimate showman but Kirsty never had, in those days, that sense of 'I need to project to the person in the back of the audience to get them to love me'. Bono almost gets in a shamanic state when he's on stage singing live, but Kirsty never really lost herself in that." Even more importantly, being surrounded by the Pogues' boisterous, blasphemous, life-enhancing creative energy also emboldened her to return to her own writing and recording with a passion that she hadn't felt for years.

CHAPTER FIVE

Designer Life

For Kirsty MacColl, a happy if chaotic home life with two young children and a music producer husband who was in demand all over the world meant there had been little energy left over for her own writing. The crowded hours of immersion in the needs and demands of a rapidly growing family – however healthy one's budget for nannies, gardeners and cleaners – meant that time for musical creativity was one of the very few luxuries she could not afford, says Frank Murray:

> Kirsty went through phases. Just prior to marrying Steve, and then after marrying him, she put her career on hold. She went where he went: if he was in New York, Kirsty went to New York. Then motherhood came along. Also, there wasn't anything like a Kirsty MacColl band, a regular touring band. It can be tough to write that hit song unless you're out there and you have a fan base that you're playing to each night. It can be really, really tough.

The frequent cameo appearances on other people's albums had kept MacColl working sporadically, but it was the success of "Fairytale of New York" that had helped to ease her episodic writer's blocks and given her renewed confidence to venture back into the studio and believe that she could again find a record company to sign her. Frank Murray credits "Fairytale" with raising her profile within an industry where many had simply written her off: "It put her back in the spotlight, it got her back on TV, and she was great in the video. Record companies started to believe in her again." The Pogues' tour had also shown record company bosses that MacColl had put her much-publicized stage fright behind her and could go on stage and give a great live performance to promote new releases.

Kirsty had also matured almost beyond recognition from the young woman who'd penned "They Don't Know" and "Chip Shop". The radical shift in life experiences and the immediate and immovable stake in the future that parenthood brings with it had endowed her with a sharper sense of political insight and a more focused and less egocentric view of the world than being young, free and single had demanded of her. MacColl had gone from being pregnant twice in quick succession, and being either housebound or travelling with her husband, to being out on the road with the Pogues, living another lifestyle with freedom from domesticity. There was so much waiting to come out in her writing that had lain dormant for too long, she suddenly realized:

Things that worried me when I was 19 seem trivial now. Your life changes when you have kids. I feel more politically aware since I've had the children, because you're more conscious of the effect that everything has on the future. I'm not saying you should go away and become Mother Teresa, but there are ways of bringing about change without burning down the House of Commons.

MacColl's children were among the reasons for her stop-start career, but by no means the only reason, says Pete Glenister: "Kirsty was never going to be the kind of mum that just palmed them off. She was involved full-time with them, and it was very difficult. There's the whole physical thing of getting up in the middle of the night, but there's also the mental thing of being in that place where all you're thinking about is the next bottle. It's hard to think about lyrics, when you're so bound up in the mundanity of it. However happy or unhappy you are, it's very hard to get into that 'head' place where you need to be to write songs. I think that was often Kirsty's problem."

Billy Bragg concurs: "When you have kids, it takes you a while to get back to focusing on what you're doing. They take up so much time, and rightly so. That's the way it should be but it can sometimes be particularly difficult for women." "She wasn't resentful, it was her own choice because she thought that kids need a good grounding," says Dave Ruffy. "And Kirsty did a great job with those boys. But as an artist, it's very difficult to put your career on hold. How soon people forget ..."

By 1987, Kirsty and Steve had moved to a large house in the affluent west London suburb of Ealing. They would host the rock and roll equivalent of a salon, with huge amounts of food, drink, music and good company. Their guests ranged from old school friends to rock stars and supermodels, and from respected stalwarts of British theatre and television to Stella McCartney, Kate Bush and assorted members of the Rolling Stones and U2.

Among the guests at a New Year's Eve party at the house was Joni Mitchell, who came along with a friend of Steve's, the former Free and Bad Company drummer Simon Kirke. Kirsty was thrilled to meet Joni and immediately commandeered her. In the course of the evening, Kirsty, in a sweet fan-like gesture, gave Joni a thoughtful gift – one of her own favourite books, in which she had written a brief inscription. The regal Ms Mitchell accepted the gift but her failure to reciprocate left Kirsty feeling very disgruntled.

"Kirsty was thinking, 'Joni Mitchell, how fantastic!'" says Steve, "But she never got anything back; not a thank you or anything. And I remember her saying, 'Bloody hell, she never gave me anything!' But it was like you don't give something to get something back! I'm sure Joni Mitchell didn't really know who Kirsty was, or that it was such an important thing that Kirsty had given her."

Jean MacColl's friends from Theatre Workshop would drop by, and Joan Littlewood was a regular guest at her goddaughter's home. "In a funny way, Kirsty had a lot of Joan Littlewood's spirit in her," reflects Frank Murray, "in her originality, in not being bound by convention, and in the way that Kirsty that revolutionized things for women singer-songwriters in Britain."

The Ealing parties would spill into the large garden, which had been planned and planted lovingly by MacColl herself. She had had an exorbitantly expensive reed bed laid out to filter the household's waste water, and was such a fervent advocate that she would later make a programme about such projects and their environmental benefits for the BBC. A large pond was home to a school of koi carp. "When you were there, you were a guest," says comedian and TV presenter Phill Jupitus, who came to know MacColl through his friend Billy Bragg. "She was very European in that way. There was a big table in the back garden by the back door, where everyone sat and always a bottle of wine on the go. You were never far from a drink at that house – and not in a bad way."

The couple had set up a small studio at home, and here they recorded a three-song demo with Pete Glenister. It contained the MacColl-penned "Free World" (among the first of what she would call her 'post-parenthood' songs), "What do Pretty Girls do?" (co-written with Glenister) and a cover of the Kinks' "Days". "Kirsty had grown up a lot," says Glenister. "She was a lot older, had lived a lot more, and had had a lot of time to write. Once she got started, she wrote really quickly." The fruits of this session persuaded Virgin Records to offer Kirsty a deal and take over her contract from Stiff, which was by then a mere shadow of its former glorious self, and would become little more than a re-issues label – albeit one with an extraordinary back catalogue.

In March 1989, Virgin released "Free World", Kirsty MacColl's first single in four years. Its theme was a biting indictment, wreathed in melodic pop, of the privations brought to so many in Britain during the long leadership of the Conservative Party Prime Minister, Margaret Thatcher, whose decade in power had made her the longest serving British prime minister of the twentieth century. Thatcher's free enterprise, monetarist strategies had seen the privatization of nationalized industries amid a swathe of legislation that emasculated trade unions while empowering big business. No part of British society was left untouched in the "greed is good" eighties, as MacColl's song reflected:

> "I thought of you when they closed down the school
> And the hospital too
> Did they think that you were better?
> They were wrong"

> —Kirsty MacColl, "Free World"

The song's anthemic chorus urged the clans to rise again, "women and men united by a struggle". MacColl could hardly claim the credit, but one year after the song's release, Margaret Thatcher resigned, ousted by her party in a leadership challenge that brought John Major to power. Thatcher left 10 Downing Street in tears, but the legacy of the Thatcher years became a permanent part of British society.

MacColl's new-found confidence then bore fruit with an album that had developed from the early demo sessions in her home studio. 1989's *Kite* was her first album under the new Virgin deal, and her first to be released in the United States, where it was picked up by Charisma. Jon Webster, then an executive at Virgin, says, "People were excited to work with Kirsty, because she was obviously a class act and the songs were really good." For Steve Lillywhite:

> *Kite* was the most complete album that we did. I set it up in a way that we got a great band together and we went into a studio and recorded everyone at the same time. Then we took the tapes home to our studio and did all the vocals without adding any extra instruments. There are different ways of making records. With some, you add everything individually; with other ones, you try to get a group performance. For this whole album, it was ninety per cent a group performance. It was the most coherent, together album.

Kite's line-up of musicians included Pink Floyd guitarist Dave Gilmour, who inspired the album's title. Gilmour, who has played on dozens of tracks for his friends and artists he admires, traditionally asks them to make a donation to charity – normally Amnesty International or Greenpeace – instead of paying him a fee. When MacColl had asked him what he wanted in return for playing on her album, the Floyd man told her, "Just send a kite to Armenia" – a reference to the huge aid effort that had followed a catastrophic earthquake that hit Armenia on December 7, 1988. More than 25,000 people died, half a million were made homeless and the country's economic and social infrastructure was devastated. Gilmour was among the musicians who organised the Rock Aid Armenia CD and video to raise funds for the humanitarian and reconstruction effort.

MacColl credited Johnny Marr with not only urging her to cover the Smiths' "You Just Haven't Earned it Yet Baby" (one of two covers on the original vinyl release of *Kite*) but also to stop making excuses to herself about why she wasn't ready to pick up her own writing again: "He suggested I do 'Just Haven't Earned it Yet'. We had worked on Talking Heads and Billy Bragg albums together, and Johnny was really encouraging. He was always saying, 'Why aren't you doing anything? Get off your arse!' He's a very energetic, 'up' person to be around."

MacColl was to later describe the poignant Smiths' song as the story of her life, with particular reference, it seemed, to the following: "If you're wondering why/All the love that you long for eludes you/And people are rude and cruel to you … You just haven't earned it yet, baby/You must suffer and cry for a longer time."

This proved the start of a strong collaborative musical relationship with Johnny Marr. The ex-Smith played guitar on several tracks on *Kite*, including the cover of "Days":

> We played for about ten hours, and it was great because we were getting
> the feeling for it, it was full on, and we started to really nail it. When we
> finally did the take, we were holding our breath as we did the last chord,
> after all that work. Kirsty had really put us through it. As the last chord died
> away, there was complete silence, then she said, "About bloody time!"

There was an irony at play here. The original recording of "Days", by
the Kinks, had also taken far longer than expected. The Kinks bass-
player, Peter Quaife, who left the band soon after, was to complain that
"Ray kept us in the studio so damn long, I was beginning to lose my
mind." Ray Davies himself recalls that a frustrated Quaife wrote
"Daze" as the title on the master-tape, then in later years Davies said of
the song in his autobiography, *X-Ray*: "I didn't realize that what I was
writing would be the most significant song of my life. The song
predicted the end of the group."

Mark Nevin, another regular musical partner, thoroughly approved of
Kite: "I heard the singles like 'Days' and 'Free World' on the radio and they
sounded good, but when I heard the album at home, listening to it and
reading the lyrics, I was absolutely amazed at how good it was." Music
critics were in agreement. Steve Lamacq wrote in the *NME* that *Kite* was:

> ... the first non-disposable Kirsty MacColl record. In a charming way that
> makes cutesy pop records like "Chip Shop" just pieces of bubblegum, *Kite*
> is a bit more serious: something more to get your teeth into. It's anti-bimbo,
> anti-yuppie, but 100 per cent positive pop. From "15 Minutes", a jazz tirade
> against starlets who kiss and tell to the Sunday papers, to "Innocence",
> taking a swipe at the "I'm all right, Jack" mentality, *Kite* paints a surprisingly
> vicious picture of Thatch's Britain while still finding room for tender
> moments like "Mother's Ruin" and "The End of a Perfect Day". Even "Free
> World" has defied the playlists with its left-of-centre political portrait. It's a
> long way from her teenage angst beginnings.

Melody Maker's Dave Jennings saw *Kite* as "a glossy, thoroughly contem-
porary-sounding piece of literate adult pop", while Roddy Thomson,
writing in the *Glasgow Evening Times*, declared it "excellent ... Kirsty has
always been willing to address what she feels is important in today's
society, and the new single 'Free World', is no exception."

The lyrical emphasis of "Free World" left MacColl open to criticism.
It's easy to be cynical about wealthy pop stars peeping above the

parapets of their sprawling homes in London and the south of France long enough to comment on social problems that have no direct effect on them. They can, after all, afford to pay for private health care and schooling to avoid the vastly over-burdened state health and education systems. MacColl, however, had stints on unemployment benefit and seen her mother struggle with work and child-care arrangements to bring up two children on her own. She said of the song:

> It's really about greed. But it's all part of the great divide between north and south in Britain, which this government has probably done more than any other to worsen. I don't know if song lyrics change people's ideas, and I'm not saying everyone should write like that. But if they can make people think at least, then the whole thing must be worthwhile. People have to take more responsibility. We're all in this together.

Regardless of critical approval, MacColl herself believed that *Kite* was the best work she had done, up to that point: "It was the first good album I'd made. I had plenty to write about because of not having written anything for a couple of years. I thought it was a landmark as far as my writing went."

In the wake of the acclaim for *Kite*, many people wondered why it had taken Kirsty so long to return to her own work. There were clearly times when the cameo guest spots had appeared more like well-timed displacement activity, an excuse to neglect her considerable capacity for creating her own work. It was a conclusion that had not escaped MacColl herself: "I spent too much time on other people's work. My ideas went completely and the longer it went before I got down to writing, the worse it got. It's such a relief to have finished *Kite*, and the best thing about it is that I don't have to apologize to anyone if I play it to them."

One of the first people she had played it to was her father. Kirsty and Steve invited Ewan and Peggy to their home in Ealing to hear the album, recalls Lillywhite:

> We turned it on and they said, "Could you turn it down a bit?" And then they said, "Kirsty, do you have a copy of the text?" They sat there with a copy of the lyrics with the volume turned down and they listened to the whole album. It was completely analytical. And they loved it. Kirsty said afterwards that this was the first time her father had ever loved anything his children had ever done. This was a father listening to his daughter's music,

and it was like a schoolteacher grading it. There was none of that, "This is brilliant because you are my daughter and I love you."

It may have been overdue praise from a father who, while loving, had seemed distant for so many years, but it came just in time. Ewan MacColl died in hospital on October 22, 1989, twelve days after Kirsty's thirtieth birthday. His health problems had first surfaced a decade earlier, with the first signs of what would become chronic heart trouble. Ailments had piled on top of each other with every passing year: digestive disorders, back pain, diverticulitis, gout, arteriosclerosis, hiatus hernia and angina. It was a heart attack that ended his final illness. Writing in the closing pages of his autobiography, *Journeyman*, nine months before his death, he had said this:

My five children: Hamish, Neill, Kirsty, Calum and Kitty. Five links of bone and flesh and blood binding me to a past in which they had no being, to a future in which I will have no being. Strange is the love you have for your children. It creeps into your life furtively, like a stray cat unsure of its welcome, and then suddenly it has occupied every cell of your being. From this time on you are never completely free of the knowledge that five living extensions of yourself are loose in a hostile world and that you are five times more vulnerable ... I would like to think that my children had some idea of the depth of my love for them, but I doubt that they will.

However, even years after Ewan's death, his eldest daughter appeared to remain ambivalent about their relationship. In an interview with a *Los Angeles Times* journalist, Mike Boehm, in 1995, Kirsty MacColl said:

It wasn't until after *Kite* that he said he thought I'd done anything worthwhile. He made all his children feel utterly worthless growing up. Everybody wants their father's support, don't they, in whatever they're doing? He wasn't very supportive for a long time. He was later on, but it was an uphill struggle. I think he was bitterly disappointed that we weren't Communist guerrillas. I find it quite hard to listen to his stuff because it fills me with really deep sadness. I know it's good, but it's associated with sad things for me.

However, Boehm noted in his article that, later in their interview, MacColl made a point of returning to the subject of her father, clearly feeling she'd been unfair and overly harsh about him. She told the reporter: "All that stuff about my dad – I did love him, even if he'd drive me crazy."

Who knows what musical treasures would have come of a collaboration between Ewan and Kirsty MacColl, had they both relented just a little? Kirsty's mother, Jean, reflected on the possibility: "Kirsty would have loved at some point to have done a song with her dad, but it just never happened. That was very sad for her and also very sad for Ewan. It would have been nice had he made the time to do something that wasn't folk or was a hybrid, to see what would have come out."

However, Kirsty had at least managed to appear, along with Hamish, Neill and Calum, with their father on a recording of one of his best-known songs, "The Manchester Rambler". Ewan had penned the song to mark a mass trespass over Kinder Scout mountain in Derbyshire in the thirties, when violence broke out as gamekeepers and police attempted to force the walkers to leave. (These mass trespass rambles would eventually force a radical overhaul of the laws denying public access to vast tracts of land in Britain and allow the "right to roam".)

The MacColl family's version of "The Manchester Rambler", recorded in 1983 at Pathway Studios in London – a studio Kirsty herself had often used – was on a 2CD Ewan MacColl compilation, *Antiquities*, that was released in 1998. The set closed with a song, mixed by Kirsty and Steve Lillywhite, that would come to be seen as Ewan's own eulogy: "The Joy of Living". He had written it in his early seventies after attempting to climb Suilven Hill on the west coast of Scotland, inland from Lochinver. As Peggy and their daughter Kitty walked ahead, Ewan stopped to rest and realized he could go no further. He felt desolate and demoralised, as if confronting his own mortality on that craggy hillside. But days later, at home, the mood lifted and the regret and despair gave way to a more reflective, less gloomy philosophy:

> "Farewell you northern hills, you mountains all goodbye
> Moorland and stony ridges, crags and peaks goodbye …
> Farewell to you my love, my time is almost done
> Lie in my arms once more until the darkness comes …
> Farewell to you my chicks, soon you must fly alone
> Flesh of my flesh, my future life, bone of my bone …
> Never lose sight of the thrill
> And the joy of living."

—Ewan MacColl, "The Joy Of Living"

Peggy Seeger would later reveal that his family sang this song to Ewan as he lay dying. Its words were a poignant testimony to much that he had loved in a full life. And, unlike Kirsty's ambivalence, Hamish MacColl felt confident of their father's love for them. He says that Ewan showed it in innumerable ways, even if at other times his behaviour mystified or disappointed them:

> He was a very gentle, warm person. I never thought that he didn't love us; he was a very loving person. When I broke up with my wife and was feeling devastated, he was just so kind and so reassuring. He didn't try to thrust any wonderful words of wisdom down my throat. But, yes, at other times he was just completely obtuse.
>
> I remember living in Hampstead in a squat. It was a real struggle. Dad was going on and on about this wonderful new TV programme called "The Boys from the Black Stuff". I remember watching the programme and thinking, "What are they complaining about? They've got nice houses, they've got washing machines and fridges and TVs and all the rest of it, and I'm living in this awful squat and we've got one toilet between ten people and water coming through the roof, and the wiring is sub-standard."

Hamish had once asked his father to lend him £2000 to buy a new car. Ewan refused. "He could afford it, he was earning a fortune, but he wouldn't give me £2000 because it was *£2000*," says Hamish, who was at the time a qualified practitioner of Chinese traditional medicine, successfully treating his father's heart problems. They had a weekly session for 18 months, and each week Ewan would try to pay Hamish £50. His son would refuse, feeling that, as Ewan had generously paid for his training course, free sessions were a way to repay his kindness: "He'd have given me £50 a week for the next five years, but £2000 was more than his working-class mentality could cope with. People would come to him and tap him for money and he'd say, 'Yes, sure!' and give them £200, but £2000 was beyond the pale."

Shortly before his father died, Hamish had signed a deal with Fly Records, which was part of a large music publishing company with some high-profile clients, among them bands like Procul Harum and T Rex and British independent broadcasters like ITV and Channel 4. Fly had planned to release a single by Hamish, and a tie-in with the broadcasters seemed like an excellent way to promote it. They formulated an idea for a documentary on the music of the MacColl family, highlighting

Ewan, Hamish and Kirsty and their half-brothers, Neill and Calum. Channel 4 expressed strong interest, recalls Hamish:

> It seemed like a really cool idea. Then I got a phone call from a producer at the BBC who said that he was making a film about the MacColl family and there wasn't enough interest to make two films so he said, "It looks as though my programme is going to get made and the Channel 4 one isn't. I've just spoken to Ewan and had a long chat with him." I phoned Dad and, sure enough, he was going with that one, which was essentially about him. He was about 74 then, and I felt, "At the age of 74, you can't even let your kids have that!" At the time, we were all struggling, apart from Kirsty. For me, Neill and Calum, our combined annual income was probably about £15,000 and we could have done with that publicity – but he wasn't prepared to do it.

Perhaps as the proverb says, the greatest mischief you can do the envious is to do well. A seam of rivalry may be inevitable and even understandable, when siblings or parents and children are in a world as intensely competitive as that of music. But it does not make for the happiest of family relationships: "Dad loved Kirsty," says Hamish, "and admired her and thought she was wonderful but, at the same time, I'm sure he was jealous. But not so that it came between them; his love conquered all."

By the time of Ewan's death, Kirsty had largely come to terms with the limitations of their early relationship. As as a parent herself by then, Hamish believes she may also have come to see how powerful and, at times, perplexing, the parent-child relationship can be: "You reach a point where you realize that it's very odd to expect perfection of your parents when you can't achieve it yourself. Some people never get there, and some people get there later on in life. I think Kirsty got there, but it was late on."

For years, people would approach Kirsty MacColl at gigs or social events and talk knowledgeably about Ewan and his music. It would frequently make her feel deeply uncomfortable, pained that she didn't know her father as well as they seemed to. "It was just very hurtful," she said. "I found it quite hard to deal with for a long time." However, her father had lived long enough to see her happily married, with two adored children, a musical career of which he was enormously proud – even if he didn't always show it – and a political consciousness that may not have been as radical as his own, but was genuine and articulate. "Kirsty was less worried about his approval," concludes Hamish, "because she was on her guard against him because of the way he treated my mother. She didn't trust him – but she loved him nonetheless."

Kirsty's partial rejection of Ewan's legacy was something Billy Bragg saw at first hand many years later, after suggesting to her that they should get together to make a folk-based album. Kirsty was at a low ebb and doing very little musically, and even appeared ready to abandon music entirely, Bragg recalls:

> I can remember sitting there one time at her house in Ealing and I thought she was just going to give up altogether. And I thought, "This is outrageous; perhaps I can think of something we could do together, because I'd love to make a record with her. I wonder if she would be interested in doing something a bit different?" So, when we were driving down to the studio where I was making [Bragg's 1996 album] *William Bloke*, I eased myself into this conversation, and I put on a CD. I don't think the singer had got a single phrase out when Kirsty said, "I fucking hate folk music!" and that was it. That was the end of the conversation.

Bragg had been inspired to risk Kirsty's ire after remembering a party he'd been to at her home. MacColl and Irish singer-songwriter Brian Kennedy had spent much of the evening serenading Joan Littlewood with word-perfect renditions of traditional Irish folk songs. Bragg had been deeply impressed:

> It was so beautiful. I thought, "If we could get that on to a record …" And Kirsty had clearly really enjoyed it. But as soon as I suggested it she rejected it, and I think it was a little of how she felt about Ewan coming through there. On one side, she loved it and was true to it. She was true to the politics and she did what she believed in, like Ewan did, and she was true to folk music because she sang those songs for Joan, but she couldn't bring herself to admit it, I think. Or maybe she felt that was Ewan's gig and she didn't want to go there, or maybe she just didn't want to be associated with it; she'd made her own career. But I know for a fact that she sang folk songs beautifully because I heard her, and it was a real shame to me.

Mark Nevin similarly recalls: "Kirsty didn't want to be seen as a folk singer. She hated folk music, so when we played at a folk festival in

Belgium where Richard Thompson was on, and maybe the McGarrigles, Kirsty wore these leather clothes and I had an electric guitar and we sang like the Ramones. She was delighted, and we just bombed." Nevin recalls few occasions when Kirsty would discuss her father and his music, "other than how she felt disappointed in him and frustrated, unappreciated by him in every way, from when she was little."

However, the nineties dawned with Kirsty displaying renewed writing vigour and in March, a new single was released from *Kite*. "Don't Come The Cowboy with Me, Sonny Jim!" was a reprise of the flippant, droll mood of "Chip Shop". Backing tracks on the song's various formats included "Other People's Hearts" co-written with Gavin Povey; a frankly ill-advised cover of the Kate and Anna McGarrigle song, "Complainte Pour Sainte Catherine"; and MacColl's own "Am I Right?" The single failed to chart, so it can have been little comfort that in an annual poll of *Los Angeles Times* music critics, *Kite* was named one of the best albums of 1990 alongside *Ragged Glory* by one of Kirsty's early heroes, Neil Young, with Crazy Horse.

MacColl was reunited with the Pogues in November 1990 for a guest appearance on the *Red Hot and Blue* charity album of covers of Cole Porter songs, put together to raise funds for campaigns to boost awareness of HIV and AIDS. Twenty artists were invited to choose a Cole Porter song and put their own interpretation on it, with the accompanying video made by leading directors. The Pogues contributed "Just One of Those Things" and interrupted their UK tour to return to London to film their video with Irish director Neil Jordan.

Kirsty had invited the band to join her to record her contribution, "Miss Otis Regrets". Jordan filmed the two videos simultaneously at the Hackney Empire in London, and controlled chaos ensued as various Pogues wandered about in a pastiche of vaudeville and music hall settings and costumes. The scene was resplendent with trilby hats, Edwardian check suits, can-can dancers and children in sailor suits, and the treatment was far more interpretive and less representational than were other bands like Erasure, whose videos were more overtly related to the topic.

Interviewed on set, guitarist Phil Chevron mused: "I wonder what Cole Porter would have thought of it all? He was, after all, the man who told Frank Sinatra to please stop singing his songs unless he could stick to the tune." Chevron would later evocatively describe MacColl's version of "Miss Otis Regrets" as being, "like an Antipodean death-ballad; she made it sound as if that had been Porter's intention all along."

Kirsty starred as Miss Otis in the video for the tune, her black lace dress and jacket in sharp contrast to her pale skin and russet hair, cut in a bob. "Normally, I'd direct any video I star in, just to have a little control," she reflected. "I just get so fed up with spending thousands of pounds and not having what I wanted on the screen at the end of the day. I produced my last few videos and directed them with a friend, so I'm not used to leaving it to somebody else."

The *Red Hot And Blue* compilation spawned some truly inspired singles. As well as the Pogues' song and MacColl's "Miss Otis Regrets", which *Sunday Times* reviewer Robert Sandall described as "a likeable, plinkety-plonkety Irish ditty". Other highlights included Debbie Harry and Iggy Pop's "Well, Did you Evah?", U2's "Night and Day" and Neneh Cherry's "I've Got You under my Skin", as well as songs by Salif Keita, Tom Waits, Les Negresses Verts, David Byrne, Annie Lennox and Fine Young Cannibals.

Around the same time, MacColl was also a frequent guest on "French and Saunders", the BBC TV comedy show written by and starring Dawn French and Jennifer Saunders which was first broadcast in 1987. Throughout the duo's 1990 series, Kirsty would appear in musical interludes in a variety of bizarre settings, invariably straightfaced as mayhem broke out around her. Jennifer Saunders says, "In those days, you had to have a song in your show. It also meant we didn't have to write so much! You could mess around with Kirsty because she was so game."

French and Saunders' anarchic sense of humour appealed to Kirsty, whose own mordant wit was one of her friends' favourite things about her. Pete Glenister, for one, regards her as, "The funniest woman I've ever met." A BBC broadcaster and DJ who was also a close friend, Janice Long, admired MacColl not least because, "Kirsty could take the proverbial out of herself, which she did loads of times. She had a sense of fun."

The "French and Saunders" series also brought Kirsty to a new, younger audience. Many had been too young to notice "They Don't Know", "Chip Shop" or "A New England" but this was the generation of TV-bred kids for whom a mix of comedy and music, with knowing pop culture references, was the perfect light entertainment. Chris Winwood, a Kirsty fan, recalls:

I was amazed at Kirsty on "French and Saunders" because normally the musical interlude in the middle of a comedy show is when you go to the loo, or go and put the kettle on. I was just glued to Kirsty singing "Fifteen Minutes" and I remember I was a bit annoyed at French and Saunders coming on and messing about with a ladder in the background, wearing sou'westers. I felt that it really intruded on the song. But it was Kirsty's humour that jumped up and hit me, when she sang about "Blankety Blank": that line really stuck in my mind. I just thought it was so funny, but so serious as well. She was quite dour and very straight-faced. It really stood out as being completely unlike anything I'd expect to see: it was such an intelligent song.

For her part, Kirsty simply said, "I was really surprised because French and Saunders invited me to go and do a number each week in that series. That was before I'd overcome my nerves about performing and I think I was just terribly, terribly nervous about it, instead of enjoying it as much as I could have done. But it was a great opportunity."

For most of 1990, Kirsty was writing new material. To her great delight, she found she had been freed from a previous weight of expectation: "With *Kite*, I felt I had to prove that I wasn't this bimbo girl-next-door I'd been portrayed as. That had been hanging around my neck like a fucking albatross for so long. I wanted to make the point that, yes, I *can* write a fucking song! This time, I didn't feel that I had to prove myself."

However, MacColl's vehemence about the "fucking albatross" of her previous image would arguably have been more understandable if she hadn't colluded with it to such a large degree. Vociferously opinionated in her romantic relationships and her friendships, she had often appeared to feel unable or unwilling to be equally assertive with her record companies and managers:

I started off much more malleable and much more eager to please, because I figured all these people at the record companies were at least ten years older than me, and they must know what they're talking about. Then after a while I thought, "If they know so much, why aren't *they* making records? Maybe I do know what I'm taking about."

Since I realized that, I've been more and more determined to do it on my own terms and not to be pushed around. Certainly, artistically, I make all my own decisions, and if people don't like the records, then at least they don't like the records *I've* chosen to make. They're not listening to something that somebody else has created and I've just done the vocal on.

By a painstaking process, MacColl had discovered that it *is* possible to have success on one's own terms within the music industry. It is not always easy but it is always possible. As she freely admitted, she had often looked for inspiration to heroes like Neil Young, friends like Billy Bragg, and women like Joni Mitchell, Kate Bush and Joan Armatrading to prove that.

After hearing the lyrical content on *Kite*, an acquaintance of MacColl's had remarked to her, "God, you must have had a shitty life!" Things hadn't been as simple as that, of course. As Tolstoy had said of family life in *Anna Karenina*, "All happy families resemble one another; each unhappy family is unhappy in its own way." However, to dispel such lingering notions of a melancholic previous existence, MacColl decided on her next album that she needed to revitalize her music – and she would harness the rhythms of dance music to do it:

I listened to *Kite* for the first time in a while, and I thought, "Well, that's really good, but I could make the next album even more enjoyable for myself if I could actually dance to it without being paralytic!" But I didn't want to make an album with computers. A lot of people think that a dance record means you have to have the bpms [beats per minute] on the sleeve, but to me a *waltz* is a dance.

MacColl hoped that the follow-up to *Kite* would throw down the musical gauntlet to those who thought her incapable of extending her reach beyond perfect guitar pop and sixties-style multi-layered vocals. To that end, she enlisted the help of a clutch of talented co-writers. All but two of the songs were written with one of a number of collaborators: her brother Hamish, Pete Glenister, Johnny Marr, Mark Nevin (who, like Marr, had also co-written with Morrissey), American pop-meister Marshall Crenshaw (whose second album, *Field Day*, had been produced by Steve Lillywhite in 1983), and the Pogues' Jem Finer.

MacColl's favoured method of co-writing was for collaborators to send each other their ideas on tape. It was rare to write in the same room together, recalls Pete Glenister: "I hadn't spent all that much time with Kirsty; we'd written a bit, but quite at arm's length. I'd bung her a track and she'd work on it. This time it was even more at arm's length than we were on *Kite*, where some of it was written with the two of us in a room. But she never used to write much that way. She would always like to have her own time and space."

MacColl had recently spent plenty of time in New York, where her husband had been recording the Rolling Stones' *Dirty Work* album, which predictably featured guest vocals by his wife. While Steve was busy in the studio, Kirsty shopped and explored Manhattan, observing the characters and scenarios thrown up by the metropolis's vibrant street life. Among them was a beaming boy from Harlem, whose smile shone out of the urban mayhem as MacColl watched him walk down a city street. She immortalized him in the dance-oriented "Walking Down Madison" (although she had actually seen him on another of Manhattan's wide avenues) on the album that she was to title *Electric Landlady*, after the Jimi Hendrix classic *Electric Ladyland*.

"Walking Down Madison" would become Kirsty MacColl's most successful release in the United States, and a hit on both sides of the Atlantic. It was co-written with Johnny Marr, who was surprised by her initial reaction: "I sent Kirsty a cassette of it, not really with the intention of her writing on it, just to get her opinion. She called me back a couple of days later and said, 'I've got some really great words for it. It's going to be fantastic!' I didn't mind but I was surprised. I was kind of intending it to be an instrumental track."

Marr had unwittingly provided the missing link for lyrics that MacColl had written in New York but which had languished, half-forgotten with no arrangement, back in London: "I couldn't find the right musical approach for ages," said MacColl. "I tried writing stuff, and asked other people to try, but it never worked until I got the tape in the post from Johnny. The minute I heard his guitar, I dug out the lyrics and sussed out the melody."

The recorded version featured a furious rap on homelessness performed by a rapper from Manchester, Aniff Cousins. MacColl had first heard him and his musical partner Colin Thorpe, who together formed the hip-hop acid jazz duo, Chapter and the Verse, on a compilation of dance music that had included their song "The Black Whip". The two rappers were inspired by their Mancunian roots, as well as the political consciousness of the best of American rap and hip-hop, to create songs about living in the urban underclass of British cities.

A further nod to urban dance music came on the CD single's next track, "Lying Down", and there were remixes of "Walking On Madison" and "My Affair" by Howard Gray, who had formed the electronica collective Apollo 440 with his brother Trevor and musician and remixer, Noko in Liverpool in 1990, and would go on to remix for U2, EMF and Pop Will Eat Itself. Trevor Gray had also provided synthesizers, keyboards and programming on "Madison".

However, listeners surprised by MacColl's house music dabblings were to be even more dumbfounded by the lush, Latin vibes of the album version of "My Affair", which Kirsty had co-written with Mark Nevin. Its breezy defence of infidelity was set to a beat that would not have been out of place in the louche surroundings of the Tropicana nightclub in fifties Havana. When Steve Lillywhite had been in New York, working with David Byrne on his *Rei Momo* album, Kirsty had been introduced to the Hispanic musicians who played on the Byrne sessions. While this hadn't been her first exposure to their music, it was the first opportunity she'd had to work with them on one of her own albums. MacColl was to describe their sessions as "very organic, and mostly live. It was such a joy playing with that many people all at once. Having spent years in the studio doing my own thing, it was just the most fun I'd ever had. I thought then that it would be really nice to do more stuff like that one day."

Pete Glenister was already in New York, mixing an Alison Moyet album, *Hoodoo*, his first major production credit. Kirsty asked him to stay on to play on her own record:

> I was the only lad from south London on the sessions. I can remember the start of "My Affair". We got to the end of the first chorus and I still hadn't started because I couldn't work out where they were, and Kirsty hadn't started singing either. We just looked at each other and started laughing. So we had to get the band to play four-on-the-floor so we knew where we all were. It was a great, fun session to do. Those guys were amazing players.

Mark Nevin missed the New York recording sessions, staying in London for the birth of his son, Wes. However, when MacColl returned, she called Nevin and played the finished version of their song "My Affair" down the phone. "When I heard it with all that brass, I thought it was fantastic," said Nevin. "Kirsty was just so excited with the tracks." However, Nevin did play on some of the later album sessions at Townhouse Studios in London:

I was a bit overwhelmed by recording at Townhouse, with Pete Glenister on guitar, Mel Gaynor from Simple Minds on drums and Steve Knight on keyboards. There were all these famous star musicians, and I had just entered this world. I was a bit overwhelmed and insecure about the whole thing because, when you're in a band, you've got your band and you know each other. You can relax like a family, but being thrown into this thing, people were much more like, "I know what I do and I can do that."

For his part, Billy Bragg was aware of MacColl's Latin explorations long before he heard *Electric Landlady*. He and Kirsty had spent a night at the Royal Festival Hall in London, at a recital of one of their favourite classical pieces, Beethoven's ninth symphony. Later that evening, MacColl had put a tape of "My Affair" into the car stereo:

She played me the first of her Latin-based tunes while we were driving round an underground car park. I was amazed. Then I saw her do a gig at the Mean Fiddler, and the band were all New York Cubans. The cost of getting them together must have been phenomenal, but she was so in her element that she really enjoyed playing with them and it allowed her to go to another [musical] place where she didn't feel so self-conscious.

One of the most affecting songs on *Electric Landlady* was "The Hardest Word". Kirsty had co-written it with her brother, Hamish, about their father in the last months of his life: "I wrote the music while Dad was dying," says Hamish. "I played it, and Kirsty and Steve heard it and said, 'That's really good.' Kirsty said, 'Can I write some words?' and I said, 'Sure.' Then Kirsty wrote the words about Dad." The moving lyrics are a poignant reminder to hold fast to those we love, before they slip from our grasp forever:

> "At war with each other, the mother, the father
> The sisters, the brothers, the daughters and sons
> Be kind to each other, your father, your mother ...
> I never know if I'm laughing or crying
> The hardest word is the word goodbye ...
> Forgive our indignity and we forgive yours
> As I am the mother, you are the father
> Entwined in each other now and forever ..."

—Kirsty MacColl, "The Hardest Word"

On its release in June 1991, *Electric Landlady* garnered generally good reviews, with some divisions emerging on whether the Latin experiment had worked. For Adam Sweeting in *The Guardian*, " ... the surprise success of the bunch is 'My Affair' where an army of Hispanic musicians under the direction of Angel Hernandez go salsa-crazy behind La MacColl's cool vocals. This is a defiantly untrendy record, which is one reason it deserves to do well."

Also in *The Guardian*, Caroline Sullivan applauded the fact that, "Rock has rediscovered its social conscience in a big way, and it's not just the province of demagogues like Billy Bragg and Sting. Kirsty MacColl, Phil Collins and Julian Lennon are just three songwriters who, unaffiliated with any politics or movement, are writing socially conscious material. These artists and many others deal with topics that would previously have been deemed too controversial for a pop tune. Unlike the un-focused punks, people like MacColl are articulate documenters of very distinct issues."

David Sinclair, writing in *The Times*, was not so convinced, however: "[MacColl's] voice has a sonorous tone and a nimble Celtic lilt, but the going is not always easy as she skates across the socially conscious electro-rap of 'Walking Down Madison', the twee folk-pop of 'Halloween' and the ghastly Club Copacabana-style cabaret of 'My Affair'. In the album's dying moments, she strikes up a maudlin duet with her old chums the Pogues on 'The One And Only', and finds her true metier at last."

The music critic for *The Independent*, Andy Gill, welcomed the album as "a far more assured and satisfying piece of work than the over-rated *Kite*. There's a pronounced Latin American presence on the wittily-titled *Electric Landlady* but not obtrusively so: apart from the straightforward samba 'My Affair', the exotic percussion and Angel Fernandez's bass and string arrangements don't define the music the way the Latin flavours did in David Byrne's Brazilian dabblings. More important ... is Kirsty's strategy of avoiding new technology and relying on real musi-cians – though it has to be said that the best track here is the single, 'Walking Down Madison'."

In *The Washington Post*, Richard Harrington found the album "emotional but also a bit slick, and such a mixed stylistic bag that it gains radio appeal at the expense of power." Its producer, Steve Lillywhite, would later concede this point, saying, "*Electric Landlady* for me wasn't quite as focused as *Kite*, and I think it slightly suffered from being 'bitty'. We used a lot of different musicians on different songs, and there wasn't that continuity."

Harnessing all of these disparate elements for *Electric Ladyland* may have been a subconscious attempt to find a niche in a market that was, at the time, dominated by either grunge rock or dance music. If so, it simply didn't work. In an age of highly specialized formats, it was possibly naïve to imagine that radio playlists would be compiled by people who have lovingly listened to each eclectic track on an album before finding a home for each one in very different programmes.

The next obvious move was to tour the album around the UK. MacColl assembled a band, and three weeks of rehearsals had got underway before Virgin announced they would not be funding the tour. At the time, they appeared to be acting in a mean-spirited and penny-pinching fashion, and Kirsty's fans pilloried the label for it. However, it appeared the situation was more complex.

Jon Webster, who was a senior executive at Virgin at the time, says disagreements with MacColl's new manager were at the heart of the problem. Kirsty and Frank Murray had drifted apart while she was relatively inactive and he was busy with the Pogues. Eventually, Steve Lillywhite asked his own manager, Ian Wright, to also oversee his wife's career. Webster found Wright difficult to deal with:

> Kirsty wanted to go out on tour, but she'd had a history of stage fright and was pretty cautious about it all. Ian Wright played on that. He came in and started talking about bringing in a horn section from New York and paying them about $1000 a week. We'd go, "Ian, a grand a week? What planet are we living on here?" I said to Ian, "We've got to get this down," but his point was, "She won't go out on tour without these people". I fired off a fax saying, "Ian, don't expect us to just roll over at the end of this. If it comes to two weeks before the tour and you put in a budget and it's this big, the answer will be 'No!'

Wright duly produced another budget, ten days before the tour was due to begin. It arrived just as Virgin executives were setting off for their annual weekend brainstorming get-together. They discussed Wright's terms and conditions and, by the time they reached their hotel on the English south coast, they'd made a decision. Jon Webster phoned Wright from the hotel to tell him that Virgin had judged his costs to be excessive and, without a significant adjustment downward, could not agree to his demands. "He said to me, 'But you've got to pay!'" says Webster, "and I said, 'No, we haven't.' His budget was something like £35,000 – a lot of money in those days."

In fact, the battlelines had been drawn in Virgin's relationship with Ian Wright even before the tour costs dispute. One Virgin insider claims that Wright would attempt to play off different Virgin people and departments against each other, until executives eventually got wise to the strategy and often simply either avoided or stonewalled him. One executive apparently decided to only ever return Wright's calls at lunchtime – when he wouldn't be in his office to take the call.

Most managers would, of course, argue that it's their job to put as much pressure on the record company as required to get the best possible deal for their client. The more pressure, the better the deal – until that strategy backfires. A famous, and favourite, music industry story relates how Steve Winwood once asked his brother, a high-level record company executive, who was the most difficult "bastard of a manager" he'd ever had to deal with. The star then promptly went out and hired him as manager.

Eventually, MacColl did venture out on a brief tour, which she partly funded herself. In its wake, "All I Ever Wanted" was released as a single, with backing tracks including live versions of "Chip Shop", "A New England" and "Walk Right Back", a song written by Sonny Curtis (who also wrote the beloved "I Fought the Law") which had been a big hit for MacColl's much-loved Everly Brothers in 1961.

The singles from *Electric Landlady* had not been successful. Even with numerous remixes, "My Affair" had got no higher than Number 56 in the UK, and "All I Ever Wanted" failed to chart at all. However, hopes were still high at Virgin that the album could restore MacColl's popularity and commercial clout, says Jon Webster:

In many ways, because she was a name, and because she had previous hits, and had had a hit off her first Virgin album, obviously an act like that was worth continuing with. The frustration was, of course, that she was hardly known outside the UK, so I don't think we ever sold many records, or if we even sold *any*, abroad. We couldn't really get the foreign companies interested. That was at the time when the world was changing. Before, everything the UK put out would be a hit in Europe. Now, they would just go, "So?"

In her early days, Stiff Records had seemed perfectly suited to an artist like Kirsty MacColl. Virgin in the late eighties and early nineties had likewise retained much of its founder Richard Branson's energetic "can-do" music fan passion while tempering it with hard-headed business acumen. Jon Webster sums up the philosophy thus:

> If you heard something you liked, bloody sign it! If someone wanted to sign Kirsty and brought the demos to an A & R meeting and we liked them, we'd sign her. It was very much not done in a clinical way. It was almost a schism between A & R and marketing at the time. The famous case was Simon Draper, the head of A & R, who saw a jazz brass quartet on an arts programme on BBC2 one Saturday night. We signed them the following week. We were all sitting there going, "What the *fuck* are we going to do with this?" He didn't care. He said, "I think they're great", and that was the motivation for signing them, not how many records we could sell.

Nevertheless, with *Electric Landlady's* sales failing to match those of *Kite*, MacColl's future at Virgin became to look uncertain. Relations had become severely strained over the disagreements on the tour budget, with lawyers from both sides entering the fray. So when, in 1992, Richard Branson sold Virgin Records to EMI for £650m to raise funds to invest in new projects under the Virgin brand, there was little surprise that MacColl was among the artists dropped from EMI's newly acquired label. Jon Webster says:

> At that point, it would have been fairly marginal. We would have paid quite a lot of money for the two albums, lots of money for the videos and the rest of it, and we hadn't actually sold that many records. So there would have been a large unrecouped balance and there would have been question marks, particularly because we couldn't sell Kirsty overseas. You get a situation where you sit and say, "Well, she has £250,000 unrecouped, and we have got to give her a £100,000 personal advance for this next record, and £150,000 worth of recording costs, which will add up to £500,000. Do we want to keep her? Do we want to deal with that manager?" And you just think, "I can't be bothered. Let him go and torment someone else."

MacColl herself tried to be philosophical: "They got rid of half the roster and half the staff as well, so it wasn't like I was alone in that. I was just really unlucky, and it was very unfortunate because it cost me personally lots of money." Her rancorous relationship with Virgin, however would not be resolved for some time, and then only with a complicated deal that allowed Virgin to release MacColl's greatest hits package, *Galore*, in 1995.

When Jon Webster later heard that Ian Wright was no longer representing MacColl, he got back in touch to try to smooth over any residual ill feeling from her time with Virgin: "I faxed her at home. I said, 'I don't know if you want to hear from me, but I wanted to tell you that all of my issues with you weren't with you, they were with Ian'. Kirsty sent back a lovely fax, saying, 'I had no problems with you at all, and I understand that he was a bloody nightmare!'"

Phil Rambow had observed MacColl's recurring problems with the music industry, and as a friend he despaired with her. As a musician, however, he had few illusions about the way the business worked:

> Kirsty had terrible record companies who couldn't understand her and couldn't deal with her managers. To be really successful, you need a certain amount of talent, you need an extraordinary amount of drive and self-belief and you need an element of luck; being in the right place at the right time. Kirsty had this concept at the beginning, which got resolved later, of, "Me and my mates, we do all this [music]," and the manager would take care of the business end of things, it was nothing to do with the musicians. She was just too detached and that held her back in her career. It was a very unsophisticated attitude, very old-fashioned, but that's the way it was then. It took an incredibly long time for her to come to terms with all that, and deal with it on her own terms. And she also had an attitude about independent labels; she never really wanted to be on an independent label. She wanted to be appreciated at a certain level.

MacColl was about to enter another dormant phase in her own music, a hiatus during which she again worked with other people on their own projects. Among them was Billy Bragg, on his 1991 album, *Don't Try This at Home*. Bragg found himself highly impressed with Kirsty's *modus operandi*:

> When we did the vocals for "Cindy of a Thousand Lives", she came into the studio and told the engineer where to put the microphone. She sang the first track, and then she said to the engineer, "Okay, I'm going to stand here now, and I want you to put this on another track and I'm going to do *this*,"

and she did it. Then she said, going to the other side of the mic, "Now I'm going to stand here and I'm going to do *this*." She did that every time; first take, half a dozen times. We were just in awe of her in the studio, she was so focused and so great and the results were so brilliant.

With the track completed to her satisfaction, Kirsty MacColl walked out of the studio and ordered Billy Bragg and his band to take her to the nearest pub.

CHAPTER SIX

Children Of The Revolution

The Cuba that Kirsty MacColl first visited in 1992 was a nation in economic turmoil. The collapse of the Soviet Union and its Eastern bloc satellite states – on which, as trading partners, Cuba was almost wholly dependent – had resonated profoundly through its society. The government had declared a state of economic emergency in 1990 in what became known as the "Special Period in Peacetime". The country had lost its international markets, eighty per cent of its income, and almost all of its fuel imports. The little food that Cuba had grown for its own consumption was heavily dependent on imported fertilizers and pesticides. Strict food rationing had been introduced, while rolling power cuts and severely curtailed public services and transport had become the norm.

The US, seeing Cuba's economic vulnerability, moved quickly to worsen Havana's woes in 1992 by tightening the existing trade embargo with new legislation known as the Torrocelli Act, which extended the trade ban to overseas subsidiaries of American firms. The Cuban ambassador to the United Nations, Fernando Remirez de Estenoz, later told the UN General Assembly that, in 1993 alone, the expanded sanctions had cost Cuba $970m in lost trade and higher import costs.

When the nineteenth-century Mexican president/dictator, Porfirio Diaz, famously remarked of his homeland, "Poor Mexico! So far from God, and so close to the United States", he might well have been talking presciently about Cuba and its own long and troubled relationship with the giant to its north; the neighbourhood bully who coveted influence and cultivated cronies in the region far beyond its own borders. José Marti, the nineteenth century Cuban independence hero, had written to a friend, "Once the United States is in Cuba, who will get it out? " Marti was by no means anti-American; he revered great American writers like Whitman, Emerson and Longfellow, dedicating some of his own work to them. For all of his admiration of those Transcendentalist authors, however, he was still a realist, and his tiny Caribbean nation had to wait more than half a century to find out the answer to his question.

The Cuban revolution of 1959, which ousted the US-backed dictator Fulgencio Batista and made Che Guevara and Fidel Castro icons of the twentieth century, continues to have a spellbinding effect on those of the Left all over the world. Even more apolitical observers can't help but be awed by the tenacity and longevity of Castro, who has seen ten United States presidents come and go. Most of them have done their best to make his life as difficult as possible; some have allegedly even tried to end it. Sadly, the most unfortunate consequence of their attempts to make life untenable for Castro through economic sanctions, diplomatic isolation and support for his opponents, is that the Cuban people have been punished simply for being Cuban.

Cultural development had been one of the cornerstones of the revolution. Castro had mass literacy and educational opportunities, a ludicrous concept to Batista and his predecessors, as a central goal. Che Guevara was to declare, "We have converted the fortresses into schools." However, by the early nineties, Cuba was forced to stop imports of books, and could no longer afford to buy paper to publish domestically.

Bookshops in Cuba had always boasted a wide array of foreign writers. From the US alone, more than 180 writers were published in Cuba between 1959 and 1982. The most popular – Hemingway, Poe, Twain and the more prosaic Ray Bradbury – had found shelf space next to writers from all over the world in fiction, politics, sport, science, poetry and biography. Despite the crippling embargo, Cuba had always encouraged the distribution of works by such quintessentially American writers.

Now, the nation that had been among the top four book producers in Latin America, after Brazil, Mexico and Argentina, was witnessing the collapse of its once-thriving book, newspaper and magazine industry. During Kirsty's first visit, the bookshops she wandered through had little more to offer her than old Marxist tracts, inferior novels that even desperate readers had left untouched, books about the glory days of the now crumbling Eastern bloc, technical manuals that were of little use because the parts needed for repairs were

Kirsty with
her father,
Ewan MacColl

Childhood photos of Kirsty

Kirsty with her
brother, Hamish,
and mother, Jean

Jean and Kirsty

Kirsty and Ewan

Kirsty during the 1980s

Kirsty in her 'Mandy Doubt' incarnation with the Drug Addix at the Venue, New Cross, south London, 1978

At the Mean Fiddler, north London, September 25, 1991

Kirsty and Jamie,
February 22, 1985

Kirsty, wearing a maternity dress that
Jean had worn when pregnant, pictured
with her son Jamie at home in Ealing,
September, 1987

Steve Lillywhite, Louis, Kirsty and Jamie

Jamie and Louis MacColl Lillywhite

On stage with Ron Wood and the Wilfs at a benefit concert for the Homerton Hospital, east London, at the Hackney Empire, February 2, 1991

With Billy Bragg at a New Year's Eve gig, Hackney Empire, December 31, 1991

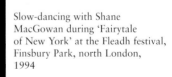

Slow-dancing with Shane MacGowan during 'Fairytale of New York' at the Fleadh festival, Finsbury Park, north London, 1994

With Cuban musicians, Raices Cubanas, at the 'I Love Cuba' benefit for the Cuba Solidarity Campaign, Camden Centre, north London, February 14, 1998

Kirsty walked off the stage after her show at the Shepherd's Bush Empire in west London on October 28, 2000, and remarked, "That was the best gig I've ever done." It was also her last.

Jools Holland was among the family, friends and fans at the memorial service for Kirsty at Saint Martin-in-the-Fields church, central London, January 20, 2001

Bono and his wife, Ali, at the memorial service

Tracey Ullman at the tribute concert in honour of Kirsty, at 'The Song's The Thing' event at the Royal Festival Hall, central London, September 23, 2002

Johnny Marr, former Smiths guitarist and Kirsty collaborator, on stage with David Gray at the tribute concert

The *Percalito*, owned by the Mexican businessman Guillermo Gonzalez Nova. The cruiser hit Kirsty moments after she came up from a dive with her sons and their dive-master, Ivan Diaz, on the Chankanaab reef, off Cozumel, Mexico, on December 18, 2000

Jean MacColl with friends, after placing a wreath at the site of the accident, March 10, 2004

Jean MacColl with a supporter of the Justice for Kirsty campaign, Fred Shortland (left) and the campaign's Mexico-based lawyer, Demetrio Guerra (right), jubilant after presenting a dossier of evidence to the Prosecutor-General, in Cozumel, March 12, 2004

impossible to get, and pamphlets declaiming many now-besieged revolutionary ideals.

MacColl's visit had been inspired by a love of Cuban music and a desire to see Castro's Cuba while the revolutionary leader was still alive, before the much-heralded changes in the post-Castro era came about. It was also a country of fellow travellers beloved by her communist father. "After the Berlin Wall came down," she said, "I decided to go to Cuba because I realized that I hadn't been to a Communist country since my trip to Poland, and that opportunities to do so were diminishing. Also, I'd been mad about Cuban music for years, and I wanted to experience it first-hand. Another reason that I wanted to go was because I associated it with my dad. He had visited Cuba in the late sixties and met Raul Castro, Fidel's brother."

Ewan and Peggy Seeger, in fact, had been to Cuba in 1968. In the same year, Ewan had eulogized the battles of the Cuban conflict and the ultimate victory for the rebels in his song "Companeros", in which he sang

"Against Batista, the Fidelistas
Courage was their only armour
As they fought at Fidel's side
With Che Guevara."

—Ewan MacColl, "Companeros"

Ewan and Peggy had given performances in Cuba. However, 35 years after the event, Seeger was sanguine about their effectiveness: "I think Kirsty did a better job musically in Cuba than we did. Our songs were a bit acerbic and hers were more easily grasped. Ewan would have been so very proud of the work she did there, and of the songs that she made there." Hamish MacColl had fond memories of his father's anecdotes of his trip to Cuba:

Dad was sitting next to Malcolm X on the plane to Havana. He was attending a huge international festival that Malcolm X was attending as well. Dad loved Cuba, but he would romanticize it anyway. Kirsty would tend to ignore any of his stories, but he was an Aquarian, so he told stories and he did tend to embellish them and you could never be sure if it was real or not. Half the time it was. But Kirsty went there because of the music, and then started learning Spanish.

So, 24 years after her father's visit, Kirsty MacColl finally made it to Havana. She travelled alone, setting out to explore the island and immerse herself in the culture and the music. That first tentative visit – she spoke no Spanish, and stayed in good hotels – was only the beginning of her passion for Cuban culture and music. Back home in London, she worked hard to improve her Spanish skills: "I couldn't stand listening to all this stuff and not being able to understand it. And when I was in Cuba I wanted to be able to talk to all people, not just to those who spoke English."

After her first visit to Cuba, Kirsty contacted the London office of the Cuba Solidarity Campaign – a non-party political, non-profit-making group that works in the UK to raise awareness of, and support for, Cuba, and campaigns against America's economic blockade. The group's director, Rob Miller, recommended some contacts in the language department at the University of Havana, and thus began Kirsty's near-decade of support for the campaign's work. "Kirsty went back and learned Spanish there, which she loved and met lots of musicians," Miller says. "She didn't just love Cuba and the Cuban people and the music; she obviously had a feeling for what was going on there in terms of the government and what they were trying to achieve."

MacColl began to work with the CSC on a number of projects, including several benefit concerts. She also attended various meetings, delegations to government ministers, and receptions. "Kirsty acted as a kind of celebrity host for us," says Miller, "and was also incredibly helpful in terms of contacts with other people in the music and arts field." Her involvement inevitably helped to raise the Campaign's profile and draw attention to its work. She fulsomely endorsed its efforts to force the lifting of the US sanctions, says Miller: "The kind of work we're doing for the Cuba Solidarity Campaign – which isn't a charity – is not a standard celebrity type of charitable cause. It's a political campaign, and we're campaigning against the American blockade of Cuba and for the Cuban people's rights to self-determination. Kirsty recognized that, and it was the fact that she was able to stand up for the Cuban people and appear on behalf of the Campaign that endeared her massively to everybody, because it's not what most celebrities would do."

Cuba and its icons have status within pop culture: the radical chic of Che, and the dazzling backdrop of beaches and fifties US cars for fashion shoots. However, it is impossible to entirely divorce politics from the image, which is why many rent-a-cause celebrities have shown no interest in Cuba, however urgent its humanitarian needs or praiseworthy its medical and educational achievements. Concerns about how this would play in their American markets is also a factor, as Rob Miller acknowledges:

> With the American blockade, it's risky for international singers and artists to associate themselves with Cuba. It can affect their worldwide work. I don't know how it affected Kirsty directly, but certainly in terms of working in the States, it can have a major impact on any career. It was a brave thing to do and people were immensely grateful to her, and proud of her involvement. We're fortunate that there are a number of celebrities who will work alongside the Campaign, and the beautiful thing about Kirsty was that she was also able to perform. People loved hearing her sing. She had such a repertoire of songs and vocal skills that she was able to take on very quickly Latin American and Cuban music, and people loved the fact that she was willing to give that music a go.

Miller has a point. Ry Cooder did not suffer a commercial backlash from his *Buena Vista Social Club* project: the album has sold more than eight million copies, won a Grammy for Best Tropical Latin Performance, and inspired Wim Wenders' much-acclaimed documentary. However, he did encounter a legal backlash. For his work in Cuba, Cooder was prosecuted by the US government for breaking the rarely invoked Trading With The Enemy Act. The star was fined $100,000 and forbidden to return to Cuba without permission.

The fine was reduced to $25,000 on appeal but it took a year of insistent lobbying from Cooder and his lawyers before Bill Clinton relented in the last days of his presidency and instructed the Treasury Department in Washington to issue an unprecedented licence to allow Cooder to resume his contacts with the Cuban "enemy". "We were on the plane the next day," says Cooder, "with the paper in our hands. The head Customs guy at LA Airport had a look and said, 'Well, I'll be damned – I haven't seen one of these in forty years!'"

During his return visit, Cooder recorded an album with the Cuban guitar virtuoso Manuel Galban, *Mambo Sinuendo*, and produced and played on Buena Vista stalwart Ibrahim Ferrer's solo album, *Buenos Hermanos*, both released in 2003. However, the licence was a temporary one. Under US law, Ry Cooder faces imprisonment if he returns to Cuba:

"It's totally impossible for me to go back until some comprehensive change occurs in the embargo. The sad thing is, these musicians are indispensable, and none of them are getting younger."

Kirsty MacColl made her second visit to Cuba in November 1994 to attend the first World Solidarity Conference in Havana. This five-day conference was organized by Cuban groups and institutions and attended by more than 3000 delegates from 109 countries, including representatives of regional and international groups. It came at the lowest ebb of the county's trade and financial crisis.

By now, the privations of the Special Period had forced the Cuban government to institute reforms that went to the heart of the communist system. There were food riots, and another exodus to Florida. In order to attract desperately needed foreign currency, Cuba had started to encourage international tourism and, in 1993, legalized the use of the American dollar. This both made use of the dollars circulating in the ubiquitous black economy, and went some way towards meeting the demand for consumer goods not available to peso shoppers.

Castro's government had also legalized small-scale private enterprise, enabling people to set up modest restaurants in their homes – *paladares* – or turn bedrooms into guestrooms, in *casas particulares* (literally, private homes). Kirsty frequented these during her later visits. They are found all over Cuba, although less so in the heavily touristed areas, where state-run hotels or those run in partnership with international hotel chains are plentiful. Staying with families in their own homes gave MacColl the chance to perfect her Spanish, and sample a more authentic Cuba than can be found in the tourist haunts of Havana and the resorts:

There weren't many tourists then, so the locals were intrigued by visitors and were always coming up to find out what I was up to. It's very easy to get a room in a family home; you just stop and ask anyone you meet and they'll know of someone with a room to let. I've found some fantastic places doing that, and you're made to feel so welcome. One place I found was a *finca*, a little farm, where they produced some of their own food. Thanks to the US sanctions, it's quite hard to get hold of proper food in Cuba. This couple kept goats and made me this amazing dessert that was a bit like cottage cheese with quince jam. I'd never had anything like it before and it was absolutely delicious. Cubans are incredibly poor, but very generous and tremendously dignified.

When a character in the Oscar-nominated 1990 Cuban film *La Bella de la Alhambra* mused, "Here, everything is resolved with drums and beer", it resonated with many Cubans. MacColl's experiences of the way ordinary Cubans lived day-to-day, and the effect of the trade blockade, gave her a focus for her political support of the Cuba Solidarity Campaign and the work it was doing. In an interview with the Campaign's magazine, *Cuba Si*, in August 2000, she said:

> I'm very impressed by the standards of education and health care in Cuba despite the lack of facilities and medicines, and I think that the Cuba Solidarity Campaign's medical aid and educational aid appeals are great ideas. Like many others though, I feel that with the US embargo there is an element of David and Goliath which makes me all the more keen to support this tiny island which has been standing fast against the megalomaniac empire for so long.

Rob Miller believes that MacColl's support for the Campaign was certainly grounded in the day-to-day reality of what she saw during her visits, rather than any naïve rose-tinted political ideology:

> Kirsty totally understood what was going on. She could contextualize the whole situation with regard to Cuba, and the fact it is an independent country and it's very proud of its independence, its sovereignty, its people, its culture and its music. She recognized that they had every right to be proud of what they achieved. She was also interested in the schooling and the health system, not just their music, and she didn't divorce the music from the society from which it came. I spoke to her about why Cuba had so many musicians and so many bands, and she was very clear that it was because the state supported musicians and artists. That's why Cuba has such a huge wealth of talent in music, arts and dance.

It's impossible to imagine a US President meeting a cutting-edge rap group while rap in the US was still considered to be outlaw music, marginalized a million miles from the mainstream territory it now occupies. However, such was the buzz about one of the first Cuban rap groups, Orishas, that Castro invited them to the presidential palace in 2000. On meeting them, he mused, "So you are the ones who have been making so much noise." In fact, rappers like Orishas, Grandes Ligas (Big Leagues) and Obsesion reclaimed a musical space for young Cubans by ignoring the *salsa* and *son* they'd grown up with and, instead, diverting the US hip-hop vibe into their own hybrid. One of Orishas' first hits was "537 Cuba", a reworking of one of Cuba's best-known and best-loved traditional songs, "Chan Chan" into a hip-hop anthem.

More recently, Castro also turned up at a Havana concert by the Welsh rock band the Manic Street Preachers in February 2001. The Cuba Solidarity Campaign had been called in by the band's management to help plead their case with the Cuban Ministry of Culture, which it must be said, was not at all familiar with the Manics' oeuvre. Cuban governmental eyebrows had been raised at the mention of their name and officials puzzled over how literally their name should be taken – after all, manic preachers and western rock 'n' roll decadence were hardly to be welcomed.

The Cuban authorities had two major fears: would the band be taking their clothes off on stage and/or taking drugs? While Rob Miller was trying to reassure the Cuban government that neither would be the case, and the Manics' left wing aim was true, Kirsty MacColl was planning another trip to Cuba. Miller asked if she could take some Manics' videos and CDs to Havana with her and deliver them to the Minister of Culture, adding her voice to supporters of the tour. Miller admits that she demurred:

Kirsty had a thing about western musicians jumping on Cuba [as a bandwagon]. That wasn't why she was into the place. Cuba goes through a number of phases of popularity, and at that time it was extremely popular. When Cuba is flavour of the month, you do get people who want to be associated with it, they want to go over there, they want to use that Cuba vibe to enhance their own position, and Kirsty was never ever like that. When she heard that the Manics wanted to go over there, she didn't particularly want to help; she didn't really see why they wanted to do it.

The reasons behind the visit were undoubtedly diverse, but not as entirely cynical as MacColl suspected. The Manics' trip was deemed a huge success and made a definitive pro-Cuba, anti-blockade statement. Both sides seemed to benefit from the resultant publicity, says Miller: "A number of other musicians who have turned down the opportunity to go to Cuba have wanted to go, but they know they are going to be under pressure from the US. They might be blacklisted; it might affect their dealings with their record company. The Manics went at their own request and had sympathies with the revolution in Cuba. It wasn't just a publicity thing for them."

For Manic Street Preachers, the ultimate photo opportunity was with Fidel Castro. The Cuban leader met the band and their entourage backstage at the Karl Marx Theatre in Havana, remarking in Spanish, "I didn't realize there were so many people in the band." The band's singer, James Dean Bradfield, expressed concern that their music might be too loud, to which Fidel asked him, "Is it as loud as war?" Later, long after leaving the stage with its backdrop of a giant Cuban flag, the band members had dinner with Castro.

Bradfield defended the Manics against suggestions from journalists that they had been too eager to glamorize the Cuban political system: "We never said it was a perfect country. It's not a perfect political agenda. But a lot of these journalists are happy to go to Goa, where some of the biggest crimes under the flag of the British Empire were committed." Manic Street Preachers' then current album, *Know Your Enemy,* included two songs that mentioned Cuba – "Let Robeson Sing" ("Went to Cuba to meet Castro/Never got past sleepy Moscow") and "Baby Elian". The latter was a song about a six-year-old Cuban boy, Elian Gonzales, who was rescued from a makeshift raft in the waters off Florida in November 1999. His mother had died on the raft while trying to reach the US. A custody battle then followed between Elian's father in Cuba and relatives in Miami.

At a press conference the day before the gig, Manic Street Preachers were officially praised for their lyrics to "Baby Elian": "Kidnapped – to the Promised Land/The Bay of Pigs/or Baby Elian/Operation – Peter Pan/America, the Devil's Playground". Kirsty MacColl, for her part, may have been dubious about the band's motives in visiting Cuba, but agreed wholeheartedly with their view of the battle for custody of Elian: "I can't understand why there was any question, ever, that he didn't belong with his father. If somebody kidnapped my children and died taking them to another country, I'd expect to get my children back. How else could it be?"

With every visit MacColl made to the country, it became increasingly clear that, along with tourism, Cuba's music had become an extraordinary economic asset. Cuban artists like Los Van Van, Arturo Sandoval, Gonzalo Rubalcaba, Isaac Delgado and Alberto Alvarez had all started touring abroad and recording for foreign labels. Some, like Sandoval, followed the lead of salsa queen Celia Cruz – who had left Cuba after Batista was ousted by the revolution – and never returned.

The new spirit of economic openness had been of direct benefit to musicians; they were able to work freely outside Cuba, forge links and contracts with recording companies, and negotiate their own rates. In return, the state would take a percentage of their hard currency earnings. The state-owned record label, Egrem, began to negotiate foreign licensing deals for its recordings, sending albums once only for sale on the domestic market out into the world and further heightening Cuba's musical profile abroad.

Cuba's rich musical heritage is a legacy of its multicultural past, its geography and its historic links with both Europe and the Americas. As one of Latin America's most influential sources of music, Cuba has spawned an extraordinarily diverse musical culture, which has in turn influenced classical, jazz, pop, rock and dance music. Composers and songwriters as diverse as Ravel, Debussy, Gershwin, Copland and Lennon & McCartney have used Cuban rhythms and percussion instruments. By the time of her first visit to Cuba, Kirsty MacColl had already joined them, with the Latin-inspired "My Affair" on *Electric Landlady*.

Ry Cooder has observed that, "Cubans live for the music, they don't live for other things. This is how they understand life." He believes that in Cuba there is a rare kind of musical honesty and integrity – untouched by, and protected from, greed and commerce by the socialist system and isolation. "I've looked for it all my life," he has said. "But I've never found it anywhere but in Cuba."

For Kirsty MacColl, music seemed to endow every aspect of Cuban life with more meaning. Music appeared to still have vitality as a life force in ways that had long since been forgotten in British society. It would not have been hard to see why her father had fought so hard to keep alive the musical traditions of British working-class communities; the songs of labour and unionism, the story-cycles, the humour and the continuity of songlines within a community.

The soundtrack to Cuba's recent history was thrilling for Kirsty. Castro's rebels had sung a merengue – *a la rigola* – in their stronghold in the mountains of the Sierra Maestra. Students sent into the fields as tomato-pickers as part of the revolutionary government's "school in the fields" programme would sing Frank Dominguez's bolero *"Tu me acostumbraste"* while they worked; the politically inspired *nueva trova* (new ballad) grew out of the revolution and emerged in the sixties as the new post-revolutionary chapter in the evolution of Cuban music. The song-form, merging the themes of politics, love, loss and longing with beautifully crafted melodies, proved the perfect synthesis of politics and romance for everyday life, and mirrored the themes of the hippies and the protest generation of the sixties and seventies that were burgeoning elsewhere.

By the mid-sixties, music in Cuba became increasingly recognized as an indispensable form of expression. The Cuban musician Rembert Egues has said, "Tito Puente, Oscar D'Leon and salsa musicians in general can thank Fidel Castro, because it was with the breaking-off of diplomatic relations between Cuba and the United States that the Puerto Ricans, Venezuelans and others took Cuban music and made salsa with it." For her part, Celia Cruz described salsa as "a little animal that gets into your eyes and ears, and when it reaches your heart it bursts out and you can't avoid it."

It was the vintage forties and fifties Cuban music that Kirsty MacColl had fallen in love with: "I collected mostly old stuff. I wasn't that into the contemporary thing, because a lot of it is like pop music anywhere. There's a lot of crap and it's not as if everything Cuban is great. But the good stuff sounded so refreshing, especially when you turned on the radio at home and heard another generation of bands trying to be the Beatles all over again. I'd lost interest in that completely."

Every time Kirsty MacColl went to Cuba, her suitcases would be full of gifts for the people she met, and children's clothes to give away. On her return trips, she would invariably be carrying cases full of Cuban records. For almost three years, she played nothing but Cuban music at home: "The kids would sit down to tea and I'd have Tito Puente blaring away and they'd say, 'Please can we listen to something else?' and I'd say, 'No, you can't!' I guess I was obsessed with it."

Celina Gonzalez became the elder stateswoman of Cuban music, following the self-exile of Celia Cruz. One of the greatest stars of Cuban country music, *musica campesina*, she rapidly became one of Kirsty's favourites. Gonzalez, who was born in 1929 to a farming family in the province of Matanzas, once famously responded to pleas from the US label, RCA Victor, that she sign with the company by saying dismissively: "Aren't you the label with the little doggie as a logo? Well, you can take that dog, cook it up and eat it."

As a young girl, Gonzalez would sing at family parties – *guateques* – accompanied by her sister and brother. At fifteen, she met her future husband, Reutilio Dominguez Terrero. They formed a duo, Celina y Reutilio, and started to perform on radio programmes and in local theatres. Soon after moving to Havana in the thirties, Celina wrote what would become her most famous song, "Santa Barbara" (or "*Que viva Chango*"), a song inspired by the most widespread of the Afro-Cuban faiths, *santeria* (from the Spanish *santo,* saint) or *regla de Ocha,* which fuses traditional African beliefs with Roman Catholicism. Gonzalez famously cancelled plans to record for the *Buena Vista Social Club* album after an inauspicious reading of her chicken bones on the day that recording was due to start.

The religion's roots are in slavery, spirit worship, god-fearing Catholicism and the cult of the Yoruba people of Nigeria (also known as Lucumis in Cuba). African slaves brought to Cuba were forbidden to worship their own spirits and deities, so devised a form of religion where they could still do so under the guise of embracing Catholicism. Each of the main Yoruba gods, or *orisha,* has its own personality, colour, chants and rhythms, and is twinned with the Catholic saint who most approximates that god's role and responsibilities. Saint Barbara, the Catholic saint who inspired Gonzalez's song, is also known as *Chango,* the spirit of war and fire, identified by the colours red and white.

There is a saying that, if you scratch a Cuban Roman Catholic, you'll find a *santeria* follower beneath the surface. The influence of *santeria* is seen on streets all over Cuba – white-garbed followers wearing the brightly coloured bracelets and necklaces identified with the religion. The musical rhythms of its rituals resound through Cuban music; the *bata* drums and *chekere* rattles can be heard in all kinds of new and traditional Cuban music. MacColl recognized this and, seeing the importance of *santeria* in cultural and spiritual life, began to study it: "I wasn't just interested in the music but the whole political scene, and I realized that to understand Cuba you have to understand the religion. If you don't understand *santeria* then the African origins of Cuban culture are closed to you."

MacColl would emphasize the "whole political scene" at the meetings with British government ministers that she attended as part of Cuba Solidarity Campaign delegations. Rob Miller has positive memories of her contribution:

Kirsty was completely honest in her views and she was extremely articulate in a direct way; she didn't dress up her language in political cleverness. She just went for it and spoke directly from the heart on her experiences in Cuba, what she'd heard from the Cuban people and why the British government should treat Cuba normally. She said that Cuba wasn't asking for anything in particular or anything special; it just wanted a normal relationship with the rest of the world. That's what was important about Kirsty's involvement in the whole thing, rather than that she was some celebrity. She often said, "Do you need me? I haven't had an album out for years!" and I'd say, "That's not important. You've been to Cuba, you've got a lot to say on the subject and it's good for us to have some-body who is as eloquent as you are, regardless of your celebrity status at this particular moment."

Within a decade of MacColl's first trip to Cuba, the tourism industry accounted for forty per cent of the government's foreign trade income. Almost two million tourists – mostly from Canada, Germany, Italy, Spain, France and Britain – now visit the island each year. Dozens of new resorts have been developed, often as joint ventures with foreign companies.

However, as tourism has grown, so too have the service industries that ensure tourists part with still more money in exchange for the diversions offered by prostitution and gambling. The revolutionary government was proud to wipe out what it saw as social evils, believing that prostitution in particular degraded and insulted Cuban woman-hood. Now, their return has had to be tolerated as part of the price to pay for economic survival. The Cuban social commentator, Juan Antonio Blanco, has described tourism as "chemotherapy for the economy"; the hard currency it brings in is essential to support the national education, health and social security systems.

On November 2, 2000, Kirsty MacColl was among several prominent figures to sign an open letter in support of the Cuba Solidarity Campaign calling for an end to the US trade embargo. It read:

Early this month, the UN General Assembly will again vote on the contin-uing US embargo of Cuba. The policy is immoral because it still denies food and medicine to children. The American Association of World Health has declared that it is causing the suffering and even deaths of Cuban children. The policy is not even working, because it has failed to weaken the deter-mination of the Cuban people to protect their independence. A year ago, this inhuman policy was condemned by 157 countries, including Britain, at the United Nations, with only the US and Israel voting against. We urge the British government to vote again against the blockade and to put pressure on the American government to end its embargo. We join with the 25,000 people in the UK who have added their voices to this campaign. It is time to end the US blockade of Cuba.

Along with MacColl, the letter was also signed by Billy Bragg, Bea Campbell, Julie Christie, Alan Fountain, John Hegley, Michael Kustor, Lizzie Lemon, Melanie MacFadyean, Rob Newman, John Pilger, Harold Pinter, Michael Rosen, David Rosenberg, Sheila Rowbotham, Mark Thomas and Arnold Wesker.

Away from the political arena, Ry Cooder's nurturing of the Buena Vista Social Club had spawned a commercial passion for Cuban music as that most beloved of music industry clichés – The Next Big Thing. The phenomenon shows few signs of lessening, and Cuban music is becoming an established part of the mainstream. Yet Rob Miller says that Cuba's culture and her people are at great risk of being hijacked by the West for promotional reasons:

It does backfire. Bacardi are a classic example, continually trying to make out they are something to do with Cuba. They are nothing at all to do with Cuba and haven't been for fifty-odd years; in fact they are anti-Cuban. Their products are not even made in Cuba and have no Cuban content at all, yet they insist that they want to be associated with Cuba. It's laughable. That can be extended to other people who have tried to claim Cuban heritage or some kind of connection. Cuba is a real country with a real, vibrant culture, and unless there is a real connection to the people, it's seen through. Kirsty recognized that and never wanted to exploit her Cuban connection at all, and did it really because she had a genuine affection for the people there and the country and the music, and the achievements of the revolution.

MacColl's love and huge knowledge of Cuban music would be put to good use by the BBC station, Radio 2, when it commissioned her to return to Cuba in November 2000 to compile and narrate "Kirsty MacColl's Cuba", an eight-part series on the evolution of Cuban music. The week before she arrived in Havana, the state newspaper, *Granma*, had carried a picture of her on its front page, taken as she handed in the petition in London supporting Cuba against the US embargo.

Working with MacColl on the programmes was producer Nick Barraclough and musicologist and journalist Jan Fairley. Their schedule was punishing; they drove the length and breadth of Cuba, with journeys fueled by copious amounts of Havana Club rum, swapping stories, songs, dirty jokes, gardening tips and reminiscences of past adventures in Cuba. "Kirsty regaled us with tales of driving, with her sons and a Cuban doctor friend, the length of the island to Santiago in the early nineties," says Fairley. "She gave hitchhikers lifts, and avoided potholes and goats in the road."

MacColl, Fairley and Barraclough recorded in people's homes, and at the new mausoleum for Che Guevara in Santa Clara. They crisscrossed Cuba to the Bay of Pigs, then back to Havana. They also interviewed dozens of people, including Buena Vista Social Club veteran Ibrahim Ferrer and young rapper Jose Luis Cortes. "Kirsty was half-hearted about Cortes until she met him," says Fairley. "By the time we left, they were talking of writing and recording a song together." Simon Calder, a British travel journalist who took part in the series, said of Kirsty: "She was the best kind of exponent of Cuban music in the West. She actually went and found it and made it accessible over here."

The first broadcast found MacColl declaring: "I'm not the commie my dad was." The series, however, demonstrated that she had an equally strong connection to, and affinity with, Cuba, its culture and its people. The series linked the fifties dance band era to the international salsa craze, early icons like Desi Arnaz to Celina Gonzalez to the global success of the Buena Vista Social Club almost 50 years later, and veered from Cuban folk traditionalists to hardcore rappers like NG La Banda. MacColl covered most of the great characters of Cuban music, not least Damos Perez Prado – who had a US Number 1 hit in 1955, only to die in obscurity after his brother took his name – and Arsenio Rodriguez, who was blinded by a mule.

The series would become her equivalent of her father's famous *Radio Ballads* series, which had been first broadcast in 1957. Working with Peggy Seeger and a BBC Midlands producer, Charles Parker, Ewan had created radio documentaries that went far beyond the genre of the usual music programming. Told in the words of working people, and in Ewan's songs, they became social commentaries about the cultural and political conditions of working-class families; the dreams and dramas of railwaymen, road-builders, fishermen, coal miners, polio patients, teenagers, boxers and the nomadic travelling community.

Kirsty's series may not have gone into such great depth about the wider political issues within Cuba's musical past and present, but she had recognized that politics is never far from the music of Cuba. This remains as true today. In February 2004, the United States government refused to give visas to several Cuban musicians, preventing them from attending the Grammy awards where all five nominees for best traditional tropical Latin album were Cubans. Only one, the piano virtuoso, Chucho Valdes, had his visa application approved, but he said he'd refuse to go if the US authorities did not relent and allow the others to attend as well. A diplomat at the United States Interests Section in Havana, which issued the letters denying the visa requests, was later quoted as saying that the decision had been taken under a presidential proclamation that allowed the George W. Bush administration to suspend entry to individuals deemed detrimental to the interests of the United States.

Among the musicians who were considered to be potential security threats were 77-year-old Ibrahim Ferrer, the veteran singer whose career was rejuvenated on a global scale with the Buena Vista Social Club, and 75-year-old salsa pianist Guillermo Rubalcaba. "I'm not a terrorist!" responded Ferrer. "I couldn't be one. I am a musician, and have always been well received by American audiences."

The Cuban Vice-Minister for Culture, Abel Acosta, accused President Bush of blocking the musicians' visas for political reasons, in order to appease the powerful and vocal Cuban-American lobby in Miami. The Bush administration's decision had been announced just as campaigning continued for the US presidential election, which was then only nine months away. "How can these musicians be considered terrorists?" Acosta marvelled. "Something as noble as music is being converted into a policy against Cuba."

Kirsty MacColl may, in her way, have highlighted the plight of the troubled musicians of Cuba, but there is still much to be done – as Ibraham Ferrer, among others, had attested.

CHAPTER SEVEN

Free World

For all that Kirsty and Ewan MacColl were universes apart in so many ways, their worldviews had far more in common than either of them would openly admit. They disagreed about many things, but Kirsty had never doubted her father's political integrity and his fight for the causes he believed in – and she admired him for it. She may not have shared her father's communism but her politics were decidedly and unashamedly left of centre. Her personal philosophy, though, was more what Billy Bragg would later term "a socialism of the heart" in his song "Upfield" than it was a card-carrying party political affiliation. "People who are socialists," says Hamish MacColl, "generally have a particular view which tends to be more caring, in the sense that you look out for others, and Kirsty was like that. That's what moved her to go to Palestine."

In 1992, the same year that she made her first trip to Cuba, MacColl also travelled to the occupied Gaza Strip and West Bank. She was part of a delegation of British actors, musicians and artists that included Julie Christie, Charlotte Cornwell, Susan Wooldridge, Richard Wilson, Simon Fanshawe, Andy de la Tour, John Gillett and John Bevan. They visited educational and social programmes for Palestinians, many of whom lived in refugee camps that had become sprawling towns, and met artists and activists.

The impoverished Gaza Strip has more than a million Palestinians crammed into its 360 sq km area, making it one of the most densely populated places on earth. The remaining part of the Strip is held by heavily fortified Jewish settlements – illegal under international law – that were set up after Israel seized Gaza in 1967. Chronic antagonism between the settlers and the Palestinian population has been a fact of life ever since. The frequent closures of the border with Israel, which prevent Palestinians from going to work in Israel and cause severe hardship and economic disruption, and the endemic poverty have made Gaza a stronghold of Islamic and radical movements. Gaza was the birthplace of the first *intifada* – the uprising against Israeli occupation from 1987–93 – and in June 1992, the newly-elected Israeli Prime Minister Yitzhak Rabin appeared to speak for many Israelis when he remarked: "I would like Gaza to sink into the sea. But that won't happen and a solution must be found."

Upon their return to Britain, Kirsty MacColl and her fellow travellers wrote a joint letter to *The Guardian* newspaper, protesting about the conditions they'd witnessed. It was published on March 16:

We had heard that fellow artists in the Occupied Territories were denied the freedom to perform and exhibit, but were unprepared for the systematic repressions which affect every area of Palestinian life. We learned at first hand of the curfews, roadblocks, house demolitions and army raids on homes. We discovered that repression of education continues – that Bir Zeit University, for example, is now in its fifth consecutive year of closure under military order. On our return we were distressed to find that one of the educationalists we had met in the West Bank – Khalil Mahshi, head teacher at the Quaker Friends School – has had his request to travel to Britain blocked by the Israeli government. Khalil Mahshi had been invited by the World University Service (WUS) and Quaker Peace and Service (QPS) to address teachers, academics and students at the WUS conference in London this weekend and at the QPS conference next week. Like all Palestinians in the West Bank and Gaza Strip, each foreign trip he wishes to make must be approved by the Israeli authorities. We appeal to the Israeli government to ease its restrictions on travel and its denial of basic rights to the people of the Occupied Territories. Such practices are a flagrant abuse of the standards of civil rights we take for granted in any democratic country.

Bir Zeit, the West Bank university they'd visited, was given approval to re-open the following month. It was the first time since 1988 that all six Palestinian universities had been permitted to function. It was to be one of the few positive things that the British group could celebrate within weeks of their return. A month after they visited the Gaza Strip, the United Nations Security Council condemned Israel for allowing the continued deterioration of the situation there, after clashes between Israeli troops and Palestinian demonstrators left five Palestinians dead and more than sixty wounded.

On August 24, *The Guardian* again published an open letter from MacColl's group, expressing alarm at the death in suspicious circumstances of a young Palestinian student at Bir Zeit whom they'd met in Jerusalem during their March visit. Twenty-three-year-old Hazem Id, from the West Bank town of Ramallah, had been arrested on June 22, and was held in the custody of the Israeli General Security Service – the GSS, better known as Shin Bet – until his death on July 9. Neither the man's family nor the Bir Zeit university authorities accepted the Israeli explanation that he had committed suicide. They'd said he appeared to be in good physical and mental condition only three days before his death, and accused the Israeli authorities of withholding information to prevent a full investigation to be conducted.

The protest letter read:

> We urge the Israeli authorities to submit to Hazem's lawyer a detailed written police report and all material evidence related to the case and to allow for an independent investigation into the circumstances of Hazem's death. The latest round of the Middle East peace talks begins today and the world expects some progress, especially with the election of the new Israeli government, towards a genuine and lasting peace settlement. We fear, though, that for the Palestinians living under military occupation in the West Bank and Gaza, the well-catalogued abuses of human rights by the Israeli military authorities will continue as before. We believe that Israel must not be allowed to continue to ignore UN resolutions and flout international law and Hazem's death must serve as a reminder that for as long as the illegal occupation of the West Bank and Gaza is allowed to continue there can be neither peace nor justice.

In its annual review of human rights in the occupied West Bank and Gaza Strip, the New York-based organization Human Rights Watch concluded that 1992 had been another year of brutality and bloodshed, in which, "The most severe human rights abuses continued on a large scale in the Occupied Territories." Its lengthy report made grim reading as it highlighted abuse after abuse, including, "The deaths while under interrogation of four Palestinians in 1992 [which] indicated no softening of interrogation methods by the General Security Service ... Evidence continued to accumulate that the mistreatment of Palestinian security suspects under interrogation was systematic."

Human Rights Watch noted that, in a public statement in May 1992, the International Committee of the Red Cross had urged Israel to end its policy of physical and psychological pressure that "constitute a violation of the [Fourth Geneva] Convention". The ICRC was particularly well informed on such matters as it was permitted by the Israeli government to meet all detainees within fourteen days of custody.

The second public letter released by MacColl's delegation had mentioned the two dramatic developments in 1992 that many believed could have brought about a transformation in relations between Israel and the Palestinians. These were the pursuit of regional peace talks, and the ousting of the hard-line Likud government by a coalition dominated by Yitzhak Rabin's more moderate Labour Party. As Human Rights Watch noted, "the most severe human rights abuses" had continued in 1992, and the few signs of hope seemed to have disappeared. A breakthrough was to come the following year, however, with the historic Oslo peace accord between Israel and the Palestinians in September 1993, which returned much of the Occupied Territories to Palestinian control.

Kirsty MacColl's pressure group stayed in touch with developments in Israel and the territories – by then under the control of the Palestinian National Authority – during the nineties, through the contacts they'd made during their visit. Another public statement came on May 25, 1996, again in *The Guardian*:

> We read with alarm your report of the arrest and detention of Dr Eyyad Sarraj. We had the pleasure of meeting Dr Sarraj a few years ago on a visit to Gaza and found him to be the most fervent campaigner for all those human rights denied to the Palestinian population living under Israeli military occupation at the time. It is to Dr Sarraj's credit that he has continued to champion the cause of human rights in the former Occupied Territories and to speak out against abuses. We look forward to hearing of his immediate release.

Julie Christie, Charlotte Cornwell, Andy de la Tour, John Gillett, Kirsty MacColl, Richard Wilson and Susan Wooldridge all signed the letter on this occasion.

However, MacColl's visit to Israel and the Occupied territories in 1992 had not taken place in a blaze of publicity. The letters, written later, highlighted specific incidents and issues and the group hoped to use their collective celebrity clout to draw attention to such issues.

One problem was that the Israeli authorities had long become inured to the constant stream of humanitarian visits and fact-finding missions to the territories that would inevitably end in criticism and condemnation of their policies. The plight of the Palestinian people under occupation had been exceptionally well-documented by international aid organizations, the United Nations' own agency, UNRWA, which had worked since 1948 to care for generations of Palestinian refugees, and in a series of resolutions passed by the UN.

The Palestinians felt that the cause of their suffering could be blamed on Israel and the support afforded by its traditional ally, the United States. For the people of Iraq, however, the source of their desperate plight was less easily defined.

By the year 2000, ten years of UN sanctions had caused deprivation in Iraq on such a scale that some of the UN's own agencies were calling for an end to them. In mid-September, a Russian plane carrying oil executives and humanitarian supplies, and a French flight with medical teams and anti-sanctions campaigners on board had breached the decade-long embargo on flights to Baghdad. A week later, a Labour Party Member of the UK Parliament, George Galloway, announced that he would defy his government's support of the measures against Iraq, and join a sanctions-busting flight to Baghdad.

Galloway had tried to organize a similar flight earlier in the year but had been prevented from doing so by objections from the United Nations sanctions committee. However, in the intervening months the UN Security Council itself had become increasingly divided over the future of the embargo. France, Russia and China maintained that the relevant UN resolutions did not ban commercial flights to Baghdad, while the United States and Britain insisted that the ban was part of a wider trade embargo. Against this background of disarray, and with several countries announcing plans to resume humanitarian and commercial flights, Galloway was adamant that it was time to act: "An embargo only works for as long as people are prepared to obey it. There is a sense that people are no longer prepared to blockade Iraq in perpetuity."

The MP announced that he was assembling a group of people to accompany him on the flight to Iraq. Among them would be Kirsty MacColl, broadcaster Andy Kershaw and two Labour peers, Lord Rea and Lord Ahmed. They planned to join a group of anti-sanctions campaigners in France, led by the French former foreign minister Claude Cheysson, and then fly to Baghdad from Paris on September 29. The Foreign Office responded to the announcement tersely: "Any proposal for a flight to Baghdad should be referred to the UN sanctions committee."

For MacColl, the blockade of Iraq and the suffering it was causing to ordinary people had a parallel with what she'd seen in Cuba. Even so, Cuba's superior health system and excellent medical training and research facilities had saved its people from the worst effects of a trade embargo, effects that were much in evidence in Iraqi hospitals and medical clinics, despite the UN's approved oil-for-food programme which allowed the purchase of food and humanitarian aid.

However. Kirsty's gesture of solidarity with the Iraqi people literally never got off the ground. The flight that had been scheduled to leave from Paris with the group on board failed to get approval from the French and Belgian authorities. Both were required, as the plane was leaving from Paris and would have been hired from a Belgian company. Activists blamed behind-the-scenes pressure from Washington but the official reason was noted as a series of technical hitches. One of the French organizers of the mission, Father Yves Buannic, was scornful: "France – the land of human rights – bends once again before the American diktat, with the complicity of the Belgian authorities. We apologize to the Iraqi people."

This, of course, was all a very long way from leafy west London, but Frank Murray sees no inherent contradiction: "Kirsty was politically motivated. But unlike a lot of people who talk a lot of politics, Kirsty actually did things. She got involved in helping people in Cuba and helping people in Iraq." MacColl clearly had a strong and heartfelt political commitment, but it was of a different hue to her father's – and rather less alienating for those around her, says her brother Hamish:

Our dad was his own propagandist. He was a communist, and he was typical of people of his era; whatever political belief he had was the right one, and everyone else was wrong. It was all about propaganda, and about manipulating and making sure that you got in there first and convinced other people you were right. Dad had a terrible habit, which I think was common at the time, of letting ideology rule his life, so that the Russians were always right, for example. He did that kind of proselytizing, regardless of the truth.

There were, however, occasions when Kirsty's father showed a rare hint of ideological flexibility. One involved Billy Bragg's efforts to rewrite the lyrics of the English version of the socialist hymn, the Internationale, at the urging of the veteran activist and singer-songwriter, Pete Seeger, who was also Peggy Seeger's half-brother. Pete Seeger and Bragg had met up at the Vancouver Folk Festival, and when Seeger decided to sing the Internationale, he invited Billy to join him on stage. Bragg demurred: "The lyrics are awful – 'Arise ye starvelings from your slumbers/Arise ye prisoners of want/For reason in revolt now thunders/And at last ends the age of cant'. I don't even know what that means!"

Pete Seeger had a novel solution, telling a surprised Bragg to "Go off and write some more, then." Bragg took up his challenge: "You can't really say no to old man Seeger, so I wrote some more lyrics that day and we sang a verse. Then I wrote the rest of it and decided to go and see Ewan and Peggy and say to them, 'Look, I'm having a go at rewriting the Internationale, what do you reckon? Is it good, bad or indifferent?' "

Bragg visited them at their home in Beckenham and ran through the lyrics several times. "Ewan was quite supportive, much to my surprise," he says. "Peggy was a bit concerned about the imagery in the lyrics, because she felt they were in some ways sexist. Ewan and I tried to talk her around, although I think I did actually change that line after we'd spoken. Then Ewan made a cheese fondue. Which was very nice, actually."

Ewan MacColl was kindly disposed towards Bragg, perhaps, because he perceived him, together with Kirsty, as being part of a maverick collection of musicians who had carried on his own legacy of dissent and debate through music. Both Kirsty and Billy were by now veterans of countless charity benefits and political campaigns through the eighties and nineties. Bragg had been one of the musicians who formed Red Wedge, a protest movement with close ties to the Labour Party which failed to defeat the Conservatives in the 1987 election. Red Wedge foundered. "That's the price you pay," reflects Bragg, "for getting your ideas on the front page of the *NME*."

Kirsty MacColl and Billy Bragg were comrades in arms from protest gigs and rallies against issues as diverse as nuclear power, repressive regimes in Latin America, war in the Balkans and the ravages of Thatcherism. Bragg recalls:

Kirsty and I would always keep meeting each other, because we were the people who'd keep turning up for the causes. If it wasn't the miners, it was Nicaragua, or anti-apartheid, or supporting the Greater London Council. There were so few of us who were willing to do that sort of thing. It was tougher for

Kirsty because it was based around live performance, and she never was that keen on performance. But when she had a cause, she was able to overcome that; she never had any reticence about getting up and singing about Cuba. She really had a different take on those sorts of gigs, and that's why I think she really felt that she was able to lend herself to those kinds of causes.

Like many of his generation, it had been the protracted coal miners' strike in 1984-85 that proved the catalyst for Bragg's activism: "It politicized me," he confesses. "It forced me to focus my humanitarian ideas around an ideology. Every time I did a gig in the north of England or south Wales, left-wing people wanted to know what my politics were: Was I just coming along to exploit this? I needed to defend myself, and argue my corner in ideological terms."

Bragg and MacColl were to unite for the miners a full decade after the crippling national strike. The once-thriving UK coal industry in Britain that had sustained hundreds of local communities had been shattered by the early nineties. However, one colliery in south Wales was refusing to accept that privatization or inevitable demise were its only choices. In 1993, workers at Tower Colliery launched an ambitious plan to buy the pit and its shallow mine under the Rhigos mountain. Bragg and MacColl were among the thousands of people who responded to an appeal for help.

Bragg organised a fund-raising benefit for the colliery and Kirsty MacColl joined him for the gig. Bragg suggested that they perform a song together, explaining that he had the perfect one in mind:

I said to her, "There's a beautiful song that would really fit this gig, called 'School Days Over'. It's one of your dad's songs. What's your feeling about that?" She said, "I don't think I could sing that convincingly." I said, "Kirsty, you'll have the miners in tears, *they'll* be weeping. *I'll* be weeping!" And, of course, it was so beautiful when she sang it.

"Schooldays over, it's real life now
The teachers all seem small somehow
Grab a job or keep on studyin',
The dole is a living death
Now they're pushin' you in at the deep end, dive in
    and hold your breath ..."

—Ewan MacColl, "School Days Over"

On the drive back from Wales to London, on a fogbound motorway with Billy's wife, Juliet, at the wheel, Kirsty regaled the couple with songs she'd learned from her father. The poignancy of the rite-of-passage lament of "School Days Over" was forgotten as she launched into the more ribald sing-a-long of "Lydia The Tattooed Lady". This good cause, at least, was rewarded: by 1995, the workers would raise enough money to make Tower Colliery the only pit in Europe to be run entirely by the miners employed there.

Despite her predeliction for helping the needy, though, Kirsty MacColl's political conscience was not a showy one. "One of the great things about Kirsty," says friend and musician Dave Ruffy, "was that she did all of this stuff, but you really had to get to know her before you knew that anything like that went on. She just did it quietly and got on with what she thought was right – an unusual thing in this day and age."

The eighties and nineties were times when pop stars frequently seemed to take on the mantle of politicians, and for the baby-boomer leaders who were taking high office, politics was the new rock and roll. In Britain, the Labour Party was rebranding itself as New Labour to avoid confusion with the strong socialist roots of the traditional Labour movement. High-profile public endorsements came from music industry figures like Alan McGee, the founder of Creation Records. And when Tony Blair's New Labour won an overwhelming election victory in 1997, ending almost two decades of Conservative rule, the new government was greeted with euphoria by most of the rock and pop fraternity.

Cool Britannia had arrived – and was duly invited to Downing Street to have drinks with Blair. The new ministers were well briefed in the ways of youth culture, with the result that even the dour Chancellor of the Exchequer, Gordon Brown, had been photographed at a Teenage Fanclub gig in 1997, describing them as "great, but obviously very influenced by Big Star". When invited to appear on the BBC Radio 4 programme, *Desert Island Discs*, Brown's musical choices included Kirsty MacColl's version of "Days", the Beatles' "Hey Jude" and "Loch Lomond" by Scottish political Celt-rock band Runrig, as well as classical works and hymns. As a footnote, when Tony Blair appeared on a separate edition of the programme and chose a song by British folk rocker Ezio Lunedei, the musician lamented: "It's not a great thing to be liked by such an establishment figure. You can't expect the kids to buy your records if they want to shock their mum. It's been like an albatross around my neck."

Predictably, the spin woven by the politicians into the musical fabric of Cool Britannia began to fray at the edges. As disaffection set in, the passionate clinch between pop star and politician began to resemble an all-in wrestling match. Less than a year after Labour's historic victory, MacColl was among the musicians and actors who criticized the new administration's policy on the minimum wage. With Primal Scream, Cornershop, the Charlatans, Echobelly and "EastEnders" star Ross Kemp, MacColl backed trade union protests against proposals to pay teenagers less than the minimum wage or exclude them from the payment entirely: "It seems an awful indictment that a Labour government could deny youngsters a minimum wage."

Alan McGee had also taken to openly criticizing Labour for its policies on blood sports, drugs and the arts. The *NME* summed up the prevailing mood in a cover feature on March 11, 1998. The music paper detailed the end of the affair between musicians and New Labour with a headline that evoked Johnny Rotten's infamous epitaph for punk: "Ever get the feeling you've been cheated?" Beneath a banner proclaiming, "Betrayed: The Labour Government's War On You", the *NME* denounced the government's policies on a range of issues including welfare-to-work schemes, university tuition fees, curfews for under-18s and the decriminalization of drugs.

The political commentator Anne McElvoy, was to later pertinently write in the *New Statesman*: "Bombast and evasion are putting people off New Labour, and we should not yet consider this problem solved. All ministers should remember the eerily prophetic lyrics of Kirsty MacColl: 'You had so many friends/They all left you in the end/'Cause they couldn't take the patter.'" McElvoy's reference implied that Kirsty's "Free World" – originally a diatribe against Margaret Thatcher's Conservatives – now had a similar relevance when levelled against Tony Blair's New Labourites. The "patter" and "spin" had already begun to drown out the voices of reason.

Of course, the role of songwriters as both historians and reporters who chronicle the political and cultural times in which they live is as old as the craft itself. The pity is that there have always been too few of them doing it well. This was emphasized by columnist David Aaronovitch, who wrote movingly in *The Independent* in June 2000 in response to the deaths of 58 Chinese people who suffocated while crammed into the back of a truck as they tried to enter Britain illegally.

The victims' bodies were only discovered when the truck's freight compartment was opened at the port of Dover. Aaronovitch recalled the grim symbolic similarity with the deaths of 28 Mexican illegal farm workers who were being deported from the US in 1948 when their charter plane crashed in a Californian canyon. The routine official description of the dead as "deportees" and the needless loss of life so outraged the legendary radical American singer-songwriter Woody Guthrie that he wrote a song in their memory: "Plane Wreck at Los Gatos (Deportees)". Aaronovitch reflected:

Perhaps, before we can frame a rational and humane policy for letting people in, we need to be reminded that they are indeed people. The Dover tragedy needs its Woody Guthrie; the dead Lius and Chens deserve somebody to remind us that they paid the price, not just for their own wish to live better, but for our exclusiveness. It's something Billy Bragg or Kirsty MacColl could and should do. Because I have seldom felt so bloody ashamed ...

The Hardest Word

O ne of the most eye-catching objects in Kirsty MacColl's home office was a print of René Magritte's painting, *Titanic Days*. One of his early works, it was painted in 1928 during what he called his "cavernous" period. This was a phase heavily influenced by his association with the Paris-based Surrealists, marked by dark themes and colours, by the macabre and melodramatic, and by often disturbing depictions of eroticism. Few were more disturbing than *Titanic Days* (or *Gigantic Days*, as it is sometimes translated). The image fuses a man's looming frame across a woman's naked body, his arms encircling her to suggest a variety of interpretations: a brutal assault, a metamorphosis of the woman into a man, or even the man devouring the woman. It is not remotely sensual, romantic, liberating or empowering.

Magritte resisted any attempt to interpret his paintings. He insisted that their only meaning was a mystery, and mystery was their only meaning: "People are quite willing to use objects without looking for any symbolic intention in them, but when they look at paintings they can't find any use for them. So they hunt around for a meaning to get themselves out of a quandary. People who look for symbolic meanings fail to grasp the inherent poetry and mystery of the image. No doubt they sense this mystery, but they wish to get rid of it. They are afraid. By asking, 'What does this *mean*?' they express a wish that everything be understandable."

It was perhaps fitting, then, that *Titanic Days* and the mysteries, puzzles and doubts within it should provide the title for, and inspire the shadowy, surreal cover of, an album that was being made as MacColl's marriage was deteriorating. The mysteries of relationships, too, so often seem unknowable. Couples who appear blessed survey their lives and see nothing but curses. So it came to appear with Kirsty MacColl and Steve Lillywhite.

The pair seemed to have it all. A whirlwind engagement, romantic-fantasy celebrity-studded wedding, the rapid embracing of parenthood, their shared fame and the riches ensured by Lillywhite's production skills had propelled them towards their future together. However, the drink and drugs excesses of the rock 'n' roll lifestyle and the self-indulgent hedonism that balanced the "work hard" ethic with an unapologetic "play hard" manifesto had placed strains on them as individuals and as a couple, and ultimately served to conspire against them.

Mark Nevin recalls that during the *Electric Landlady* sessions, he couldn't keep up with the pace of recreational drug-taking: "Kirsty and Steve just got so incredibly stoned. They would be so stoned, and I'd join in but then I just couldn't play. I couldn't even think, I couldn't even see."

Steve Lillywhite is painfully honest about his own shortcomings and endearingly willing to take the blame for the break-up of their marriage, although many of their friends believe the pressures on both of them made a break-up inevitable. Steve says:

We did start growing apart because Kirsty started getting less drug-influenced. Some people get to a point where they go, "This is getting boring," and ease off, and other people go, "I want more!" I think I went into the "I want more" scenario. Kirsty just started doing less and I think my self-confidence started getting eroded. A relationship is like a balancing act, especially when people get married too young. I very much felt inferior to Kirsty; she was so powerful a person. We just started drifting apart and I shrank into my own world of, "It's time to have a drink now". It was definitely my actions that made the marriage fall apart.

Lillywhite entered a period of rehab in 1997 and has had neither drink nor drugs since. When a relationship is under severe strain, though, it's not always just the big issues that cause it to erode even further. Something as seemingly simple as musical preferences can also add to the tensions, adds Lillywhite:

One of the reasons our marriage was not so successful towards the end was that Kirsty had a *need* to listen to music, a physical *need* to acquire music, which I don't have at all. I love music but I see it as a job. She would be there playing records, while I never played one record in our whole married life. It was always her choice. I remember being so influenced by her. She didn't like a lot of things that were deemed successful and I was very influenced by that, and quite rightly so. There were a couple of money-making things that I could have done but I was thinking, "I can't do this, Kirsty would hate it!"

What had seemed an engaging balance between Lillywhite's easy-going, sunny-surfaced Peter Pan charm and MacColl's depression, dark moods and self-doubt gave way to frustration and resentment. Steve's extraordinary success and gilt-edged profile within the music industry only served to highlight his wife's opposing fortunes. For some in the business, MacColl had come to be seen as an adjunct of her husband, benefiting from his contacts, production clients, manager and opportunities. The intermittent nature of her own career, the lack of continuity with record companies, the lingering hangover from the "Chip Shop" and "They Don't Know" connotations of old and her seemingly constant cameos in other people's work, rather than wholehearted devotion to her own, had done little to portray MacColl within the industry as a solid, attractive long-term investment who would deliver the goods and shift those units.

Preliminary work on the planned follow-up to *Electric Landlady* had already begun by the time Virgin terminated her contract. MacColl and Mark Nevin, who'd just finished co-writing with Morrissey and was without a record deal himself, revived the writing partnership they had fostered for *Electric Landlady*. Nevin recalls: "Kirsty said, 'Let's get a band together', so when we started to make *Titanic Days*, it was to be as a band. We were doing it for quite a while, writing songs, until Kirsty's manager [Ian Wright] said, 'This is going to be really hard, it will be like starting again if you do it as a band.' So we did it as Kirsty MacColl."

Nevin and MacColl, however, did retain one element of the band concept – the name Baboon Farm, under which they co-produced most of the album. The name had come to them during a promotional trip to Denmark where they'd seen a reference to said primates on a farm mentioned in a Sunday newspaper. They adopted the name as their own; Nevin swears it seemed hilariously funny at the time.

After two Kirsty albums and several singles produced by Steve Lillywhite, it had seemed inevitable that he would also produce MacColl's new album. So, although her husband's existing workload and their strained relationship seemed to preclude that, MacColl waited for him to be available – and waited still longer. Finally, she opted for a new producer, Vic van Vugt, and co-production with Nevin. In the end, Lillywhite produced just one track, "Angel", but he did mix the entire album.

"Kirsty felt a bit insecure about standing on her own," says Nevin, "and in a way *Titanic Days* was funny, because we did it without Steve for the first time, so that was a big step. Then he came in and mixed it. He's such a brilliant mixer that it went onto a new level … but it was half a step away from Steve because he didn't produce it."

Titanic Days was Kirsty MacColl's most mature and darkest work. It mirrored the disintegration of her marriage in a bleak lyrical landscape covering loneliness, violence and depression, but with some of the most melodic music that she had ever produced. Long, drink-fuelled sessions in London's media hangout, the Groucho Club, were interspersed with equally long drink-fuelled sessions in the studio. The mood was exacerbated, says Mark Nevin, by the fact that his own domestic circumstances mirrored those of Kirsty: "We were just so unhappy. We would just blot out all our feelings, not just the pain, but everything. We would just numb everything because I think we both knew that our marriages were about to fall to pieces, and that was a horrible thing."

MacColl was to later describe *Titanic Days* as her "sad divorce album" but it was also Mark Nevin's. His relationship with his wife, Eve, was disintegrating and the closer he and Kirsty worked together on the album, the closer the parallels seemed. This was mirrored in many of the songs they wrote together. Among them was "Tomorrow Never Comes" which they recorded in a single day, with Nevin playing the organ, guitars and bass:

That's my favourite song on the album, and I think it was Kirsty's as well. We were both about to get divorced. Our lives fell to pieces when that album came out, and it was as though the album was saying, "Tomorrow never comes". It was saying, "Keep trying and trying, and tomorrow is going to be better," but tomorrow never comes, and at the end of the day you give up, don't you? It's like banging your head against the same old brick wall. In a way, it's almost like the album is a concept album, although it was never meant to be that.

The malaise that depression brought with it was temporarily nudged aside by the frustration of the opening line of the first song on the album,

"You Know It's You". It read: "I want to shake up this world and not feel so useless." The last song they wrote for the album was the moving "Dear John", an elegy for a failed marriage and so painfully autobiographical that MacColl refused to include it, says Nevin:

> She did the demo in my house. She came over and I put a tape on and she stood next to me so I could hear and she had the words in front of her and she was like a little girl. She sang that song and it was like we both knew then that was it, we had to go through it.

In tears, MacColl told him, "I can't put that song on the record; I can't play it to Steve."

Ten years and two days after their wedding, on August 20, 1994 – while they were on holiday at their home in the south of France – Kirsty told Steve she wanted a separation. He recalls, "She said, 'Look, Steve, it's not working.' So she kicked me out." They discussed the impact on their sons, then aged ten and eight, and decided that the boys' ages might actually make it easier for them to adjust; they were old enough to understand that both of their parents loved them very deeply and nothing would get in the way of that, but they were young enough not yet to be in the midst of the teenage years that can often bring their own set of problems. The couple also sought advice on practical ways to ease the transition for their sons.

The separation, says Lillywhite, was a relief in some ways – but it did not always feel like it. "I spent the next year wanting to come back and absolutely not doing one thing to make her want me to come back. My actions did not mirror my intentions. I wanted her to have me back without me changing at all, because I felt, with my 'poor me' attitude, that she deserved to have me back as her husband! But she had other ideas and she was absolutely right, of course; it was the right thing to do." When the news got out and journalists asked for comments, the couple were at pains to emphasize that nobody else was involved. In an interview shortly before their marriage ended, Steve had said with gentle understatement, "She's brilliant, and sometimes she's not very happy."

The album *Titanic Days* was two years in the making, by which time MacColl had secured a deal with the ZTT label run by veteran producer and former Buggles star Trevor Horn. In the US, she was with IRS. The album was preceded, in December 1993, by a single, "Angel", which was released with multiple remixes, including one by Apollo 440.

In February 1994 the album finally appeared, and again showed MacColl's hard-to-categorize range of musical taste, inspirations and influences. "Angel" had a Happy Mondays' vibe, while "Soho Square" and "Titanic Days" were both gorgeous pop songs. MacColl and Nevin employed knockabout rockabilly on "Big Boy on a Saturday Night" (its titular hero surely a close relative of the guy who worked down the chip shop), Latin breeziness on "Last Day of Summer" and then turned to lush, orchestral neo-classicism for "Don't Go Home". Then, as previously noted, there was the sly unequivocal good-girl-turns-bad message and declaration of independence of "Bad", which contained one of MacColl's most revealing personal observations:

> "I've been the token woman all my life
> The token daughter and the token wife ...
> I've been an awful woman all my life
> A dreadful daughter and a hopeless wife ..."
>
> —Kirsty MacColl, "Bad"

The critics gave *Titanic Days* a mixed reception. *Rolling Stone* reviewer Armond White acclaimed MacColl as one of the best songwriters in British pop: "From the sauntering bossa nova of 'Last Day Of Summer' to the ethereal funkiness of 'Angel', the album is a veritable hit parade of clear-eyed pop sentiments. MacColl's sophisticated *modus operandi* – the unexpected mesh of hooks and dread – is her particular speciality: getting a melodic grip on melancholy and on every romantic's confrontation with the abyss."

The *Washington Post*'s critic Mark Jenkins was less impressed, declaring of the album: "Smoothly consistent and entirely listenable, it nonetheless lacks the highs of her previous work ... the songs feature the expected MacColl passion, empathy and wit, yet few are grabbers ... Too bad more of these songs don't have tunes and arrangements as sharp as MacColl's words."

In the UK, *The Times*'s Paul Sexton described it as "a gloriously harmonious mélange of frustration and melancholy ... [but] it would be wrong to assume that MacColl has become some embittered misanthrope with a brimming inkwell of vitriol." *Record Collector* reviewer Mark Paytress highlighted the personal and political themes on *Titanic Days*, saying, "MacColl may not dress up her words of social discomfort in rock's traditional revolutionary language, neither does she pander to the simple skills of the sloganeer, preferring instead to weave her cultural metaphors (most impressively on the title track) into songs of a distinctly personal nature." Paytress concluded that the album had, "a slightly more open feel than the previous two albums, perhaps a result of Steve Lillywhite's role being restricted to the mixing desk."

But the album was a one-off deal with ZTT and, while it scraped into the UK chart at Number 46, the lack of promotion or radio play meant it was unfairly doomed. Dave Ruffy, who co-wrote "Just Woke Up" and played drums on several tracks, says, "*Titanic Days* just disappeared. It didn't really get known and it's such a great record. Some of her best work is on it. But she wasn't in a good way. It was a very unhappy time for Kirsty."

On June 11, 1994, Kirsty played the one-day Fleadh festival in Finsbury Park, north London – the annual music festival run by London-based Irish businessman Vince Power, who had made his Mean Fiddler Music Group one of the UK's biggest live music promoters. Over the years the Fleadh has stretched its original brief of showcasing Celtic music and the Celtic diaspora to include Bob Dylan, Neil Young, Crowded House, Suzanne Vega and D:Ream. Visibly nervous, MacColl played for barely twenty minutes in the Acoustic Tent, away from the main stage where she'd later join Shane MacGowan and his post-Pogues band, the Popes, on "Fairytale of New York" in a duet with MacGowan that was described by the *Evening Standard* music critic Max Bell as "splendidly ramshackle". In a review in *The Times*, Louise Gray remarked, "The one shadow was cast by Shane MacGowan, a character who could illustrate the tortuous tie between muse and booze. With its themes of bitterness, booze and the loss of love, MacGowan's song was chilled by his evident decline and the overall effect was one of immense sadness."

Less than a month later, on July 13, MacColl was back at a favourite London venue, the Mean Fiddler in Harlesden, and three days later at the Phoenix Festival in Stratford-on-Avon. Appearing with a full band, MacColl's set-lists were almost identical for both shows and mixed songs from *Titanic Days* with her previous hits including "Chip Shop", "They Don't Know" and "A New England". Both sets featured a raucous cover of the Ramones' 'I Wanna Be Sedated'.

The following year, plans were made for a US tour. Mark Nevin, as co-writer, co-producer and guitarist on much of *Titanic Days*, was an obvious choice for the touring band. However, things were not to be quite that straightforward. During a visit to New Orleans, Nevin had been browsing in a huge record shop when he was thrilled to see *Titanic Days* trumpeted in promotional material. Until he looked more closely:

> They mentioned Kirsty's new album and it was, "Kirsty collaborated with Johnny Marr on her new album." My name was not mentioned once; it was just Kirsty and Johnny Marr. He didn't play guitar, he wasn't even on the album, he didn't ever come down to the studio. I played on all of the tracks, I co-produced all of them, and yet it was looked at as a Kirsty and Johnny Marr album. I was furious.

Back in London, Nevin's mood did not improve when MacColl's manager posited the view that, given the tiny budget available for touring, Nevin should not take it amiss if he wasn't paid to do the tour, given that his co-writing credits would ensure he had a healthy share of the publishing revenue. He was wrong, as Nevin explains: "I was really short-changed, and then on top of that they'd turned around and said, 'Would you do it for no money?' It was just like the last slap in my face. I didn't want to go away on tour anyway, because my marriage was falling to pieces and we had a baby."

Nevin and MacColl went out for dinner one night. Nevin believes Kirsty knew then that he didn't want to go on tour under those conditions, but was hoping that he would change his mind:

> She could sense that I was going to say that I wasn't going to go on the tour, and so she was saying, "I'm so glad you're coming on this tour." Kirsty said, "I don't know what I would do if you weren't there, you're like my rock," because she used to get so nervous about going on stage and we were like this real team. We just had to look at each other and we'd be laughing. She said, "I'm so glad you're coming, it's going to be great."

Mark Nevin couldn't face telling MacColl the truth. He paid the bill – about £30 – and they said their goodnights. "I was terrified," he admits, "because Kirsty was not someone you wanted to be on the wrong side of." Perhaps recovering some fortitude at home, Nevin sent MacColl a fax that tried to explain his decision. She responded by sending him an acerbic cartoon postcard, together with £30 and a note that said, "Here's your thirty pieces of silver".

For MacColl, her falling-out with Mark Nevin was much more than a professional disappointment, or a simple matter of a musician not wanting to go through the upheaval and disruption of a tour when his home life was disintegrating. It was one of many slights – real or perceived – from friends that she had come to rely on when she desperately needed emotional support and understanding. Although they resolved the issue of the tour – and what had seemed, to her, a heartless way of telling her, by not confronting her in person – their friendship was to be fractured still further when they were both reeling after the end of their marriages.

MacColl and Nevin's times together deteriorated into maudlin mumbling, getting drunk and stoned, and making each other even more miserable – hardly the role of good friends, but not surprising given that they were both so unhappy and needy. Nevin began to realize that the friendship was doing neither of them any good:

> Kirsty rang me up and said, "You are avoiding me". I said, "Yes, I am avoiding you, I feel like I really need to have some space from you at the moment. I need to sort myself out, and every time we get together we always end up getting out of our heads and I need to stop doing that and be a bit more conscious and work out where I've gone wrong in my life." Kirsty said, "We don't have to do that", and I said, "We don't have to but we always do, don't we?"

MacColl then told her friend about a strange dream she'd had the night before, in which they were both performing "They Don't Know" on the Eurovision Song Contest. In the dream, Nevin had his own guitar and his own photographer. In re-telling the dream, Kirsty said to him, "I thought, 'What has he got a photographer for? He's only the bloody guitarist!'" To Nevin, the comment – and the imagery – was emblematic:

> I said, "That's exactly it! I want my own photographer! I don't want to stand next to somebody else like I did with everyone, like I did with Brian Kennedy, like I did with Morrissey. I'm always the bloke on the side. I need to do things for myself; it's nothing against you personally, it's just there's stuff I have to make for myself."

Kirsty told Nevin that she understood his dilemma. However, Nevin doubts that this was the case, given her closing words: "Don't call me."

At a time when she most needed her friends – with her marriage at an end, her sons now both boarding at the exclusive Bedales public school – Kirsty MacColl's future stretched in front of her and it seemed to promise little joy. "She used to get so depressed," says Mark Nevin. "You wouldn't want to be around. You'd just give up." However, not everyone did. The fact that Nevin gave up on her hurt Kirsty deeply, when she felt she had been a good friend to him and helped him recover his musical career after Fairground Attraction imploded under the weight of the tensions between Nevin and singer Eddi Reader.

MacColl's close friend Fuz Boniface recalls, "Kirsty had a lonely time, because some of her relationships had gone wrong and others were not working out. She had a couple of years of being quite down. As much as she was a brilliant laugh, she had her depressive side." Another close friend, Pete Glenister, saw this side of MacColl mirrored in many of her songs, despite the image that the public had of her: "She had quite a few miserable songs. I think they were some of her best, and for the people who really liked her they were the things that spoke to them most. People don't know about them, they think of her as the girl who did 'Chip Shop' or the girl in 'Fairytale'. They never saw the vulnerable side of her. And she was very vulnerable."

MacColl's friends were split into those who felt powerless to intervene, those who tried and were rebuffed, and those who persisted, remembering how the woman underneath all of that pain had an extraordinary capacity for warmth and generosity, laughter and revelry. This was a woman who once stunned into silence a large table of noisy, drunken boors in an up-market Chelsea restaurant by launching into a pitch-perfect German song from the thirties, deducing that it was the only way to shock them more than they were shocking the other diners with their bawdy songs and insulting remarks. Brian Nevill, who was with her that night, recalls, "You could really have a laugh with her. Kirsty decided to do one of those things that would just shock you – and she could do it, she had the talent and the knowledge and the balls to do it. She was like, 'So, you think *you're* funny … !'"

MacColl had always been unstinting in her kindness to friends, and her empathy for waifs and strays. While still with Steve Lillywhite, she would frequently offer friends the use of their house and car in the south of France. She had always kept open house in their Ealing home and no special occasion would go unmarked without a lavish gift. However, this sensitivity also left her feeling vulnerable, and in her darkest days, says Brian Nevill, she sometimes felt abandoned by some of her friends who she'd expected to support her as she'd done them:

> You had this really funny, really nice person, but don't mess her around. She would be the person who would deal with a situation. If someone was ill or in trouble, or if something looked like it was going to go off, if something needed to be dealt with by someone who had the bravery to deal with it, Kirsty would be the one who would do it. That was a big part of the character that she was. That was juxtaposed against this person who could also be very timid about how she came over, someone who was easily hurt.

With her emotional energies at such a low ebb, Kirsty MacColl's songwriting once again subsided into the background as other projects bubbled to the surface. The novelist Patrick McCabe had approached MacColl to write a song to accompany the talking-book edition of his novel, *The Butcher Boy*, and in early 1995 she released it as a CD single, along with the old stand-by "A New England", "Irish Cousin" which had been co-written with Mark Nevin, and MacColl's own "Caroline". There were further singles, including "Days" – which was enjoying a renaissance after being reissued to take advantage of its use in a Sony television advertisement – to support the June release of a career-spanning, 18-track compilation album, marketed as a "Best Of" by Virgin under the title *Galore*. The release of *Galore* would end the acrimony that lingered over the end of her relationship with the label, and serve as a reminder to the industry and the record-buying public that MacColl's intermittent career could be distilled into some moments of real magic.

MacColl herself chose the tracks carefully. She included all of the "big" hits, along with some street-cred additions like her duet with the Lemonheads' Evan Dando on their version of Lou Reed's "Perfect Day". The names of those former Smiths gods, Morrissey and Marr, were represented by the choices of "You Just Haven't Earned It Yet, Baby" and two songs MacColl had co-written with Marr, "Walking Down Madison" and "Can't Stop Killing You". The latter was just one of a surprising three choices from the recent, much-neglected *Titanic Days*.

No "Best Of ..." compilation ever pleases every single fan. However, there was no doubt that many of MacColl's fans had hoped to hear songs like her 1983 single "Terry" revisited. The *Washington Post* criticized the track selection in its review of *Galore*, which described MacColl as "a Scottish folk rocker" who had recorded "such charming British singles as 'They Don't Know'." It continued:

> MacColl devotees could rightfully argue about the selection. "Elvis" is the only song from the never-released-in-the-US album *Desperate Character*, and there's no "Terry", no "The Hardest Word", no "What Do Pretty Girls Do?" Such fans can hardly resist the collection, however, if only for the utterly delightful "Caroline". The other new track, a duet with Evan Dando on Lou Reed's "Perfect Day", is inessential. But for those unfamiliar with MacColl's distinctive mix of tunefulness, compassion and wit, *Galore* is a fine introduction.

Writing in the *Los Angeles Times*, critic Mike Boehm said: "*Galore* seems like a savvy attempt to give MacColl a boost toward the Stateside success that has eluded her on her three previous US releases, all of them critically esteemed but slow-selling. With the Adult Album Alternative format newly established, and perfectly tailored to MacColl's combination of a mature songwriter's vision and a distinctive dusky-toned alto of many hues, this somewhat early look backward – MacColl is in her mid-thirties – makes business sense."

For the sleeve of *Galore*, MacColl jokily borrowed an idea from her copy of the Shangri-Las' *Greatest Hits* album, and modified it. Where the sixties girl band members had invited journalists to offer comments on their beauty, talent and general genius, MacColl solicited musician friends to contribute to the sleeve notes to *Galore*, thinking it would make more interesting reading than something written by "some journalist that nobody has heard of."

MacColl's celebrity endorsements were certainly fulsome and loving. Bono defined her as, "Red hair, sharp tongue, she should be Irish, but I think of Kirsty MacColl as one in a line of great English songwriters that include Ray Davies, Paul Weller and Morrissey ... the Noelle Coward of her generation." Morrissey lent an appreciative, "Kirsty is a voice gradually added to a body. She has great songs and a crackin' bust." His former Smiths cohort, Johnny Marr, wrote, "Writing songs with Kirsty has always been a joy for me. These strange stories of people, relationships and life, with the wit of Ray Davies and the harmonic invention of the Beach Boys. Only cooler."

MacColl didn't just bring the estranged Morrissey and Marr together on the page. She did the same with David Byrne and his former Talking

Heads colleagues Chris Franz and Tina Weymouth, with whom he was not on speaking terms. Byrne offered a pithy, "The voice of an angel from a mind and heart inflamed by Thatcher's England". Franz and Weymouth, who had worked with Kirsty in their Tom Tom Club incarnation as well as in Talking Heads, said, "Together we roamed the streets of Paris, rocked the nightclubs of London and rolled the mean streets of New York City. When you hear these songs of Kirsty's, you're going to want to hang out with her too."

Billy Bragg and Shane MacGowan traced their friendship with MacColl back to its roots, with Bragg concluding, "Unpretentious, inimitable, writes like a playwright, sings like an angel." MacGowan noted that they had bonded over their shared propensity for drinking champagne, " … and it turned out that the shy, frightened-looking girl with classical red-haired Gaelic beauty was funny, charming, intelligent and a real gas to talk to. We became good friends and she was soon boosting my ego and hypocritically lecturing me about my excessive drinking while keeping me up all night slugging champagne."

McGowan further waxed lyrical about Kirsty's songwriting, her gift of interpreting other people's songs and her harmonic range, before stopping himself in mid-flow by saying, "Sorry if I sound like a bloody jazz critic". He closed by posing the question that anyone who has ever considered the full scope of Kirsty MacColl's career has asked themselves: "Why isn't she massively successful?"

In the same liner notes, MacColl herself dryly acknowledged the compliments with a message that would have unbearable and prescient poignancy in years to come: "Special thanks to my friends who contributed liner notes and made it possible for me to revel in the glory without the inconvenience of actually dying." She later joked that, "I thought you had to die before you got tributes like that, and frankly, I wasn't prepared to put myself out that much!" She had expected, " … something weirder. I didn't expect them to write such eulogies." MacColl's own liner notes ended thus: "As always, my greatest love goes to Steve, Jamie and Louis."

The typical Kirsty MacColl fan tends not to be a hardline supporter of the American blockade of Cuba, but if there were any among them, the sleeve art of *Galore* would have left them in no doubt about whose side she was on. The back of the cover featured a photograph of MacColl in a Castro-style military cap lighting a huge Cuban Cohiba cigar – with a burning US dollar bill. American fans, then, knew they couldn't expect a ringing endorsement of President Bill Clinton's continued support for trade sanctions against Havana when Kirsty embarked on a brief tour of the US in 1995 with guitarist Pete Glenister, bass-player Marcus Williams and drummer Roger Johns.

During the tour, *Los Angeles Times* writer Mike Boehm, a long-time fan, interviewed MacColl. He asked whether the emergence of the Adult Album Alternative radio format, with playlists that provided a natural home for her music, was a factor in the energetic promotion of *Galore* in the United States. She answered with a shrug: "There might have been some thought of that, but it wasn't from me. I can only concentrate on the music. I find the business side incredibly tedious. I think if you want to be a big star, you have to play big-star games and I can't be bothered. It's a very sick business and I don't enjoy it."

Back home in Britain, *Galore* peaked at Number 6 in the album charts. At the time, it was competing with some of the biggest names in eighties rock and pop – Bruce Springsteen's *Greatest Hits*, Radiohead's *The Bends*, Annie Lennox with *Medusa*, Celine Dion's *The Colour of Love* and Blur's *Parklife*. It became the highest-ranking of any of MacColl's albums, staying in the chart for 27 weeks. However, even this was not enough to secure a new recording contract. "*Galore* was a gold album," says Phil Rambow. "It was on Virgin, but would they give her a record deal? No! It was unbelievable."

Even labels which respected Kirsty MacColl's work knew that they would struggle to manufacture an image for a voluptuous, opinionated, thirty-something mother-of-two in a pop market-place crammed with lip-synching girl bands, anorexic nymphets and teenage tabloid fodder. So they simply didn't try, MacColl realized: "Every time things have got bad, I think, 'Oh, no, this is terrible,' and feel dreadful for a few months. But then afterwards, I just really want to kick arse, and get up and say, 'I'm going to show them!' And that's usually when I come up with my best stuff."

Dave Ruffy confirms this self-assessment, claiming that Kirsty always managed to emerge from those low points by remembering what was really important to her: "This is a bullshit business, it always has been," he says. 'The only way you can carry on doing it is by not getting cynical. You've got to remember why you liked it in the first place. Kirsty really knew that." James Knight, with whom Kirsty would become involved in 1999, believes that her refusal to compromise on what she believed in also contributed to her troubles within the industry:

Kirsty didn't toe the line; she was just straightforward. She would have hated it if she were huge. She struggled with being famous and then not being famous. In order to be famous, you have to do a lot of shit that you don't want to do, and she got dicked over on several different occasions and by several different record companies who pulled tours or tour support or just bullshitted her basically. "They Don't Know" coming out during a distribution strike is a typical example. If there hadn't been a distribution strike I think her career would have been completely different, but I don't think necessarily better.

MacColl herself was, by now, used to barren spells in her recording career. This time, it was to be two or three years before she would even attempt to write again, but she tried to be sanguine at this latest setback: "If you've got nothing to say, I'm a great believer that it's better just to shut up. You don't *need* to make an album a year." And Kirsty MacColl made herself a promise. She vowed that she would not make another album until she had something happy to write about.

CHAPTER NINE

Maybe It's Imaginary

"I was as sure as that I was alive," wrote the British psychoanalyst Marion Milner in 1934, "that happiness not only needs no justification, but that it is also the only final test of whether what I am doing is right for me." Milner, writing under her pen-name of Joanna Field, concluded in one of the earliest explorations of her pioneering work on creativity, *A Life Of One's Own*, that, "happiness is not the same as pleasure; it includes the pain of losing as well as the pleasure of finding." Even a happy life, said Carl Jung, cannot be without a measure of darkness and the word "happiness" would lose its meaning, were it not balanced by sadness.

By 1995, Kirsty MacColl had had enough of sadness and was ready to balance out the equation with some happiness. A decade earlier, a music magazine, *Debut*, had asked Kirsty where she would like to find herself ten years hence. She thought about it for a moment then said, "I think I'd like to be in a beach bar in Spain." It was to prove to be a beach bar in Brazil.

A life-long Londoner, MacColl's love affair with Latin culture was to transport her over thousands of miles and an incalculable cultural distance. Her musical fling with Latin-inspired pop with "My Affair" on *Electric Landlady* had turned into a passionate and enduring relationship as she explored Cuba and then made her own discovery of Brazil. She had met a Portuguese teaching trainee through her Spanish language classes. He was in London to do his training and was looking for somewhere to live. Kirsty offered him a spare room in her house in return for Portuguese lessons. "We had all overdosed on Cuba," she said, "so then I went totally Brazilian." With the same passion that she had shown for Cuban music, MacColl collected the classics of late sixties and early seventies Brazilian music, including Milton Nascimento, Gilberto Gil and Jobim.

The next step was to visit the country that had so heavily influenced generations of musicians, from Carmen Miranda's Hollywood films of the forties to Paul Simon's 1990 album *The Rhythm of the Saints*, and from international jazz to hard rock. With good Spanish and basic Portuguese, MacColl had become so enamoured of Latin culture that she was even considering giving up music in order to do a degree in Latin American Studies. Lavishly decorated South American folk art adorned every room in her house. The sounds, the colours, the textures, the attitudes and the essence of Latin culture was so vastly different to buttoned-up Britishness that she found it quite irresistible:

> I think what a lot of people like about it – and it's not just Cuba, but a lot of Latin America – is that it's very open emotionally. It's not just intellectuals who are poets; people are quite romantic and poetic in their lifestyles. I'm not saying that everything is perfect and they have great lives and are dancing all night, but the way they deal with life is much more directly emotional than the way we deal with things in northern Europe, where people don't like letting on how they feel about something. You get on the Tube and everyone just ignores you. People are much more open there, and will actually talk to you.

This revelation was, MacColl decided, "like a sudden liberation of my brain. I'd spent so long being unhappy in a very British way, and suddenly there was all this new stuff! I'd made a very melancholy album in *Titanic Days* and I didn't want to do that again. People would say, "Oh it's that miserable British woman, depressed again!"

In fact, some people had been saying exactly that. Many friends who were well versed in Kirsty's quixotic moods were nonetheless deeply concerned about the level of her depression after her marital break-up. There had been tearful late-night phone calls, feuds that would flare up out of nowhere, and her aching anxiety about a future stretching ahead of her. She was now without a loving romantic relationship and without a record deal; at her bleakest moments, she refused to accept that there would ever be a prospect of either one again.

MacColl's "sad divorce record" had been made and that chapter of her life was drawing to a close. The initially amicable separation from Steve had threatened to turn nasty over lawyers' arguments regarding the divorce settlement, but even that was being resolved. Whatever friction it had caused between the couple was put behind them in a phone call that was overshadowed by an event in which neither would have imagined they'd have any interest – the funeral of Diana, Princess of Wales, on September 6, 1997. Lillywhite says:

I phoned Kirsty for some reason and we were both crying over the phone. Diana's funeral was very moving. And for Kirsty – this is what she inherited from her dad – one individual death is of no great consequence, especially someone with a silver spoon in their mouth. It did not rate against the plight of the Palestinians or the Cubans. But she was actually quite moved by this. I said to her, "Look, Kirsty, this is terrible, we're bickering and fighting. Imagine if one of us died like that." We were saying, "Imagine how Prince Charles must feel, having not made amends for their children's sake. If you've got children, you may not want to like the other person but you have to have a relationship that works because of your children. You have to be able to relate to each other and make it work on a certain level. So we made a pact. We said, "Just in case something like this happens to one of us, let's make sure we are always civil with each other." And from then on, we never really had an argument. It brought us together in a way of closure. We just felt, life is too short; we both have two children whom we love so much.

Now, there were no expectations and no limitations; Kirsty was free to do anything she liked. Her depression may once have anchored her to the spot but as she began to emerge from that, it became a catalyst. Her travels to Cuba and Brazil reinforced that it was still possible to be inspired about music in particular and life in general. As she considered making another album, MacColl became enamoured of the idea of recording with the best Latin musicians she could find in Havana and New York, just as she had done on "My Affair". She then thought a little further:

What's the point? Other people have gone there and done a purist thing, which is fine. But Cuba doesn't need Kirsty MacColl doing that. So I decided to introduce elements of the stuff I'd really enjoyed into my next batch of songs. Then the Buena Vista Social Club thing became really big and I was pleasantly surprised, because I realized it wasn't just me who was getting turned on to it.

MacColl flew to Brazil for the first time in 1997, in search of further inspiration, and didn't have to wait for long. The first new song came to her in a plane high above the Brazilian rainforest. "Celestine" had lines like, "She's hot, she's hot, she's hot, she's just a wild and wicked slut", prefiguring the return of the good-girl-goes-bad who'd appeared on "Bad" on *Titanic Days*. "Look out, world," the subtext appeared to run, "I'm about to be bad."

MacColl arrived in Recife, Brazil's fourth-largest city and the capital of the north-eastern state of Pernambuco. The city's many canals, bridges and tiny one-way streets have led to it being christened "the Venice of Brazil". A thriving international port, it is a mixture of modern high-rise apartment buildings and lovingly-tended colonial churches, and boasts a rich legacy of folk art and craft, music, dance, sculpture and painting.

Once in Recife, MacColl managed to borrow a guitar to work out the chords to "Celestine". With bossa nova rhythms, acoustic guitars and percussion arrangements reeling in her head, she was eager to get into a studio and record it. Kirsty found a tiny studio and was introduced to three local musicians who, she was certain, could translate what she was hearing in her head into a brilliant bossa nova. What she hadn't allowed for was the enormous regional variations in Brazilian music, reflecting the vastness of the country itself – the fifth largest in the world and covering almost half of South America.

While *bossa nova* dominated in Rio, *fórro* – which she would later describe as "mental, high-speed accordion music" – was more common in Recife, as it originated in the backcountry areas of the north-east. The music, and the dancing that so often accompanied it, were fast and furious, and traditionally played by a trio of *sarfona* (accordion), steel triangle and drum. The name *fórro* is said to be derived from the English expression "for all" – the inclusive term for the dances organized by British companies in the area in the nineteenth century, who would hold social events "for all" their British and Brazilian workers.

The other surprise awaiting Kirsty MacColl was the slavish worship that the local musicians had for mainstream British guitar rock, rather than Brazilian music:

> It was funny trying to boss people around in a language I was crap at, espe-
> cially when they all want to be in Dire Straits and you want them to sound
> ... Brazilian! They'd turn up with rock guitars and syn-drums and I'd really

want something more acoustic-y and they were like, "Oh, we want to be in
Dire Straits", and I'm going, "I can get rock in London; I came here for
something different."

After what she would later describe as "two of the most educational
days of my life", Kirsty left the studio with the basic track exactly as
she'd imagined it.

MacColl continued her travels in Brazil over the next few weeks. She
explored Rio de Janeiro – known to Brazilians as *Cidade Maravilhosa*, the
Wonderful City – and its extraordinary surroundings of rainforest-clad
cliffs, not to mention its 70 kilometres of the most famous beaches in the
world, Copacabana and Ipanema. Kirsty was also thrilled to get tickets
to see one of the great Renaissance men of Brazilian music, Caetano
Veloso, perform. A revered poet, songwriter, painter, video director and
musician, Veloso pioneered the modernist movement in Brazilian music
in the sixties; he was eclectic, innovative and heavily influenced by the
African culture of his birthplace, the north-eastern state of Bahia.

MacColl's excitement, however, was rapidly tempered by the reality
of deep disappointment. "He was playing in the basement of a shopping
mall," she said. "It was absolutely massive and the tickets were very
expensive. I was really excited. Then he came on with just an acoustic
guitar and no band and played this set. I felt really let down."

Kirsty visited Salvador, the state capital of Bahia, and a city which
lays claim to some of Brazil's best-known musicians, including Veloso,
Gilberto Gil (who was elected Minister of Culture in 2003) Gal Costa,
Maria Bethania and Moraes Moreira. The city is reputed to have so
many churches that you could attend mass in a different one each day
for a year, and is home to arguably the most vibrant African influences
of any Brazilian city. Far less glamorous and cosmopolitan was Aracaju,
the capital of Sergipe state. A brief visit was enough to a city that was of
little interest to most mainstream tourists, understandably unimpressed
by the modern building boom funded by the area's oil wealth.

When she returned to London, MacColl was determined to make her
own brand of Latin-inspired music rather than anything for the genre
purists or the fans of the *vida loca* bump-and-grind of Latino pop stars
like Ricky Martin, or even the Western take on world music as interpreted by David Byrne. It would combine what she loved about Cuban
and Brazilian music, without having to totally assimilate their structures
and disciplines. It would be an album that would appeal to her existing

fans and woo non-believers who'd only ever thought of her as the "Chip Shop" girl or the woman they vaguely thought might have sung that Christmas song with the Pogues. "I didn't want to turn off people who've been with me for years by singing in Spanish," she said. "But maybe it can introduce some of them to this music, and also attract a new audience that hasn't necessarily been into my kind of songwriting before."

When MacColl eventually felt ready to bring in some collaborators to work on the ideas, she chose seemingly unlikely cohorts to help create what would become an individualized Latino hybrid: her two close friends, Dave Ruffy and Pete Glenister. Ruffy reflects that, "The great thing about Kirsty was that she was very, very generous. Inviting me to produce was a tremendously generous thing to do. I really appreciated it. When I did a few acid house tunes, she said 'I really like that, can I use it?' " The trio began work, in Glenister's studio in Bermondsey in south London, and Kirsty's home studio in Ealing.

For Dave Ruffy, who'd come through punk as the drummer in the Ruts, the prospect of Latin drums and percussion at first proved daunting: "I'm a self-taught drummer. I came out of punk rock, so I never went down the jazz route of getting lots of lessons and learning lots of chops. At that point, I thought, if she's doing these Latin things, I'm really busking it here. So I had my first ever drum lessons. I didn't want to look like a complete charlatan!"

Much of the early work was done on computer, apart from the vocals, some guitars and fragments of brass and percussion. "It was all done on a sample base," says Ruffy, "in a dance music way, using a library of sounds. It was a lot of fun and we spent a lot of time on it." They worked to a strict schedule, putting in eight-hour days from Monday to Friday for six or seven months. Currently without a record deal, they were nonetheless confident that the work they could produce would be strong enough to clinch one, says Ruffy:

With the industry then and now, it's almost impossible to get any development money. You've got to have the confidence to get on with your work, and the belief in it to say, "Whatever money I fork out, it'll be all right because I believe in this thing." The whole thing about this game is confidence, and if you're not doing really well, it's hard. It's a very hard business.

They were confident, but they had few illusions about the task ahead. This was a new musical departure for MacColl. It had been some time since her last studio album and, in the public consciousness at least, she had seemed to fall from sight and sound in the intervening years. Britpop now ruled the charts and radio playlists, and MacColl could find nothing new that inspired her in the least, except for occasionally listening to Beck CDs. In her view, nothing remotely compared to the Latin music in which she had become immersed. She was convinced that her instincts were right, but Pete Glenister knew that persuading a record label would be a much tougher proposition:

> When we started working, we were up against it. We felt we had to come up with some "clothes" for the project that would get attention. There were already quite a few good songs but there wasn't anything that could really pull it together. There were a few songs that weren't written from that Latin point of view at all, there were written as straight-up songs. We arranged them that way just because we got on a roll and got really excited. There was a way we could do that by essentially chopping up bits of Latin records. We felt we had to make a contemporary record with contemporary production values. And I remember Steve Lillywhite saying afterwards, "It's almost a pop record." And it *was* almost a pop record; at least some of the tracks were, the more single-y tracks like "In These Shoes?". Kirsty did a brilliant job on that.

As the months went by, Kirsty and Pete recaptured the mood of their New York sessions for *Electric Landlady*, where half the rhythm tracks had been recorded with Latin musicians. However, while Kirsty had vowed, after releasing *Titanic Days*, that she would never make another record until she was happy again, she had started this new project feeling sad, uncertain and unhappy, says Glenister: "Kirsty was in a very dark place when we started. She was really miserable. They were dark days. There are some quite light songs, but most are very dark. They're all done with great bravado, but they're all written from a place of hurt."

A careful ear to the album that was to become *Tropical Brainstorm* shows exactly that. "Wrong Again" was among the songs recorded live, and Kirsty's vocals are audibly strained as she tries to hold back the tears. The heartache and rejection she'd just experienced when a brief and ill-advised fling had gone badly wrong was painfully clear in her words:

> "I feel empty, I feel deceived
> You shouldn't have done that to me,
> I was fine 'til you came along,
> I'd grown used to being alone."
>
> —Kirsty MacColl, "Wrong Again"

Kirsty had written the song the day after the break-up and was recording it a mere 24 hours later, the emotion still obviously raw. "You can hear it on the first verse," says Ruffy. "You can't get much more real than that. That's what moves you about music, when it's for real."

"Wrong Again" was one of several songs clearly written from the point of view of a woman of a certain age who was single after a long marriage. However, this auteur was evidently far brighter and less self-obsessed than angsty Bridget Jones singletons, even if she did appear to be equally unlucky in love. MacColl had insightful humour to her credit. When a much-anticipated date went wrong when the man in question neglected to mention that he was married with three children, MacColl wrote one of the funniest-ever songs about faithless men.

As the live broadcast of a football match between England and Colombia unfolded on the wide-screen television in a pub where she met the man for a drink, his friend confided in MacColl that she was being duped. She left the pub in tears. In the studio the next morning, Dave Ruffy asked, "How was your date?" Kirsty played him the song that she had just written about it, "England 2, Colombia 0":

> "You lied about your status
> You lied about your life
> You never mentioned your three children,
> And the fact you had a wife,
> Now it's England 2, Colombia 0
> And I know just how those Colombians feel."
>
> —Kirsty MacColl, "England 2, Colombia 0"

Kirsty found some ideas for other songs during a week-long writing workshop organized by EMI Music Publishing at Huntsham Court, a nineteenth-century, neo-Gothic hotel near Tiverton in Devon. The fifteen songwriters gathered included Suggs from Madness, Chris Difford of

Squeeze, Graham Gouldman (10cc), Kenneth Crouch (Prince, Tom Petty), Richard Drummie (Go West) and Motown great, Lamont Dozier.

Each morning songwriters worked in groups of three: that evening, they performed the song(s) they had written. On the first day, MacColl's group equalled the workshop record of writing four new songs between breakfast-time and dinner: "I was terrified," MacColl admitted, "because I had had writer's block for three years. But on the third day I wrote 'Designer Life' with Kenneth Crouch, which ended up on the record. I also met Graham Gouldman there, and later we wrote 'Treachery' for the album."

The EMI-run workshop was the brainchild of Chris Difford, who had once attended a similar ideasfest organized by music manager and IRS label head Miles Copeland. By the end of the week in Devon, MacColl reflected, "You could say we're all just sitting around, getting pissed and slapping each other on the back, saying 'Aren't we great?' But so what? We've made a connection. It's the international music of lurve."

The writing workshop gave MacColl much-needed impetus and, as always, the collaborative process stimulated her own ideas. As the *Tropical Brainstorm* sessions continued, its creators began thinking about pitching it to a record label.

By now MacColl had a new manager. In 1996 she had been taken on by HRM, the artist management division of Hit & Run Music. HRM was run by Kevin Nixon, a long-time Kirsty fan, who became her manager. In 1999, Nixon left HRM to set up his own company, Major Minor. Kirsty went with him to the new company. Nixon negotiated a deal with Richard Branson's V2 Records and, with some record company money behind them at last, MacColl, Ruffy and Glenister were able to get the Latin musicians they wanted, including Oscar Puente, Chucho Merchan, Bosco de Oliveira, Felix Gonzalez and Luiz de Almeida.

They went into Air Studios in London to mix the album and the mood was incredibly optimistic. Kirsty's insecurities about her career seemed to have been consigned to the past, reflected Pete Glenister: "When she felt she had something that was good she would stick by it and would defend it to the end. With *Tropical Brainstorm*, she wasn't insecure about that. She'd made the right record. It was in our minds when we were recording it, that we were doing the right thing, and it was good. But there were always great doubts about how it would be received and how the record company would treat her." MacColl and cohorts had indeed made exactly the album they had set out to make.

Dave Ruffy proudly described it as "Latin music by way of south London."

Released in May 2000, *Tropical Brainstorm* was an Anglo-Latin pop hybrid and a celebration of music and life. "I didn't want to create an authentic sound, first of all because I'm not Celia Cruz and a lot of people like my music, and mostly because of the lyrics," Kirsty said. "I didn't want to try and fail at being Buena Vista Social Club. I wanted to succeed at being Kirsty MacColl." The consensus view was that she had succeeded. Many critics regarded *Tropical Brainstorm* as the highlight of a musical career that had by now spanned over twenty years. It seemed that a creative and commercial renaissance was now widely expected.

Writing in *Straight No Chaser*, Max Reinhardt observed: "The highway to musical hell is strewn with debris, especially those albums made in exotic climes and aimed at rescuing the maturing rock star from a faltering career. Not surprisingly, *Tropical Brainstorm* navigates its way effortlessly and gracefully through those rock star cliché quicksands and stands tall as a twenty-first century triumph of lyricism, wit, magical realism, melody and rhythm."

In the soundbite jargon beloved of reviewers, Fiona Shepherd in *The Scotsman* declared the album "Buena Vista Social Club meets Billy Bragg" while Tim de Lisle in *The Mail on Sunday* trumpeted it as "Paul Simon meets Bridget Jones". Nigel Williamson, in a feature for *Folk Roots*, looked more extensively at the work as a whole, avoiding reducing it to a simply formula: "Although MacColl has made an unashamedly popular album, her love of both Cuban and Brazilian music is profound and her knowledge of its traditions impressive."

The Guardian's Caroline Sullivan noted that Latin vibes were *de rigueur* in certain musical circles at the time, and added: "She'll be accused of cashing in on the current Latino fad. There's an opening track full of tourist-brochure cliché … creating the impression of a less sophisticated (yes, really) Geri Halliwell's 'Mi Chico Latino'." However, Sullivan astutely concluded that, "This isn't a Latin album as such. Its conventional pop structures mean that it's hardly authentic Cuban, but rather a portrait of a determined woman, with Latin textures added as dramatic enhancement. As such, a winner."

Of the reviewers who saw MacColl's new album as part of some newfangled fad, Barry Didcock in *The Sunday Herald* was less willing than most to be forgiving: "I blame Ricky Martin. Why else would a forty-year-old Englishwoman throw up her respectable pop/folk credentials for an album full of Latin moves? She aims for a sort of Kurt Weill effect, all barbs and high camp, while the music blends bossa nova, salsa, and several other foodstuffs into a stew which contains more than a splash of tango but is far from fizzing."

The acclaim for *Tropical Brainstorm* was not limited to the critics and fans. Kirsty's old friend Billy Bragg invited her, with her band, on to his BBC Radio 2 show, and loved their set: "She'd really got it. She was writing songs, she'd overcome the obvious difficulty of having kids and breaking up with Steve and she managed to channel that into the songs. *Tropical Brainstorm* was a great album, I was so happy when I heard it."

The album even won over Hamish MacColl, who had felt that some of his sister's past work was not as good as she was capable of creating: "Probably as a result of my dad, I was an intellectual snob in a way, and although I admired a lot of the stuff that she wrote, it wasn't until the last couple of albums that I thought, 'That was fantastic, that was really good.' I thought they were a world away from where she had started with fairly average pop."

Broadcaster Phill Jupitus declared "In These Shoes?" to be "the sexiest song that's been written in the last ten years." He saw the album as a whole as easily MacColl's most accomplished work: "The scope and ambition of that record ... for a girl, a little punk from Croydon, to write something of the sweep of *Tropical Brainstorm* beggars belief, and you just knew that it was the beginning for her; she'd experienced this renaissance."

However, by the release of *Tropical Brainstorm*, its songs detailing dangerous liaisons and disastrous affairs ("Wrong Again", "England 2, Colombia 0"), cyber-sex ("Here Comes That Man Again"), wanton women ("Celestine", "In These Shoes?", "Us Amazonians"), one-sided obsessions ("Treachery") and love-sick longings ("Autumngirlsoup") were hopelessly out of sync with their creator's emotions. Kirsty MacColl had fallen in love again, and all of the old clichés about the transformational power of true romance had come true.

MacColl had met James Knight, an accomplished saxophonist, when he was giving her son, Louis, saxophone lessons at Bedales School. Knight, then 26, had an impeccable musical background. He'd grown up in Harrogate, North Yorkshire, and taken music lessons from the age of five: first the piano, then clarinet, then the saxophone. After seven years at a music school in Manchester, he went to the US where he spent a year studying at the prestigious Berklee School of Music in Boston. Returning to Britain, he was accepted at the Royal Academy of Music, graduating with a degree in jazz. His musical passions ranged from punk to the Beach Boys and Steely Dan – virtually identical to MacColl's own.

Kirsty had booked James to play sax on sessions for a couple of *Tropical Brainstorm* tracks. She was really pleased with them and invited James to join her and some friends at a gig; by the evening's end, it was just the two of them. The pair saw each other again a few days later, when James was in the studio while MacColl was mixing "Wrong Again". Listening to the lyrics would have left him in little doubt of what he was getting into – or what behaviour she wouldn't tolerate. Knight was fifteen years younger than Kirsty, but this seemed irrelevant from the moment they met. The more time they spent together, they more they were struck by how similar they were. A weekend in Seville sealed the romance.

James and Kirsty felt incredibly lucky to have found each other when they did. The timing was right; they were both ready for a totally committed relationship. Kirsty, especially, was just ready to have *fun* with someone else who loved to stay up all night, play music and talk for hours on end – to have someone who was totally on her side, after so long on her own. Knight says they inspired each other and never stopped being amazed at the similarities between them. They appeared to share the same strengths, weaknesses and insecurities:

It's the only relationship I've ever had that was on a level footing, and on the outside I think, to a lot of people, it must have looked like the most un-level relationship in the whole world. But it was certainly the only relationship I've ever had where it was absolutely totally perfect because there was no hierarchy. I wasn't trying to hack away at anyone, I wasn't trying to do anything and it was just the right thing to do, and it was so easy, and we just slipped into it so easily.

Knight recollects the couple only ever having one argument: "It was when Kirsty was really drunk and she went to the wrong house on the way home. I said to her, 'No, we're next door', so she went to try and clock me and missed! She was mortified the next day; she didn't remember anything about it."

Working so closely with Kirsty, Pete Glenister and Dave Ruffy had watched the relationship begin. As protective male friends are wont to do, they insisted on knowing whether James's intentions were honourable. Assured that he was as smitten as Kirsty, they gave him their blessing, says Glenister: "The thing that really turned things around for Kirsty was meeting James," he says. "That changed her life. I did say to him that Dave and I were suspicious at first. We thought, 'Oh no, she's going to get really hurt by this!' But they had so much in common and they were very similar people." Any misgivings about the age difference disappeared rapidly: "James has got an old head on young shoulders," says Ruffy. "Kirsty felt she could trust him, that he was a strong person and that she could rely on him. He's for real."

After years of being single, or having unsatisfactory dalliances, Kirsty MacColl's life was transformed at the age of forty, at a point when she'd all but given up hope of falling in love with a man who felt the same way about her. With James, there was no pretence and no holding back, and for the first time in many years, her insecurities, bleak moods and anxieties evaporated. The couple's overwhelming physical attraction was matched by an equally stimulating intellectual connection, not to mention their shared passion for all kinds of music. Both of Kirsty's sons already knew James as a friend, given the informal regime at Bedales School and Louis's sax lessons, and they welcomed him without hesitation into the family home.

When Knight joined the band on the *Tropical Brainstorm* tour, there were inevitable concerns that a cloying couple-y atmosphere might make things awkward for the others on the tour bus. However, it simply wasn't a problem. "James handled it really well," says Pete Glenister. "Both Dave and I liked him and that makes it a lot easier. And he's just a brilliant player. Because he was in the horn section, we could let them get on with their bit." The three men got on well and Knight could see what a difference the working relationship with Glenister and Ruffy had made to Kirsty's work in the studio: "Dave Ruffy's probably not really got enough acknowledgement, but he was there the whole time. He was like a best mate and he's a fantastic bloke; he's so positive and up, he's a great person to have around and work with. I think he was an enormous influence on Kirsty and he's been played down, not for any reason other than he didn't actually write the harmony or something."

The live shows in 2000 were some of MacColl's most successful and most enjoyable. However, her first gig of the year, in February at the London Palladium supporting another Stiff veteran Ian Dury and the Blockheads, was tinged with sadness. Dury was terminally ill with colon cancer and the show was to be his last. He died at his home in Hampstead, north London, on March 27. During the filming of a BBC documentary the previous year, Dury had been asked how he felt about the prospect of dying. "I don't worry about it," he had replied. "I don't think about it. I don't think it goes on afterwards. I don't care if I'm immediately forgotten; I don't care if my work floats down the tubes. I don't give a shit. I'm not here to be remembered, I'm here to be alive."

In his memory, a bench was placed in Poet's Corner in Richmond Park, where he had often taken his children to play. The bench is marked, "Reasons to be Cheerful", and two shiny blue solar panels on each armrest provide a suitably Dury-esque interlude for anyone with personal-stereo headphones. Plug into one side and you hear "Reasons to be Cheerful" and other Dury songs; plug into the other, and you hear an interview with him.

In June, Kirsty again shared a stage with the Blockheads when she performed "Hit Me With Your Rhythm Stick" at a Brixton Academy tribute show in Dury's memory. The show raised funds for the CancerBACUP charity, which Dury had supported vigorously before his death. Many observers perceived links between MacColl and Dury, not least the extraordinarily vibrant music-hall tradition informing the work of the most literate of their generation of British musicians: "It's a common touchstone with Kirsty and with Ian," says Phill Jupitus, "that allusion to the music-hall, or to Noël Coward. That is who they're up there with: it is like Noël Coward at his very best."

Yet that tradition owed nothing to the social revolutions of the sixties and seventies and the rock and punk they spawned. The debt lay, rather, to the industrial revolution of more than a century earlier. By the mid-nineteenth century, the industrial revolution had not only transformed the working life of the British working class beyond all recognition; it had also transformed its social life. Music halls grew out of the taverns, pleasure gardens, saloons and theatres that had offered music and a range of entertainments since medieval times.

Music-hall performers based their music and comedy on the charac-ters their audiences saw in everyday life, and this accessibility was the key to their success. As Peter Leslie wrote in *A Hard Act To Follow: A Music Hall Review*: "The police, the rent collector, the bailiffs, mothers-in-law, the drunken husband and the shrewish wife, the spendthrift who had gambled away his pay before he got home Friday night – such were the dragons slain by these seedy St Georges. Patriotism and the more chauvinistic aspects of Victoriana were pandered to and at the same time subtly ridiculed; the rednecks were kept happy and, for those with the wit to see it, the satire was there."

That satire is also there in the work of Kirsty MacColl and Ian Dury, of Morrissey and Billy Bragg, of Shane MacGowan and Elvis Costello. These are the contemporary wordsmiths who are the true inheritors of the best that music hall bequeathed: the wit and humour, the populist touch, the sophisticated structure that looks deceptively simple, the sexuality and innocence. Underlying it is the knowing wink that lets the devoted punters in on the joke, and never makes them the butt of it. A subtle anarchy is employed to undermine and threaten targets as diverse as a faithless Latin lover, a corrupt corporate number-cruncher, a repressed public schoolboy, a homophobic adolescent thug or a sensation-starved housewife.

"Kirsty MacColl was in a very clear tradition," says Bono, "which is much stronger than the family line or her father. In particular, the musical tradition is very English, and it's music hall, it's Noël Coward. You start to see that everything does add up. When I say 'music hall', I'm referring to some of the influences around that time. These were enormous influences on the Beatles, which is never written about the Beatles – the huge music-hall influence after the war." It is, indeed, not hard to imagine a George Formby arrangement of "There's a Guy Works down the Chip Shop Swears He's Elvis". "Had Kirsty played it with a ukelele," concurs Bono, "nobody would have batted an eyelid."

There were copious clues to this influence. At times of equipment failure on stage, or in need of entertainment on a long journey, MacColl would often launch into the old songs her father had taught her. "Lydia The Tattooed Lady" was a special favourite. Billy Bragg marvels at the influences that merged in the MacColl muse:

It was an incredible background to come from, and I think some of that Stratford East stuff, the music hall, permeated some of what she did. A mate of mine once saw her in America. Halfway though the gig, the equipment had stopped working, something untoward had happened, so they couldn't play. Kirsty just led the crowd in verses of "Have you seen Lydia? Lydia The Tattooed Lady." She had that music-hall vibe about her, and so does Morrissey, and I feel a bit of affinity towards that as well. I don't know if that's something in common with our generation, but there's a certain amount of pub-singing in what we do; not in a bad sense but communal singing, getting beyond the performance into the general having-a-laugh of it, the moment. Kirsty was great at the *moment*; she lived for the moment.

Thanks to James Knight, those moments were now bringing her more happiness, inspiration and confidence. MacColl's anxiety about being on stage had never entirely left her. She had tried to ease it using beta-blockers, but Knight came up with another solution. He reconfigured the normal layout for the band on stage so if she started to feel shaky, his reassuring presence was just a few feet away:

We had a long conversation about it, and I said, "I can't cure it, but I will be standing next to you." I would always spend two or three minutes on my own with her before she went on, away from everybody else, and just calm her down and she'd be fine. It's like anything; it's a repetitive thing. If it's in your brain, it might not even be there any more, but you conjure it up just because that's the process of going on stage. You shit yourself with nerves and then go on stage and that's just how it's always been. It's very hard to break that cycle.

Knight quickly diagnosed that the roots of his partner's stage fright also lay in the autobiographical nature of her songs; she felt exposed and uncomfortable when so much of what she was singing about was intensely personal:

It's like you've got your whole life in the songs, and she was so brutally honest about what she was singing about; she very rarely made anything up. It wasn't a lack of confidence with her voice, it wasn't lack of confidence with her music; it was the fact that what she was saying was so acutely personal, and often very painful as well. But that's how she expressed herself.

Phil Rambow was at two shows during the tour, and describes the change in MacColl as remarkable: "*Tropical Brainstorm* was a great album. Kirsty had a great band and she was one of the UK's great artists. She was in love; she'd finally found everything. She had the artistic success; on an aesthetic level, she could do exactly what she wanted to do. She had the best band anyone had ever dreamed up, and everybody loved her. She could have done anything. She'd grown up; she'd become a mature woman and a great artist."

MacColl's former bandmate Lu Edmonds saw Kirsty play at London's Jazz Café: "I was just standing there, looking at her and thinking, 'I really look forward to when Kirsty is 75, she's still going to be up there on that stage hassling the world'." The last gig on the tour was at the Shepherds Bush Empire in London on October 28, 2000. As Kirsty left the stage, she told Pete Glenister, "That's the best gig I've ever done in my life." Glenister had had the same feeling about the entire tour: "It was great, and the last gig was the best gig that we ever did. I was so pleased about that. The band played really well, it was just fantastic. I came off and I remember thinking, 'Well, maybe we'll never ever play again.'"

Tropical Brainstorm reached Number 39 in the British album chart, but this was no guarantee that Kirsty MacColl's career-long problems with record companies were at an end. V2 dropped her from the label. It was a puzzling decision. The album had been cheap to make and it had recouped its costs. "In These Shoes?" had appeared on an Adidas sports shoes advertisement, a Playstation football game, several TV programmes, including the hit American series "Sex and the City", and a Bette Midler album. Pete Glenister is scathing about the decision:

> I think Kirsty was very hurt when V2 dropped her. She couldn't understand it. I can't believe that she could make a record like that, it was relatively successful – their biggest record that year – and then they dropped her. She didn't fit the template; they wanted Liberty X. The politics involved in getting a record out are so labyrinthine. For an act to stay in the same place, over a long period of time, given the way that the personnel in record companies keeps changing these days, is almost impossible.

Billy Bragg simply describes V2's decision as, "the story of Kirsty's life. I was outraged by it."

Despite the disappointment of V2's decision, MacColl was already making plans for a follow-up. "I think there will be a *Tropical Brainstorm Mark II* at some point," she said. "But I don't think I could ever make two records that sounded the same right after each other. So the next one might be a heavy metal thrash album. One on which I can play lots of loud electric guitar very badly." Nearing the end of a hectic year – one of the happiest of her life – Kirsty decided she needed a holiday; a brief glimpse of summer in the bleak English midwinter.

The *Tropical Brainstorm* tour and promotion, plus the recent visit to

Cuba for the BBC's 'Kirsty MacColl's Cuba', had been exhausting. Her sons would be coming home from boarding school for the Christmas break; they were only just getting over the death of a schoolfriend and it was also a chance for a family holiday. Jamie and Louis were both teenagers by now and the appeal of using their holiday time to go away with their mum and her partner, rather than their teenage friends, would soon wear off.

Kirsty chose the Mexican resort island of Cozumel, which she had visited before. The island had achieved fame among the international scuba-diving fraternity after the French oceanographer and filmmaker Jacques-Yves Cousteau made a documentary extolling its virtues in 1961. He showed that the surrounding waters are home to an extraordinary diversity of sea-life and spectacular coral reefs. However, in 1998 the environmental organization Greenpeace had urged the Mexican government to control tourism in the area. Greenpeace claimed that the tourist industry, and the increasing boat traffic in particular, was causing intolerable strain on local eco-systems and damaging the reefs that are its main tourist attraction.

Nevertheless, the authorities on the island had become increasingly eager to expand its reputation beyond diving expeditions, and as a place for a stopover for wealthy Americans on huge cruise ships and divers. They wanted to embrace eco-tourists, and families who wanted an alternative to the over-crowded, over-hyped tourist trap of nearby Cancun. It was hardly a deserted paradise, then, but it was as good a place as any to escape the English gloom.

Kirsty, James, Jamie and Louis left London on a flight to Cozumel on Monday December 11, 2000, looking forward to ten days of scuba-diving, swimming and sunbathing. They planned to cram as much as they could into their brief holiday before returning, tanned and reinvigorated, in time for Christmas Eve and family festivities at home in Ealing. Kirsty had even been organized enough to decorate the tree early, leaving the presents piled up beneath the tinsel, waiting for their return.

CHAPTER TEN
Hard To Believe

There is a peculiar agony left among those who mourn a premature or accidental death; the persistent feeling of being cheated, of being haunted by the incessant *why*, raging at the sheer injustice of it all, at the random nature of events and the odds-defying conjunction that brings them together. Just a few months after the acclaimed release of *Tropical Brainstorm*, many of the writers who had heaped praise on her new album were writing Kirsty MacColl's obituaries.

None of the familiar rock 'n' roll lifestyle caveats or the "live fast, die young" occupational hazard clichés applied; there was no air of inevitability that so often accompanies the announcement of a well-known musician's sudden death. There was simply a deep and abiding sadness at the painfully premature loss of one of the few truly original characters in British pop music, a woman who was also a mother, daughter, sister, friend and lover.

The facts seemed clear, at first. On the afternoon of December 18, Kirsty, an experienced diver, was diving with Jamie and Louis and their dive-master, Ivan Diaz. They were in a protected maritime national park just off the Cozumel coast. The four had just come to the surface after exploring the Chankanaab coral reef and were about to return to their support vessel nearby. Suddenly, they were approached by a speeding powerboat named the *Percalito*. Within seconds it had careered over them.

The powerful boat's propellers hit Kirsty with their full force; her death was almost instantaneous. They also glanced against fourteen-year-old Louis. As the sea water around them swirled deep red, the boys struggled back to the dive-boat where the crew members and the dive-master, aston-ished at what they had just seen, tried to comfort them as the boat returned to shore. Ivan Diaz recalled, "Louis kept asking, 'How is my Mummy?' It broke my heart when I turned around and told them both, 'I'm sorry, boys, your mother is dead'." Both Jamie and Louis began to cry, and I tried to hold them but I was sobbing too. It all seemed to happen so quickly."

The *Percalito* was owned by Guillermo Gonzalez Nova, the multi-millionaire chairman of one of the largest companies in Mexico, Comercial Mexicana. The family-run company operates a chain of restaurants and almost 200 supermarkets, some as part of a joint venture with the American firm, Costco. On board the boat that killed Kirsty were Gonzalez, his two sons Luis and Gustavo, Gustavo's wife, Norma, and their baby daughter. Back on land, statements given to the port authorities and police by the four adults confirmed that a deck-hand, 26-year-old José Cen Yam, had been at the controls of the boat. As the investigations began, the British Foreign Office announced that it had offered consular assistance to the investigation. A police spokesman initially said: "It appears the woman was in an area that is reserved for divers. She received head injuries. We are still investigating."

Back at the hotel, James's immediate priority was the boys:

I remember bits of it with great clarity, and other bits of it I have absolutely no idea at all. My main concern was the kids. If I had been on my own, I don't know, I probably wouldn't have survived it. They know that I love them; they knew that I loved them already; they trusted me, and they still do. Jamie said to me, "What's going to happen to us?" and I said, "Nothing is going to happen to you. You can go home, and you can go to school, and you can come home at the weekends, and I'm going to look after you, and that's it." And after that, he settled.

As he comforted the boys back at their hotel, James phoned Jean MacColl to break the news. "I was making a cup of tea when the phone rang," she says. "James could barely get the words out. I think he was numb with shock. He said, 'I'm sorry, there's been a boating accident and Kirsty is dead.'"

Steve Lillywhite was among the first to hear the news. He was in New York, a city that since 1996 had held out the promise of new beginnings in both his personal and professional life. While keeping a foothold in London for Jamie and Louis, Lillywhite had set up home in New York with his partner, Patty, whom he'd met in 1996 and with whom he has a son and daughter. As soon as Steve heard about Kirsty's death, he tried to arrange a flight to Cozumel, only to find that flight schedules meant it would be many hours before he could get there.

Without hesitation, his friend Chris Blackwell, the legendary founder of Island Records, put his private jet at Steve's disposal and he left immediately for Mexico. From there, he returned to London with Jamie and Louis. They arrived home just two days before Christmas. Jean was at the house to greet them. "I saw their figures walk up to the door," she thinks back. "We just held each other. That Christmas Eve, the house was packed with friends, who were wonderful to us."

Kirsty had put up the Christmas tree before the party had left for Mexico. When they were alone after their Christmas Eve guests had left, the family finished decorating the tree. Turning off the lights, they lit a candle for Kirsty. Each played their favourite Kirsty song. When "Fairytale of New York" was played, Jean remarked about the quality of the CD-player sound, compared to her own creaky cassette player at home. Jamie and Louis laughed. "I realized why the next day," says Jean. "Kirsty had bought me a CD player for Christmas."

MacColl's management company, Major Minor, issued a short press statement: "Kirsty MacColl was a bright, fun-loving person as well as a talented singer and writer who was loved by anybody and everybody she came into contact with." The official announcement of her death was greeted with an air of disbelief at an accident that seemed so random and so unexpected. It made national news headlines in Britain; obituaries also appeared in the international media, including *Le Monde*, *The New York Times*, *The Washington Post*, *Rolling Stone* and National Public Radio in the United States.

The tributes to Kirsty MacColl were immediate, heartfelt and loving. Shane MacGowan said of her: "She had a lot of demons in her life, but she never put it on to others. She was full of fun, full of laughter; she could cheer you up if you were down. Her death was a terrible shock for me. And it's a great loss to many people. She achieved her potential but I'm sure the pop business never marketed her properly or gave her a proper chance." Bono remembered Kirsty, "as just a really brainy, funny girl whose songwriting came from all different traditions. I just remember her humour. She was really funny. Her death just makes you feel very sick, thinking about her kids." For singer-songwriter Tom Robinson, "Kirsty was a human being first and a pop star second. She had enough talent to have hit after hit after hit, but she chose to put her family first. She deserves respect for that." Writing in *The Spectator*, Marcus Berkmann said:

> Pop stars tend to die earlier and more pointless deaths than most people, but the end of Kirsty MacColl still came as a shock. For one thing, she was never quite a star, despite the acres of press coverage she received the following day. Then there was the manner of her death. Drug-addled mediocrities like Kurt Cobain polish themselves off in a haze of adolescent self-hatred, but it's the genuinely talented songwriters who lose their lives protecting their children from arseholes in speedboats. I can't remember a pop death that left me feeling more numb and angry. It's a fetching irony that someone who spent a career writing songs about macho idiots should eventually be run down by one. What MacColl offered above all was a fierce intelligence, and there aren't many of those in the music industry.

In the London *Evening Standard*, Matthew Norman wrote, "I cannot remember a celebrity death that provoked such genuine if understated sadness, partly perhaps because, for all her talent and success, she didn't have an aura of celebrity ... the loss of both her and Ian Dury – two left-wing ironists (and you can imagine what a crowded field that is in pop) who inspired more affection than any other British performers you can think of – in the same year seems as tragically wasteful as the incongruous manner of her death."

In *The Daily Telegraph*, Sandra Laville praised MacColl for rising above "a world increasingly criticized for rewarding style over substance. Kirsty MacColl was the antithesis of a pop star. She shied from the media, hated commercialism and put her children above her fame. Her inventive, intelligent lyrics and powerful voice earned her the unstinted praise of her musical peers." On the other side of the political spectrum, the World Socialist website carried a lengthy tribute written by Liz Smith:

> To the tens of thousands of fans she built up around the world, she will best be remembered for her acerbic wit and treatment of everyday occurrences and feelings in a brutally honest but sensitive way. She possessed that rare ability wholly absent in many contemporary artists – to speak the truth and, in doing so, make all those who listened to her songs feel that she was one of them.

Writing in the *New York Daily News*, Jim Farber said, "As pop's answer to Dorothy Parker, MacColl wrote abut love's awful happenstances and life's tragic whims, leavening her pessimism with a desert-dry wit and an underlying faith that together made her one of music's most honest scribes ... Nobody in modern pop has written songs with more life in them. And that life will not die."

Kirsty's fans were stunned. There was no fan club as such, but the Freeworld website – better known as www.kirstymaccoll.com – that had been set up by one of her fans, Alan Officer, in December 1995, and the Yahoo chatroom forum devoted to Kirsty had taken the place of an official fan club. Many people turned to these sites for comfort. Chris Winwood, a long-time fan, heard the news from a friend who called him at work to tell him:

> At the time I hadn't lost a friend of my age or someone I was close to, but I really did feel that I knew Kirsty. At that time, I was listening to her music every day. I remember watching the news that night and being quite emotional. The phone was ringing, because people had seen it on the news. I turned the computer on and I had a hundred e-mails, most of them from the chat group; people not knowing what to do or what to say. You could just tell that people were crying into their keyboards as they were typing. It was such a shock.

The BBC announced that it was delaying the broadcast of "Kirsty MacColl's Cuba", the series of radio programmes that was due to be broadcast on December 20 – two days after her death – until it could discuss with Kirsty's family whether they wanted the series to go ahead. The BBC production team said, "We are devastated at her loss, which is a tragedy for her family and has robbed the world of a major musical talent. She will be much missed." "Kirsty MacColl's Cuba" was eventually broadcast from January 31, 2001.

Kirsty MacColl's funeral service was held in early January. A private affair for family and close friends at Mortlake Crematorium in London, it started with a brief address by a humanist celebrant, followed by tributes from other close associates including Ronnie Harris, Kirsty's long-time friend and accountant. Her mother's recorded oration was a moving reminder of the early years of her longed-for "autumn child", born in an October over 41 years previously, when the leaves had turned as russet-coloured as the baby's hair: "You brought me great joy and great happiness, and I loved you. I love you still. I remember my autumn daughter with great pride and great privilege."

The sound of the Beach Boys' "Good Vibrations" filled the chapel, and was followed by one of the last songs that Kirsty had written with James. The words of "Good for Me" arguably showed how the singer had finally come to accept that she deserved as much happiness as she could find in life: "Where can I find the words to describe the way that I feel with you at my side ... Everyone agrees that you are good for me ... Yes I think I deserve you, yes, I think I really earned you ..."

On the day of the funeral, however, there was sadness that the family tensions of the past, and the enmity that Jean MacColl still felt for Peggy Seeger, had resurfaced at a time when both of Ewan's families were mourning their loss. Peggy Seeger says she regrets not being able to attend the funeral with her children, Calum and Kitty, but she knew that none of them would be made welcome:

> They were not asked to the funeral, nor was I. I was told not to come. With Calum and Kitty, it was virtually the same, even though Calum had worked with her and Kitty had lived in her house for a year. Neill was asked. I know there was a lot of grief at the time and you never know what happens under these circumstances. But Neill asked us whether he should go and we said, "Yes, you're our representative", so he went and my kids waited outside the gates. It was not good. It was a time when we could have been pulled together, but weren't. I still, to this day, don't know why, because I went around to see Jean the day after I found out. She and I had a long talk, but things are never hunky dory ... I had never realized that it would be a rift the way it is now. The families don't see each other and the boys don't see their cousins. Kirsty was the one who was pulling it all together. Kirsty was the lynchpin between the two families.

A public memorial service was held on January 20, 2001, at St Martin-in-the-Fields, a beautiful 300-year-old church in the heart of London. Kirsty MacColl would no doubt have approved of the choice. For many centuries, different incarnations of St Martin's have held an unashamedly non-traditional and often radical role within the confines of the established Church, from offering a lending library in 1680 to its unique modern-day Social Care Unit for London's homeless and its respected Academy orchestra, which was set up in 1959. In further evidence of its colourful past, the legendary mistress of Charles II,

Nell Gwynn, is interred there, as is the notorious highwayman Jack Sheppard.

It was a fittingly colourful venue for fans to mingle with musicians as well as Kirsty's many non-celebrity friends when they crowded into the church, just off Trafalgar Square, at 11 o'clock on a bitterly cold Saturday morning. Bono and Adam Clayton from U2, assorted Pogues including Philip Chevron, Jem Finer and Spider Stacy, musicians including Nick Lowe, Billy Bragg, Johnny Marr, Holly Johnson and Jools Holland, broadcaster Phill Jupitus, actors from Jean and Ewan's Theatre Workshop days and British film and TV stars were all among the congregation.

Opening the service, the Reverend Nicholas Holtam said that, although Kirsty's death had been deeply shocking, there was much to celebrate about her life: "Many of her songs touched the big questions of life." Jean MacColl told the mourners that she had lost both a daughter and a best friend: "Kirsty is still with us," she said. "She is still touching the hearts of all the people she loved." James Knight described the enormity of her loss: "The space left by her is bigger than the universe we live in."

For his part, Phill Jupitus told the congregation that, "I count myself extraordinarily fortunate that there were some fragments of my life that have been imbued by Kirsty MacColl." Jupitus had prepared a short oration, but as he walked from his pew to the altar, decided instead to just tear up his notes and speak from the heart, musing about her famous hospitality, and the everyday moments of friendship. Jupitus had been shaken badly by Kirsty's death, only finding out about her accident when a reporter from the *Daily Express* called him at home to ask for a quote about MacColl. "Oh, she's great," enthused Jupitus. "She's dead," replied the journalist.

Amid all of the loving tributes and anecdotes at the memorial service, no one could escape the feeling that MacColl's death was a terrible injustice to those who'd loved her. "I liked, at the memorial service, how angry Jean got," says Jupitus. "She was so angry; it was not right that it had happened. It was wrong. It was as if she was saying, 'I don't want to stand here being lovely about it; I'm going to be fucked off that it happened.' That was one of the most moving things."

Music, inevitably, provided the perfect counterpoint to the overwhelming sadness. Billy Bragg sang "A New England", and Kirsty's band was joined by Holly Johnson to perform "Don't Come The Cowboy With Me, Sonny Jim" at the end of the service. As he left the church,

Bragg told reporters that it had been a tough year for all those who loved witty songwriters, due to the deaths of both Kirsty and also Ian Dury, some months earlier. Bragg paid tribute to MacColl's activism on behalf of Cuba, saying, "I considered her not just a friend, but also a comrade. While others just sing about issues, Kirsty always got involved."

For Bono – who had read the lesson at Kirsty's and Steve's wedding, and been friends with them for years – attending the memorial service somehow brought Kirsty into sharper relief as a person: "I'm so happy I got to the service. That meant a great deal to me. I was very aware of how much you don't know about someone, that you can be quite close to them but you don't really know someone unless you know their family and their friends. So I couldn't say I knew Kirsty until she was taken away, and I met her family and friends, and then I really got a picture. I came away from that feeling like I had spent a lot of time with her, more time with her than I did, and I was really glad to be there."

People who had worked with MacColl at her many different record companies were also among the mourners. "The memorial service was very sad, obviously," says former Virgin executive Jon Webster. "But it wasn't full of people who were there because they *thought* they should be there, it was full of people who were there because they *wanted* to be there." The celebrities and industry figures, however, only made up part of the congregation. Chris Winwood was among the many Kirsty fans also there:

> People had come from all over the world. It was an amazing experience to meet other Kirsty fans. In some ways, that was a real boost for Kirsty MacColl fans, because there never had been any fan club or any organized thing in the past. The website, the chat group and the fanzine had all begun to pull people together and help them to connect with other fans. It hadn't been possible in the past. After the service, we went to the pub and had a sing-song and talked about Kirsty's music, and it was just so nice to talk to other people about Kirsty.

BBC Radio 2 broadcast a tribute to Kirsty MacColl on the day of the memorial service. DJ Johnnie Walker, who had known Kirsty for years, hosted the programme, which was called "Thank You For The Days". The one-hour show featured contributions from musician friends like Billy Bragg and Johnny Marr, who talked about her commitment to both motherhood and music; Phil Chevron of the Pogues, who discussed extracts from the last project Kirsty was working on, a musical with Chevron and Ronnie Drew of the Dubliners; Pete Glenister; Holly Johnson, and Paul Conroy, veteran of Stiff Records.

The programme was produced by Nick Barraclough, who just a few weeks earlier had been in Cuba with Kirsty, working on their music series: "It was such a joy working with Kirsty. Her energy, her passion for the music and her appetite for hard work and fun made the news of her death a devastating blow to me personally. This tribute programme reflects how well-loved she was in the music world and, along with Kirsty's Cuba series, captures the wonderful spirit she was. I hope both will stand as fitting tributes to her."

The Cuba Solidarity Campaign issued a statement paying tribute to Kirsty's work for the organization, describing her as a true friend of Cuba and saying, "The untimely death of Kirsty MacColl is a terrible loss for all those across the globe who support Cuba's rights to national sovereignty. Our sincere condolences go out to her family and friends." Within days of Kirsty's death, her management had got in touch with the CSC to discuss possible projects that could be launched in her memory. They agreed to set up a fund to be administered by the CSC for the benefit of Cuban music schools and their students. Work began immediately on preparing an information sheet to be distributed at the memorial service and sent to contacts throughout the music industry. Many of them gave generous contributions to the fund, says CSC director Rob Miller:

> It was very clear that Kirsty was so into Cuba and it seemed like a wonderful way of helping preserve her memory and also of using her memory to further an aim that she would strongly believe in, which was to help young musicians in Cuba. The music fund itself is very much geared around the fact that Cuba has this brilliant breadth of talent yet it's being eroded by the blockade, which is stopping the importation of basic things like violin strings or piano wire or musical instruments. It also highlights the stupidity of the blockade that affects ordinary people who just want to play music. How ridiculous can that be in the modern world? It's something that Kirsty would be proud of. We're very hopeful that the fund will do well and will forever be associated with Kirsty and that's a lovely testament to her.

The south London-based Goldsmiths' College, part of the University of London, established a scholarship in Kirsty's name. The college, best known for its arts faculty alumni including artists Damien Hirst and

Gillian Wearing, designer Mary Quant, actor Colin Welland and Blur's Damon Albarn and Alex James, is also renowned for its work on contemporary culture and ethnicity. Goldsmiths' set up the annual Kirsty MacColl scholarship, which provides tuition fees for a student to undertake an MA in Culture, Globalization and the City. Seven months after MacColl's death, the acting head of the college's Centre for Urban and Community Research, Dr Les Back, launched the scholarship:

> I think many people were moved very deeply by the injustice of her death. What's special about Kirsty MacColl's career is that she never really bowed to musical fashion and the image-driven ethos of the industry. She was a storyteller, an ethnographer of private troubles and triumphs. Her songs focus on the mundane details that are often overlooked or deemed trivial. She wasn't ideological and didn't indulge in political sloganeering. But she was a great listener and that comes out in her songwriting. The conversations she overheard resonate in her music like so many sonic portraits of city life.

The first recipient of the MacColl Scholarship was a freelance radio producer, Sally Brewer, who had graduated from Goldsmiths' with a first in Anthropology in 1999. The scholarship made it possible for her to return. "Like many other students," said Brewer, "especially those with children, I'm struggling with a huge burden of debt. So while I've worked for the last couple of years, often freelance, I'm actually worse off than when I left Goldsmiths'. The scholarship means a massive vote of confidence and the lifting of a financial burden that might have sabotaged my academic success."

It was an inspired move by Goldsmiths' to put money in Kirsty's name into a project that she would doubtless have supported. It was also apt that it was Goldsmiths' that chose to honour Kirsty's memory in this way; her father's own collection of sheet music and publications on British and Irish folk music are held in the college library.

On Sunday January 7, 2001 – less than three weeks after her death – Kirsty MacColl had been due to unveil a plaque in Ewan's memory at the Working Class Movement Library in Salford. Friends and fans of Ewan's had been invited; memories would be shared, his songs would be sung, and there would be a performance of "Meerut", one of the early street theatre pieces performed by the Red Megaphones. The event, "The Joy of Living", was intended as a celebration of Ewan's life and music.

However, as Kirsty's family mourned her death, the event was postponed until the September of that year. Peggy Seeger attended and unveiled the plaque; words were said in Ewan's honour, tales told, and laughter shared. But with Ewan long gone and Kirsty's loss still so raw, the most moving moment came when two of Scotland's most acclaimed traditional folk singers, Alison McMorland and her husband, Geordie McIntyre, showed why they were among those who had taken on the mantle of tradition-bearers and folk-revivalists from Ewan himself. They had recently recorded Ewan's song "The Joy of Living" with their daughter, also called Kirsty, but in Salford that day, their rendition of the song became a homage to both Ewan and Kirsty MacColl:

> "We'll sing of the hurt and pain
> And the joy of living."

> —Ewan MacColl, "The Joy Of Living"

CHAPTER ELEVEN

All The Tears That I Cried

As the tributes to Kirsty MacColl accrued back in her native Britain, the police and port authorities in Cozumel continued to gather evidence. The pathologist who carried out the autopsy concluded that Kirsty MacColl's death was the result of a tragic accident. Dr Pascual Piccolo noted, "The danger of this type of dive is that the boats continually drift because they are not allowed to put down an anchor in the reef. As a result, the divers can lose their bearings and, in this case, Miss MacColl had no time to react. Unfortunately, it's one of the risks of coral diving."

Several people, including Kirsty's sons, had said the *Percalito* was travelling at high speed, possibly up to twenty knots; so fast that its bow was forced high out of the water. They said it was also well within the national park zone, which bans all boats except divers' support vessels. In his testimony, the diving instructor, Ivan Diaz, described seeing the boat heading directly towards them as they watched, powerless to stop it: "Kirsty pushed Jamie away from her and I tugged at Louis's wetsuit as we all became engulfed in a white wake of water," he said. "As the swell broke, Louis and I were swept to one side; when I resurfaced, I noticed Kirsty's body was floating face-up in the water. The normally light-blue sea had become cloudy all around her and I immediately feared that the worst had happened."

Kirsty's elder son, Jamie, told police that he felt slightly disoriented after coming to the surface, but he could see his mother close by:

She seemed to be motioning and pushing me away from her side as I glanced through my mask. The next thing I remember is feeling something glance off the side of my head, hitting the left side of my shoulder, body and elbow. I started to call out to our boat for help and to come and pick us out of the water. Suddenly I could hear shouts coming from all around, and my mother's body seemed to be just floating in the water.

Jamie's brother, Louis, simply said that he remembered hearing some-body screaming, "Be careful!" just seconds after they surfaced.

Diaz told the police that he had no doubt that Kirsty had saved Jamie's life by pushing him away: "She was a very brave lady to do that. She was just caught up at the wrong place at the wrong time. It's too late now but that boat should never have been going so fast inside the reef." A spokesman for Diaz's employer, Papa Hog's Scuba Emporium, said, "The dive master, who was in a boat, waved at the other boat to go around, but it was too late. He could not do anything. Kirsty could not get out of the way. We are very shocked and upset; it is a dreadful thing to happen."

The authorities in Cozumel, however, soon began to notice discrep-ancies between some of the witness statements they were gathering. Guillermo Gonzalez Nova denied that his powerboat was even within the restricted area, and both he and Cen Yam also disputed the allega-tion that the boat was travelling too fast. They said that its speed would have been no more than one knot.

It emerged that Cen Yam had never before taken the controls of the powerful boat, bought by Guillermo Gonzalez in 1994 for the equivalent of £127,000, and had no qualifications to do so. His job was simply to carry out routine maintenance on the boat. Jean MacColl was later to question whether Gonzalez would have entrusted the safety of his own family and control of an expensive twin-engine boat, capable of speeds up to 33 knots, to an unqualified deck-hand.

Cen Yam told investigators that he had taken a seaman's course; when questioned on basic points, however, he appeared confused. While insisting that the boat was only travelling at one knot, he could not explain nautical speed and didn't seem to understand exactly what a knot was. He also stumbled over simple arithmetic and the difference between left and right. Cen Yam was released on bail, and a spokesman for the Mexican Attorney-General's office said the case was being treated as negligent homicide.

As an experienced scuba-diver herself, Kirsty had done all she could to ensure the safety of their expedition. The day before, she had gone to the long-established dive shop to ensure that the boys had some preliminary training with an experienced instructor before setting off. The official Mexican government guide to Cozumel advises accordingly: "For diving the coral reefs, walls and drift diving, Cozumel's guides are invaluable for their knowledge of the area. Most diving in Cozumel requires qualified, professional and competent guides."

However, it also soon emerged that the dive-master on Kirsty's fatal trip had failed to display a marker buoy; nor was the dive boat flying a warning flag that conformed to international regulations. It was also discovered that the dive boat should have had one extra crew member on board to conform to crewing standards. Papa Hog's Scuba Emporium is owned and operated by a Canadian couple. The owner, Mike Gerus is a diving veteran of more than 30 years, and national training director of a Canadian diving association, IDEA. He and his wife opened the dive shop in 1991, and expanded their operation in 1998. Their publicity literature boasts: "You can depend upon Papa Hog's and our dive-masters to safely do your dives the way you would want ... our staff of dive-masters are some of the finest you'll find in Cozumel."

The dive master employed by Papa Hog's, Ivan Diaz, would later allege that, after signing his initial statement for the port authority captain, he was called back by another official and asked to sign a blank piece of paper. Diaz says he was told that officials would "take care" of his statement. He says he refused to sign the piece of paper. Diaz also later alleged that one of Gonzalez Nova's lawyers had remarked to him, "You do know who you are dealing with, don't you?" Jean MacColl says that, in late 2003, Diaz contacted her to say he was so concerned for his safety that he was no longer in Cozumel and had given up working as a dive master.

When port authority investigators presented their findings, they ruled that José Cen Yam had been negligent and had violated maritime navigation laws; that Gonzalez Nova should not have allowed him to take control of the *Percalito* and that the boat had indeed been within the protected national park at the time of collision. The investigators also found the dive company at fault for infractions over the warning flag, marker buoy and crew numbers.

On the basis of the findings and police investigations, José Cen Yam was charged with the killing of Kirsty MacColl. After lengthy court proceedings, he was found guilty of negligent homicide. Appearing before Judge Fidel Gabriel Villanueva Rivero in a Cozumel court in March 2003, Cen Yam was sentenced to a prison term of two years and ten months. Under Mexican law, such sentences can be commuted to a fine of one peso for each day of the prospective imprisonment. Cen Yam, not surprisingly, accepted this option and was freed after paying a fine that amounted to little more than £60. The judge also ordered him to pay compensation of £1,450 to Kirsty's sons.

This decision outraged Jean MacColl, who believed that Cen Yam was little more than a scapegoat. Kirsty's mother maintained that Gonzalez Nova, as the owner of the boat, should have accepted ultimate responsibility. The Mexican court disagreed, however; within the Mexican system, the judicial process had done its work. At the time of writing, no one other than José Cen Yam has been charged in the case, and no further charges are pending.

The decision did give impetus to the campaign that Jean MacColl had launched during the proceedings, frustrated by the apparent lack of progress in bringing any charges against Guillermo Gonzalez Nova. With the support of some of Kirsty's friends, she'd set up the Justice for Kirsty campaign in order to highlight the case. The group launched a website and urged supporters and Kirsty's fans to contact several organizations – including the US-Mexico Chamber of Commerce, the Professional Association of Diving Instructors, the British Sub-Aqua Club and the Divers Alert Network – in the hope that they would be galvanized into action, given the enormously lucrative diving industry in Cozumel. A sample letter provided by the campaign stated:

We have read with great interest the story of the composer and singer Miss Kirsty MacColl's death while diving off Cozumel in Mexico on 18 December 2000, and are saddened to learn that the guilty have not yet been brought to justice. I hope to hear from you that you are actively assisting in the search for justice for the MacColl family. And for the army of fans worldwide who, like us, after two years are baffled that the guilty have not been brought to justice. It appeared to be an open and shut case. Help us understand why it has become protracted. Let us know how you are helping the family to get to the truth. We hope that you can help secure a conviction and show worldwide, your organization cares. It is important.

The response to the e-mails was hardly overwhelming, however. Few people reported even being able to get through to the joint Chamber of

Commerce. The Professional Association of Diving Instructors eventually began sending out a stock response:

> Thank you for bringing the matter of Kirsty MacColl's tragic accident to our attention. While thousands of divers safely enjoy the beautiful reefs of Cozumel each year, we understand how the circumstances of Kirsty's death raise questions about public safety in the island's waters. As we are unfamiliar with the details of the investigation by the Mexican authorities, we have made contact with the leaders of the dive community in Cozumel and asked their assistance in pressing the government to resolve the issue and publicly address the concerns you've raised.

Jean approached many of Kirsty's friends and musical collaborators, asking them to support the campaign. Some were happy to do so, either by getting involved directly or responding to pleas for donations and publicity. But others were more circumspect, feeling that it could ultimately end in deep disappointment with little, if any, likelihood that the campaign's original aim of bringing the boat's owner to court would ever be realized.

One described it as a "quest for retribution that is SO not what Kirsty was about. But I was made to feel that in some way I didn't care enough about her if I didn't get involved, and I resented that."

Still others believed that the considerable sums of money being spent on the campaign, primarily in lawyers' fees, should instead have gone to causes that Kirsty believed in and supported – among them, children's charities and Cuban causes – or simply, remained as part of her estate, which initially funded the campaign. There, it would have been used exactly as Kirsty herself had intended, going to the principal beneficiaries named in her will – Jamie, Louis and her partner, James. Irrespective of their father's wealth, Kirsty had left clear instructions that her own financial success should benefit their sons as well, yet their legacy had been eroded somewhat by the cost of launching and sustaining the campaign. Phil Rambow explains:

> Anybody's death in tragic circumstances like that polarizes people. At the end of the day, a person died in Mexico, hit by a boat that was where it was not supposed to be – a boat owned by an incredibly wealthy guy, and a lot of people won't say anything because he's really powerful. Then a deck-hand gets fined £61. People who aren't famous die in worse circumstances

but the point is that it's unfair. It's not just justice for Kirsty; it's justice for anybody. It's something that will make the world a better place, if people can be made accountable for their actions.

The campaign was revitalized by the involvement of Fred Shortland, UK director of the children's charity, Casa Alianza. The charity had worked tirelessly to highlight the issues surrounding the ill-treatment and human rights abuses of children in Latin America, and had won high-profile human rights cases that established recognized precedents in human rights law. While there may have seemed little in common between the deaths of poverty-stricken, neglected and brutalized children and the publicity surrounding the death of a well-known, wealthy British singer-songwriter, Shortland was drawn to the Kirsty campaign, seeing her death as another example of injustice and the campaign as a quest for fairness.

Shortland had also had a passing acquaintance with Kirsty. They'd met on a couple of occasions; the last time they had spoken had been at one of her concerts in London a few months before she died. They had a mutual friend in a sound engineer, Glynn Wood, who had worked with Kirsty many times. Wood's partner, US singer-songwriter Suzanne Vega – a long-time supporter of Casa Alianza – also shared an agent with Kirsty. Shortland had read about the family's campaign in Vega's website chatroom and when, in early 2003, the campaign organizers put out an appeal for volunteers with specialist knowledge, Shortland contacted Glynn Wood and asked him to pass on his good wishes to Jean MacColl, together with an offer to help in any way he could.

A decade of experience in lobbying, campaigning and working with governments and their judiciaries soon proved invaluable – especially as fees for private investigators and bills for lawyers in New York and Mexico mounted to exorbitant levels. The money was haemorrhaging from Kirsty's estate, and donations to the campaign, which included generous sums from high-profile supporters, could do nothing to reverse the financial decline. "I felt very strongly," says Fred Shortland, "that the family and estate should not be paying huge bills. It should be the responsibility of the state of Mexico to investigate the proceedings."

Shortland believed that the British government, too, should be taking more of an interest in the controversial death of one of its citizens. He initiated contact with the consular section of the Foreign Office and asked officials to make an application for an appointment with Baroness Amos, who was then head of the consular section. The officials refused, saying they had neither access to, nor control of, her diary. A request to at least try for an appointment was met with identical intransigence. "They were not interested at all," said Shortland. "Their only interest was in damage limitation, once we had mentioned the documentary that was being planned and the campaign."

It was, perhaps, surprising that Baroness Amos's officials were so dismissive of these requests to bring MacColl's case to the attention of their boss. She was, after all, a politician whose career had been built on a platform of promoting justice and equality. Formerly chief executive of the Equal Opportunities Commission, when she was elevated to the House of Lords, Amos joined the Labour Party's front bench as a spokeswoman for women's issues, international development and social security. In May 2003 she became the first black woman to serve in a British Cabinet, when she was appointed Secretary of State for International Development, after Clare Short resigned over the war in Iraq.

However, it was only after making representations to the Secretary of State for Latin America, Bill Rammell, over what Fred Shortland described as "an absolutely disgraceful response", which he says was unprecedented in a decade of his dealings with the Foreign Office, that officials within the consular section relented and got in touch with the British Embassy in Mexico and the consulate in Cancun. Just a week later, important documentation on maritime hearings into the case suddenly appeared and was made available to Jean MacColl and her lawyers.

The British government did not intervene directly in the Kirsty MacColl case as it proceeded through the Mexican courts and reached its conclusion there, nor could it be seen to be interfering in the judicial process of an independent nation. However, quiet diplomacy appeared to have paid dividends. Later, when Jean MacColl was making plans to go to Mexico, the Foreign Office expressed renewed interest in the case. "The Foreign Office asked for new details of the case from my lawyers," she said, "And they say someone will work with us out there."

It would have surely been deeply unusual for the controversial death of a high-profile British citizen not to be discussed within the portals of power in the UK government. However, given the efforts that both Mexico and Britain have made to establish closer ties since President

Vicente Fox was elected to lead a country with the ninth largest economy in the world, it is perhaps not surprising that Britain is protective of that relationship. Tony Blair had visited Mexico within months of Mr Fox's inauguration in July 2000, and in November 2002 the Mexican leader made a reciprocal visit to London.

Speaking after the two men held talks, Mr Blair said he was delighted at the status of the bilateral relationship between their nations. He highlighted three areas of even closer co-operation: "The first is our bilateral relationship, which is both trading, economic, but also political. The second is in relation to Europe and Latin America, which is an enormously important relationship for both of us and for the wider world ..." The third area was "on the big issues, like Iraq or world trade."

For his part, President Fox spoke optimistically about the economic relationship that was of great importance to the two countries, and said that in a meeting with business leaders earlier that day, "We heard from them that after gross, there is more than $3bn worth of British investment in Mexico; now they are planning in these next two years an additional investment of $1.5bn ..." This is clearly a very valuable economic relationship and one that the two governments are eager to protect. Posing awkward questions about the death of a British celebrity holiday-maker in Cozumel may, therefore, not be very high on a Whitehall bureaucrat's list of priorities – and certainly not of those far higher up the political ladder.

There was a further setback when initial plans fell through for the making of the documentary about Kirsty's death, just days before her mother had hoped to travel to Mexico, with the film crew in tow, to confront Gonzalez Nova in late 2003. The campaign had been relying on just such a programme to raise awareness about the case and fuel an outcry that would add to the pressure on the Mexican authorities. Efforts were redoubled to find a broadcaster prepared to take on the project.

As time passed, the prospect of bringing direct legal action against Gonzalez Nova was receding. Jean MacColl's initial aim of bringing him to court began to look increasingly unrealistic.

While legal reforms in Mexico did allow foreigners to present claims in Mexican courts with rights equal to those of Mexican citizens, there were still major issues to be resolved. Providing specific proof of alleged negligence by Gonzalez Nova would not have been easy and, even if it had been proved to the court's satisfaction, a conviction may not have resulted in a custodial sentence and could merely have been commuted to a fine. This would certainly be no hardship for a man of Gonzalez Nova's considerable wealth.

Launching civil litigation was a possibility but Mexico is not known as a litigious society in the way that the United States – and, to a growing degree, Britain – has become. It is an expensive and very lengthy process, there are no punitive damage awards and both parties must pay their own legal fees and costs. Even if Jean MacColl had considered it seriously, the issue of the statute of limitations under Mexican law had not been explored fully; deadlines came and went for various stages of the investigative and judicial process. Lawyers acting for the estate had earlier launched a civil claim for damages in Guernsey, where the *Percalito* was registered. That claim was later settled in the estate's favour.

The Napoleonic Code governs much of Mexican law – judges rather than juries decide all cases, and the campaign group feared that a residual culture of impunity might not have been destroyed entirely by the willingness of President Fox to make the judicial process more transparent since his election ended seven decades of one-party rule by the PRI. In his inaugural address, the new president had promised to tackle his country's long-standing issues of human rights abuses and in the months that followed, his administration took a number of steps to fulfill that promise. But by 2002, the international organization, Human Rights Watch, was calling for greater improvements. "Vicente Fox wants to be a global player," says Fred Shortland. "He's made lots of noises about human rights ... we're hoping he'll put pressure on the Attorney-General and the president of the Supreme Court to see this process through."

The aim of the campaign then subtly changed to applying pressure on the Mexican authorities to agree to a judicial review of the entire case. The campaign group even launched a postcard petition, calling on supporters to send the card to President Fox. Each postcard urged the president to implement an immediate judicial review; to investigate why the boat's owner was not charged and brought to trial; to ensure that those found responsible are sentenced according to the gravity of the offences, not just given what was described as token fines and sentences, and to guarantee that local authorities implement meaningful controls to ensure the safety of all divers in restricted areas.

Supporters of the campaign were also asked to contact other senior figures in the Mexican and British governments – among them, the Mexican Minister of Foreign Relations, Dr Luis Ernesto Derbez Bautista; the deputy minister for human rights and democracy, Mariclaire Acosta (for years one of Mexico's most outspoken human rights advocates) who had been appointed to the newly created post by President Fox; and the British Foreign Secretary, Jack Straw, as well as the British ambassador in Mexico City, and the Mexican ambassador in London. The postcard campaign appeared to be having some effect and, in early 2004, Jean MacColl was told she would be permitted to meet Mexican officials to discuss the issue.

After months of anticipation, Jean MacColl left London in the first week of March 2004, bound for Mexico at last. Travelling with her was her friend, John Dalby. They were soon joined by other members of the campaign group including Fred Shortland and photographer Charles Dickens.

Their first stop was Cozumel, for what would be the most emotional moments of the journey. Just before sunset on March 10, the group boarded a motor-launch at the harbourside at Playa Corona to take the short trip out to the site of the accident. Also on board was Ivan Diaz, the dive-master who had been with Kirsty, Jamie and Louis. Jean got to her feet and leaned over to place a large wreath of flowers on the surface of the water, above the coral reef. The words "Kirsty: Goodbye to an angel" were written in white ribbon stretched across the wreath. "Kirsty," she sobbed, "why did you have to die?" John Dalby read a verse from one of Kirsty's songs and each member of the group dropped a single rose into the water. As the white ribbon unfurled and the roses floated after the wreath, the small boat returned to shore.

Jean MacColl later remarked, "Even as we sailed out to the reef where Kirsty died, I could see boats zipping in and out of diving zones and ignoring speed limits. It seems to me that not only are rules regarding the safety of divers routinely ignored in Cozumel but that in Mexico, if you are rich and powerful, you are above the law."

Whatever the merits of her argument, this may not have been the most conciliatory line to take when, two days later, she and Fred Shortland were joined by the campaign's Mexico-based lawyer, Demetrio Guerra, at the Federal Prosecutor's office in Cozumel. They had a dossier of documents, which they believed provided important new evidence in the case. Their attempts to present the new evidence appeared doomed when an official refused to accept the documents that were being thrust on him so unceremoniously. "They didn't want to accept the papers at first," said Jean, "and tried to throw us out."

Guerra eventually persuaded the doubtful official to at least take a cursory look at the file. Three hours later, the new material had been read by the Federal Prosecutor himself, who had agreed to consider it further. The campaign group interpreted this as a first step towards a fresh inquiry. In a statement to supporters the group said, "We believe the Federal Prosecutor will feel compelled to notify Jean that he accepts the evidence and will start a new investigation."

Time will tell. It has not been easy for Jean MacColl's investigators and lawyers to get strong, independent and irrefutable evidence. Ivan Diaz has made a number of allegations about comments he says he overheard Gonzalez Nova making to police, after the accident, which he says were at odds with the version he overheard José Cen Yam make soon afterwards. While admitting that he could not see who was at the controls of the boat as it sped down on top of them, Diaz has said, "I don't think it could have been Cen Yam, because right afterwards I got a look at the *Percalito* and I saw him jumping from the front to the back."

Given that Diaz was talking about something he said he saw immediately after the impact, when he would have been at best badly shaken, if not in a state of shock, Gonzalez Nova's lawyers could cast serious doubt on this. But another witness, Felipe Diaz Poot, the captain of a second dive boat in the area at the time of the accident, the *Nazareno*, is also reported to have given similar evidence to Diaz on who was nearest the controls of the boat.

When her Mexico trip was first mooted many months earlier, Jean MacColl spoke of going there to confront Gonzalez Nova himself. By the time she was actually in Cozumel, this goal had changed somewhat. Instead, two journalist friends who were in Cozumel with her were despatched to Gonzalez Nova's home. They were told that neither he nor his two sons who had been on board the *Percalito* were at home at the time. But another son (named as Geraldo by a *Mail on Sunday* journalist, and Genaro by one from *The Times*) told them, "My father is a good man, a great man. Just ask anyone around here. It was just an accident. All they want is money. Some people are sick." Jean admits that some other people also felt that money was among her motives: "In Cozumel, people were a bit unsure of us at first. A lot of people thought I just wanted to ask for money – but money isn't going to bring my daughter back."

Mr Gonzalez Nova's lawyer was quoted by the *Mail on Sunday* as saying that his client had no reason to meet Jean MacColl, given that he was simply a passenger on the boat at the time of the accident. The lawyer, named as Joachin Soles Ribera, insisted that José Cen Yam had been at the controls, just as the court that convicted him had concluded. Before the group members left Cozumel, they saw the *Percalito* – moored in the harbour and ready for use.

On March 15, Jean MacColl took her fight to Mexico City and the very centre of government. While initially hopeful of a meeting with President Vicente Fox himself, the group was eventually welcomed by one of his officials, Laura Carrera Lugo, at Los Pinos, the presidential residence. When Ms Carrera Lugo encouraged them to pursue the case, "as it would help fight corruption", Fred Shortland admits they were both surprised and delighted: "The statement was made in the context of our campaign objectives where we indicated that we had faith in the Mexican judicial system but should it fail us again we would have no choice but to pursue the matter through the Inter-American Commission in Washington and the Inter-American Court of Human Rights. The basis would be that we had exhausted due legal process in Mexico and the case would be against the Republic of Mexico. To our surprise she indicated that if we had to do that and it was our right to do so, it would be in the interests of Mexico and would help them in their fight against corruption and impunity."

Polite talks at the presidential palace were followed by discussions with the Minister of Tourism, Rodolfo Elizondo Torres. He is reported to have promised to examine safety conditions for divers. Mr Torres' concern was hardly surprising given President Fox's comments, when announcing the new minister's appointment in late July, 2003: "Tourism is clearly a factor in the development of the nation. Millions of jobs and many communities the length and breadth of the country, in addition to major foreign currency flows, depend on it. I am sure that Rodolfo will be up to discharging this new responsibility with the efficiency and sensitivity the citizens' mandate demands of us."

While in Mexico City, Jean MacColl also held talks with the

Attorney-General, General Rafael Marcial Macedo de la Concha, who, according to the *Mail on Sunday*, told her that he would monitor the case.

As the two-week visit drew to a close, the Justice for Kirsty campaign committee issued a jubilant statement to its supporters, describing the trip as an unmitigated success:

> The committee has been heartened and bolstered by the reception they received. The Mexican authorities have been unswerving in their pledges and determination to help, and the Justice for Kirsty party have been suitably convinced that there will be some real change in Mexican law enforcement that will endeavour to protect against any possible re-occurrence of the tragedy that befell the MacColl family. The Ministers have been attentive, compassionate and understanding, all of which has been of great comfort to Jean.

Arriving back in London on March 20, Jean MacColl was confident and combative, saying the visit had been a great success. She declared to a BBC London camera crew waiting at Heathrow airport that she was now certain that José Cen Yam was not behind the controls of the boat that killed her daughter.

The next phase of the campaign would have to focus on replenishing the campaign's depleted coffers after what had become a prohibitively expensive fight, with the newly-added costs of taking several people to Mexico to be taken into account and plans for the continuation of the protracted battle in Mexico. Retaining lawyers in the US and Mexico, private investigators in Mexico and paying other expenses cost the estate more than £100,000 in the first year, and in early 2003, Jean MacColl had appealed for public donations to help boost the fund by a further £100,000.

On February 1, 2003, a group of performers had staged a variety concert at the Theatre Royal in Stratford East, in memory of Joan Littlewood, who had died almost five months earlier. On February 2, friends of Littlewood – including British actresses Sheila Hancock, Miriam Karlin and Barbara Windsor – attended a private gathering, where more contributions were made. On December 7, Jean MacColl had been among several Theatre Workshop figures, past and present, who took part in a discussion on the company at the Theatre Museum in Covent Garden. Leaflets about the campaign were distributed and t-shirts sold to raise funds.

U2 had agreed to help publicize the campaign on their official website. A message called on their fans to support the campaign, saying "Kirsty was a friend of U2 since their earliest days. The campaign to get justice for the late singer-songwriter, Kirsty MacColl, is gathering pace." Throughout, Bono has been a great supporter of the Justice for Kirsty campaign:

I think what's missing is a sense of her being a truly great British artist and England should be fighting for this, making sure that everything is done right and that she is not to be trifled with now. You judge a country by how it treats its artists, just like how it treats its nurses or its elderly. This is how we judge a culture. England is still full of fine engineers but it's not famous for building bridges any more; there are some great inventors in England still, but it's not famous for its inventors. But England has been at the cutting edge of pop culture for forty years and its artists are the greatest in the world, and they shouldn't be put on the periphery of things. They should be brought into the midst of it and just treated a bit better.

In the early hours of April 30, 2004, almost six weeks after her return from Mexico, Jean MacColl received word from her Mexico-based lawyer, Demetrio Guerra, that the Federal Prosecutor in Cozumel had issued a subpoena for the dive-master, Ivan Diaz, to give further testimony in the case. "This", she said, "is the beginning of justice".

CHAPTER TWELVE
The One And Only

You have to have total faith. I want to write better songs, make better records. I want to do everything better and better and better until I die. That's all.

—Kirsty MacColl

Soho Square is one of those London surprises that you find by accident, looking for a short-cut to the mayhem of Oxford Street or trying to follow directions to the local post office or to a publishers' office or the global headquarters of Sir Paul McCartney's company. It is the last vestige of the fields that covered the area until the Great Fire of London in 1666, and for a time after it was laid out in 1681 as King's Square – in honour of Charles II, whose statue still stands – was once the most fashionable address in London. It is clearly no longer that.

But it is still a *very* London square, as likely to be used by fashion victims styled to within an inch of their lives, as inelegantly wasted junkies, roadies setting up at the nearby Astoria, Eurotrash students, elderly residents of Soho and families having a picnic. It was here that one long-time fan, Chris Winwood, decided there was no better place in London for a memorial to Kirsty MacColl.

A simple park bench was somehow the perfect choice. This would be a utilitarian, everyday object that would be used and enjoyed for years to come, just like the one immortalized in one of MacColl's most poignantly beautiful songs, "Soho Square". Sitting in a nearby pub, surrounded by other fans after Kirsty's memorial service, he had concluded, "This has got to go on; she can't be forgotten. With people who are so full of passion for Kirsty's work, I was sure there could be some mileage in it. That was the inspiration for it." Winwood contacted her management company, Major Minor, and they agreed that it was a great idea. "I was aware that, once Kirsty had gone," says Winwood, "she could be forgotten. It was unlikely that there'd be any more unreleased stuff. People have to be kept interested in Kirsty; they have to know that she existed and not forget her."

A submission was made to Westminster Council, which approved the application and agreed to erect and maintain the bench. After an intensive fund-raising drive, it was unveiled on Sunday, August 12, 2001. Unseasonable summer rain fell on 150 family members, friends and fans of Kirsty MacColl, who sheltered under umbrellas, the surrounding trees and the curious Victorian-built mock Tudor shed in the centre of the square as the song "Soho Square" was played. Chris Winwood welcomed them by explaining why he had chosen this course of action:

> We wanted a permanent, lasting memorial, not just another blue plaque on a wall. With the officials I spoke to almost falling over themselves to be helpful, cash started to arrive from fans. There was cash, cheques, hundred-dollar bills and rare bootleg CDs. People sent what they could afford, and everyone wished they could send more. Even though I collected the cash, braving the woman in Thomas Cook [currency exchange] with twenty one-dollar bills three times in one week, this is the fans' gift to Kirsty's memory. As we're not able to produce a cash-in CD of songs everyone already has, we brought one of her best songs to life. We chose the inscription, a quote from the song, and we're so excited to see so many people here now, united in one way or another by our love of Kirsty.

Jean MacColl also paid tribute to the fans' thoughtfulness, and their innovative approach to keeping her daughter's memory alive. She told the gathering:

> I'm so thrilled to see you all here. Your love, affection and kindness and your solidarity has been so supportive of all the family, and I do thank you, really, from the bottom of my heart. It helps a lot. You've been most generous, and I'm sure Kirsty would be amazed at how many friends and fans she had, and I can't thank you enough. I think this is a wonderful place, and I'm sure she's looking down and having a little smile somewhere, and I shall come and sit on the bench. If I get down, this is where I shall come.

The unveiling of the bench provided the perfect opportunity to highlight another tribute to Kirsty – the fund that had been set up in her name to provide musical equipment for Cuban schools. Steve Wilkinson, of the Cuba Solidarity Campaign, held up an oversized cheque for £11,200 to represent the money raised so far for the Music Fund for Cuba:

> Kirsty was an avid supporter of Cuba, and the gains of its socialist revolution. In October last year, I had the great privilege of going with Kirsty to hand in a petition to the Foreign and Commonwealth Office of 25,000 signatures against the American embargo of Cuba, where I can tell you that Kirsty was a very direct, outspoken and courageous advocate of the cause which we support. This money which has been raised by you all and many others is going to buy oboes, French horns, double bass instruments, cellos and reeds and strings for all of those things which will be going to 23 music schools in fourteen different provinces right across Cuba.

Jean MacColl presented the £11,200 cheque to the Cuban ambassador to Britain, José Fernandez de Cossio, who attended the ceremony along with his wife, Tania Domingues-Rosas, and the deputy ambassador, Oscar de los Reyes. The ambassador accepted, saying, "I just want to say thank you on behalf of the Cuban people. This very touching and very moving gesture, it goes directly to the students and to the professors and to the teachers."

With the afternoon's formalities over, most people ventured to a nearby pub for more singing and reminiscing. This lasted only until the barman, apparently overcome with lack of emotion, warned that any mass singing would involve a mass barring: "If you touch that guitar, I'll ask you all to leave!" With the words of "A New England" ringing in his ears, the party moved on to a more welcoming bar, and the start of what would become a tradition – a Soho Square Kirsty Fest, held every year on the Sunday nearest her birthday, October 10.

There was, furthermore, an additional deep-rooted connection to Soho Square that the fans and friends had not been aware of. Across the square from Kirsty's bench, Ewan MacColl had once opened a folk club, the Singers' Club. Run jointly with *Sing* magazine, Ewan and Peggy Seeger held the first meeting, at 2 Soho Square, on June 25, 1961. For many months beforehand, they'd sung in the same building with the Ballads and Blues Association, until they split with the association's manager, Malcolm Nixon, over disagreements on artistic policy.

Outlining his five-point manifesto for the new Singers' Club in *Sing* magazine, two months after the new club opened, Ewan MacColl had declared:

> It is necessary to rescue a large number of young people, all of whom have the right instincts, from those influences that have appeared on the folk scene during the past two or three years; influences that are doing their best to debase the meaning of folk song. The only notes that some people care about are the banknotes. We are determined to give top traditional singers a platform where they will be protected from the ravages of the commercial machine. Finally, we need standards. Already the race for the quick pound note is on in the folk-song world. "Quaint" songs, risqué songs, poor instrumentation and no-better-than-average voices, coupled with a lack of respect for the material: against these, we will fight.

This was a typically uncompromising and ideological approach to a battle that Ewan believed that he was fighting against all that would diminish and deride the music he treasured. His clarion call to resist these dark forces that perpetrate "quaint songs, risqué songs, poor instrumentation, no-better-than-average voices" could as easily have been his daughter's more subtle campaign in the pop world.

Another opportunity to celebrate Kirsty MacColl's life came in September 2002. The music promotion company, Serious, was organizing a week of events celebrating the craft of songwriting at the Royal Festival Hall in London. Pete Glenister and Dave Ruffy were approached to discuss devoting an evening to the work of Kirsty MacColl as part of the event, "The Song's The Thing". They agreed to take on the role of musical directors.

Glenister and Ruffy contacted James Knight and between them began putting a band together and drawing up a wish-list of artists that was to eventually include Johnny Marr, David Gray, Tracey Ullman, Eliza Carthy, Evan Dando, Roddy Frame, Brian Kennedy, Mary Coughlan, and Boo Hewerdine. They felt that the timing was right – enough time had passed for such an event to be purely celebratory of Kirsty's life and music, rather than in any way commercialized or seen as a quick and exploitative cash-in. "I'm really glad we did it," reflects Glenister. "It was a great night, but it was so hard to do; it was hard emotionally but it was quite cathartic, so it was good for all of us."

The band came to resemble a one-off super-group, made up entirely of musicians who had worked with Kirsty. Many of the *Tropical*

Brainstorm players and band-members – Knight, Glenister, Ruffy, Michelle Drees and Ben Storey formed the house band, along with Neill MacColl, Julian Cox and Liam Kirkham. Guests Boz Boorer, Jem Finer, Omar Puente, Phil Rambow and Spider Stacey joined them at various intervals. The band members had two weeks together and during that time ran through the entire show, as well as the individual performances with each artist. Tracey Ullman flew in from Los Angeles the day before the concert and went directly to the Festival Hall to start rehearsing.

The final dress rehearsal on the day of the concert went well, but the band were rehearsing up until the moment the doors opened, says Glenister: "The physical thing of getting through it, rehearsing a band and working with all of these different artists, was a logistical nightmare; the most difficult thing I've ever done. It was a very emotional night. It was only when we got through the first two-thirds of it, we could think what it was really about, and not just worry about who was coming on next."

Everyone involved was determined that the mood would be uplifting and celebratory, not maudlin and mawkish. Phill Jupitus was chosen as the perfect MC to ensure that the pace and mood never flagged. "It wasn't a sad thing," says Dave Ruffy. "That's why we had Phill. It was very light-hearted. All of the emotion was in the songs, you didn't have to play it up." Jupitus called on his arsenal of Renaissance Man skills; he was a stand-up comedian, rock 'n' roll poet, walking music encyclopaedia, radio show host, TV personality and, not least, friend of Kirsty MacColl's. He was even to add "singer" to the list, opening the show with "Fifteen Minutes" before welcoming the audience to what he said would be a night of "Kirsty-oke": songs that Kirsty had either written or recorded, performed by a stellar line-up of musicians.

Throughout the evening, the introductions were peppered with reminiscences and observations about Kirsty. "It would have been disrespectful of me," says Jupitus, "to play any sort of emotional ticket. But you just remember random things about her, you get chatting backstage with people and you're remembering things that happened, all the great stuff. There's a roomful of people that loved her. I can't add to that love and so all you can do for them is just talk about memories."

The first guest, Christine Collister, had chosen one of the newer songs, "Us Amazonians". However, classic late eighties MacColl followed in the form of Boo Hewerdine's spirited "Free World" and Roddy Frame's "Innocence" (accompanied by Eliza Carthy) and another recent song,

"Wrong Again". Former Lemonheads singer Evan Dando was among the less likely musicians to appear in a Kirsty MacColl tribute line-up, but their duet on "Perfect Day" had been inspired casting and Dando reprised the song that night, following it with an effortless prince-of-the-slackers version of "He's on the Beach". Eliza Carthy swept onto the stage in an outfit she'd had made for the occasion – a skirt decorated with a Warhol-style screen print of Kirsty's face – for "Mambo de la Luna" with Christine Collister, and then a solo "England 2, Colombia 0". "This is a good one," she promised, by way of introduction.

Irish singer Mary Coughlan's sardonic world-weary delivery wrapped itself around "In These Shoes?", "Head" and "Bad" as if they'd been written especially for her. Her countryman Brian Kennedy's inspired choice of "Dear John" showed that the specifics of gender, sexuality and relationships are irrelevant in the best-crafted songs – they become universal. He performed "Angel" and "Don't Come the Cowboy with Me, Sonny Jim" before his friend, Mark Nevin, sang "Soho Square", the song he'd co-written for *Titanic Days*. Christine Collister returned to the front of the stage for "My Affair", before the audience's tumultuous welcome for Johnny Marr and a guitar god version of "Tread Lightly" which also employed Marr's much-under-rated vocals.

The former Smith stayed on stage to play guitar on "Walking Down Madison", the song he'd co-written with Kirsty. David Gray, then the toast of transatlantic pop charts with his hugely successful *White Ladder* album, performed the song. Tellingly, Gray had interrupted a promotional trip to the US to return to London for the show. Years earlier, as a singer-songwriter with a small but devoted following, he had been the support act when MacColl toured the US, and it was heartening to see Gray's eventual triumph. This "overnight success" had required a decade of recording and performing, almost as many record companies as Kirsty MacColl, and very similar experiences with them.

Marr's version of "You and Me, Baby" was followed by the appearance of former Pogues Jem Finer and Spider Stacey for "Fairytale of New York", performed as a duet by Mary Coughlan and Mark Nevin. MacColl and MacGowan had so made the song their own that it's hard for anyone else to match their chemistry, but Coughlan and Nevin gave it their best. One of the most hyped appearances of the night was that of Tracey Ullman, who told the audience that for the first time in almost twenty years, she was about to perform "They Don't Know". As the applause subsided at the end of the song, Ullman paid tribute to MacColl's writing: "Thank you, Kirsty MacColl, for giving me that fabulous song to sing." All Ullman had ever added to the original, she confessed, was:

> ... a short pink lurex mini-skirt, and I had Paul McCartney in the video, and it was Number 2 and we couldn't knock bloody "Karma Chameleon" by Boy George off Number 1. Bastard! But I was Number 1 in Norway for eight weeks ... rockin' the fjords! And it was Number 1 in a few other countries too and, without doubt, it launched my career in America ... it was my calling card. I want to thank you, Kirsty, and we miss you.

With that, Ullman introduced the co-writer of "Chip Shop", Phil Rambow, as almost all of the musicians crowded onto the stage for the sing-along finale, romping through one of MacColl's best-known songs. It was a rousing end to a lovingly crafted tribute, about which Adam Sweeting in *The Guardian* wrote: "The caustic, anti-sentimental Phill Jupitus hit the perfect note. He ridiculed hecklers mercilessly, and aimed powerful jets of scorn at the staidness of the Festival Hall. MacColl herself would have fled in terror from the idea of a maudlin, Oscar night-style ceremony. Laconic wit and self-mockery were far more up her street, a fact appreciated by the evening's participants."

For Tim de Lisle in the *Mail on Sunday*, a newspaper for which Kirsty had written several music reviews, "The evening glowed with British stoicism. The performers were so resolutely cheerful, it brought a tear to the eye."

While noting that the printed programme had included a clumsy inaccuracy about the date of Kirsty's death, the *Evening Standard* critic John Aizlewood reserved special ire for Tracey Ullman: "The results, inevitably, were mixed, although only Tracey Ullman's ghastly self-aggrandizing speech in the encore struck a truly jarring note. Instead, the performers who knew Kirsty spoke briefly and touchingly of her talents and personality." Aizlewood concluded that "Kirsty MacColl would surely have been delighted" with the tribute. Paul Sexton in *The Times* agreed:

> Kirsty MacColl didn't do showbiz and she would have screamed at anyone waxing sentimental at her wake, so she would have approved the sentiment of this uneven but heartfelt tribute by her peers. The songwriting

varnish she lovingly painted on everyday scenes made MacColl a tune-wallah of the people, for the people, and this gathering underlined that her compositions would continue to live large.

From the first song to the finale, the tribute evening had provided a time capsule of MacColl's song-writing gift and the extraordinary diversity she'd displayed over two decades, realized Dave Ruffy:

So many people were saying, "I had no idea she'd written all of those great songs." It was that British thing where she underplayed everything so much, even to her friends. I knew Kirsty quite well before I even knew how good she was, because she did hide her light under a bushel. When we did the concert, it was gut-wrenching in a way when you realized how hard-hitting the lyrics were.

Phil Rambow, who had known MacColl for twenty years, described the entire evening as "a learning experience. The value of her music is going to be around forever. That's a legacy of quality." For Phill Jupitus, it had been a chance to highlight the fondest memories of Kirsty and the best of her work: "Seeing all the work there, and other people doing it, the quality of the songs just came out. It was a really lovely evening, because the crowd were so into it and the band were really into it, everyone kept saying, 'We kept expecting her to be there, it was like it was her gig and she wasn't there.' It *was* her gig, and she wasn't there."

For Mark Nevin, too, the event had taken on the ambience of one of Kirsty's own parties, with the music, the people, the humour. "It felt like, when is she going to come?" he says, "especially at the party afterwards, because that was so much like one of her parties at her house with so many people. They were all the same people we'd known for ages, all there together." For writer Matthew Westwood, a friend of Kirsty's, "It was sad, but uplifting as well. It was great to be there, watching the reaction of the audience and at the party after, the reaction of the people who knew her and loved her. There was joy there. She would have wanted everyone to be having a laugh and having a party and that's what happened. It wouldn't have been able to happen two years earlier."

The concert was broadcast the following night on the BBC digital radio station, 6 Music. James Knight had found the evening difficult but cathartic:

It did go really well. I'm happy that it's done; it was necessary to sort of put it to bed, because it was going to happen at some point. Doing it with a load of people who really loved her as well was obviously very painful and we just really went for it. But certain songs were extremely difficult, and it's not that I hadn't listened to everything, because I listened to everything the minute I got back from Mexico. I listened over and over again for two weeks, because I knew otherwise I wouldn't be able to listen to it ever again.

A few months before she died, MacColl had told a journalist, "Whenever I go into the studio, I always operate on the principle that I might get hit by a bus tomorrow. I'd hate the obituaries to read, 'And her last album was her not-very-good album'." James Knight says his partner did sometimes feel that she wouldn't live a long life:

She had this idea that she wasn't going to be around. It was almost like she put everything in order before she died; she had somebody who would look after her children in a way that she would have wanted, which is all I can do, and still have the best eighteen months of her life, which is more than some people have in their entire life. It's better to have that total bliss for eighteen months than a lifetime of mediocrity.

One of the songs that Kirsty MacColl had written for *Tropical Brainstorm* was about going to the sea and turning into a mermaid and disappearing. It was never released. Johnny Marr spoke for friends when he once said: "I miss Kirsty terribly. I always sensed a patronizing attitude towards her. She was self-critical, but she didn't suffer pretentiousness and preciousness in people. She was tender and sensitive and those qualities come out in her work."

However, everybody took heart from the fact that the last year of Kirsty MacColl's life had been among the happiest she'd ever known. "It always fell back to her," says Billy Bragg, "after the record companies dumped her, or the guys dumped her, or the band got too expensive. That was why it was such a shame, because she seemed to be in such a good place with her sons and with James and the new band. That to me just adds to the tragedy of it all."

Steve Lillywhite recalls the sadness he felt when Bono told him he could barely remember so many things about his mother, who had died when he was 14. It was so painful for Bono's father that the family tried to ease the pain by just not talking about her and, eventually, much of her was lost to the past. Steve is determined that his sons won't ever feel that depth of disconnection with their memories.

Kirsty MacColl's legacy will be lasting – in her work, her family, her friends, her fund-raising, her politics. Most especially, though, for her sons, Jamie and Louis. In her 1918 novel *My Antonia*, American author Willa Cather wrote: " ... it is no wonder that her sons stood tall and straight; she was a rich mine of life, like the founders of early races." Kirsty MacColl, too was a rich mine of life, in all of its joy and sadness. "The dead don't die", wrote D.H.Lawrence in 1923; "they look on and help". And therein lies what comforts and sustains us all.

Soho Square, London, October 27, 2005

The pigeons in the park and the windows seem to show nothing of what they're doing in the same old game...

Epilogue

Soho Square, London, October 12, 2003

Your name froze on the winter air

The pigeons in the park and the window-cleaners in the building opposite stop what they're doing as the sound of more than 150 voices singing her best-known songs echoes around the square. A tiny Japanese boy, no more than two years old, stands behind a guitarist who has crossed the Atlantic and travelled several thousand miles to be there. The child watches, entranced, then begins to dance to the music before his family realize that he's not among them and call him away. Two police officers stop to ask what's going on. Reassured that the only disorder may be in the lyrical recall, they leave with a pamphlet.

An empty bench in Soho Square

Bunches of yellow and red roses and tall, pink gladioli have been tied to a park bench that only the day before bore yellow tape and a warning sign: "Wet Paint". Children's drawings have been anchored down with pebbles. A tiny cake, with marzipan icing and a tartan ribbon, has been left carefully by the red roses; she would have been 44, two days ago. A shining brass plaque fixed to the bench reads, "Kirsty MacColl 1959–2000. One day I'll be waiting there, no empty bench in Soho Square."

And we'll dance around like we don't care

The sky is an unbelievable blue. It is one of those stunningly clear, just barely chilled days that only autumn can produce. As pigeons wheel above and into the oak trees, or across to perch on the roof of the mock-

Tudor folly in the centre of the square, tourist couples pause to ask what's going on. It's far too sedate for a protest, although it is that, in part; though not the kind they would recognize or understand. It is a celebration and a commemoration and a ritual of remembering. The drunks, derelicts and crackhead kids that often drift through the square en route to who knows where – the flotsam and jetsam of the urban life she often wrote about – are nowhere to be seen today.

On this same city square, in 1961, her father's voice would have rung out from windows flung open, heard across the green just as these voices – including those of his two grandsons – are being heard today. Close by, in another leafy square in the heart of the city, there is a tree planted in his memory.

> *And I'll be much too old to cry*
> *And you'll kiss me quick in case I die before my birthday*

Back in Soho Square several hours later, with family, friends, fans and photographers long gone, there is only one bench that is empty, but for the offerings of roses and pictures, of pebbles and cake. A small lilac candle has appeared on the bench; it had been burning, but the wind has snuffed it out. All else remains as it was, the same but different.

> *And I'll be painting stars up in the sky*
> *Before I get too old to cry before my birthday*
> *I hope I see those pigeons fly before my birthday*
> *In Soho Square on my birthday.*

—Kirsty MacColl, "Soho Square"

Appendix 1

The Electric Landlady (by her tenants)*

I invited Kirsty MacColl's fans, through the Freeworld forum (www.kirstymaccoll.com) and the Yahoo chat group (kirstymaccoll@yahoogroups.com) to encapsulate their feelings about what she means to them, and nominate their favourite Kirsty song. The responses that I received were heartfelt:

Kirsty just wrote the best songs and sang them with those angelic harmonies, floating in and under, acerbic, tough/tender leads and lyrics.

Favourite song: *I could not name a favorite tune as I am amazed by her variety of tunes. For the moment, perhaps, "End of a Perfect Day" sums it all up best.*

Carol, USA.

Kirsty to me was a songwriter and a poet. Her lyrics were quite possibly the most beautiful, poignant and funny I've ever heard. Although her voice was beautiful, her main appeal was her skill as a lyricist.

Favourite song: *"You and Me Baby".*

Rachel Krengel, UK

I had a very tough childhood, which I managed to drag myself out of when I was 13 and voluntarily placed myself in the care of the local authority. Mum was an alcoholic, and had other mental health problems. I spent my whole childhood in children's homes and with foster parents, and by the age

* With thanks to Bono for the title suggestion.

of 13 it was all too much for me. I discovered Kirsty not long after that and her music helped me a great deal, particularly her Kite album. I think her lyrics, along with others such as Joni Mitchell, Billy Bragg, Sinead O'Connor, Joan Baez and Nina Simone, helped me become who I am today.

Favourite song: "He's on the Beach" (especially her stripped-down version of it on *What Do Pretty Girls Do?*).

Dylan Lancaster, UK

For me the eighties were a bit frustrating. I was in my twenties and had a great time, but I didn't like most of the mainstream rock bands that got airplay. The electronic sounds of New Order, Pet Shop Boys, Spandau Ballet, Depeche Mode and so on just sounded bland and depressing to me. I preferred the music from the sixties and seventies. But the great thing was there were a few brilliant singer-songwriters – if you knew how to find them. My favourites were Elvis Costello, Lloyd Cole and Kirsty MacColl.

It was an age when the world was turned upside down and the mediocre talents got most of the attention. In due course, though, I'm sure that Kirsty will be recognized as the finest singer-songwriter of her generation. Like Bob Dylan, Joni Mitchell and Ray Davies, she combined the ability to compose beautiful, original melodies with verbal inventiveness and genuine wit. She wrote about real people and real situations – you could place yourself there. But she never set out to impress with cleverness; she always remembered that the melody's the thing.

Favourite songs: "Caroline" and "On the Beach" (In both, there is an infectious pop tune that appeals on first hearing but never tires. There's also a real story of pain, regret, love and affection, and personalities that come to life as much as in a great novel).

Philip Whiteley, UK

Kirsty was my rescuer from secondary school. I have Asperger's Syndrome and dyspraxia and I found school very daunting as I find communication so hard because of this. Discovering Kirsty's music was like a big hug coming out of the speakers. I was so upset when she died. She inspired me to write songs of my own, though my songs are not very good, and I wrote one about her when she died. I think it is such a shame that so many of Kirsty's albums remain unreleased. Britain is such an ominous place! Kirsty wrote beautiful words of fire against society and was warm as the sun.

Favourite song: *"Don't Come the Cowboy …"* is my favourite – eloquent love that should never change.

Mark Alexander, UK

I love Kirsty because she combined a beautiful voice with the best lyrics ever. She had a superb line in wit, and she could also turn out very moving songs like my favourite, "You and Me Baby". The warmth and compassion of the lyrics, the affirmation of the strong emotional bond between the two friends who, we sense, have been through a lot, together with Kirsty's lovely, haunting vocal, make it one of her most affecting recordings.

Favourite song: *"You and Me Baby"*.

Jess Cully, UK

The first time I heard Kirsty MacColl was on American commercial radio. For a few weeks in the fall of 1993, "Can't Stop Killing You" had a couple of spins on a station in Atlanta, Georgia, that had recently switched formats from Top 40 to "alternative". They had to fill up a playlist with something other than grunge (already on its last legs by that point), so it was that I heard it one afternoon in the kitchen while avoiding homework. The song was crisp and economical compared to the stuff I'd just heard previously, and I was hooked. I scribbled down an approximation of her name and the album's title after the DJ recapped his plays, and bought a copy of Titanic Days *a few weeks later. And the rest, as they say, is personal history.*

I wouldn't say that "Can't Stop Killing You" is my favorite song of hers; part of the charm and strength of Kirsty's work, at least to me, is that my favorites are always changing depending on the most capricious of reasons (mood, weather, memory, you-name-it), and yet there is almost always a song that fits. That being said, you'd still be hard-pressed to pin the gist of this song to anything you'd want to remember. But it is the song that hooked me, "the lightning that strikes you just before you hear the thunder," I'd guess. And that is a memory I'd like to stay with me for a long time.

Caroline O'Reilly, USA

If Kirsty's songs had a theme from beginning to end it was, more than anything, about reportage and storytelling. Sometimes she was reporting how she was feeling and sometimes what she'd seen; sometimes the stories were true, and sometimes they weren't. But always, there was That Voice that blossomed from roots in her soul and said ... someone understands, someone knows, someone has been there. Going back to Sinatra for a moment, I once read someone say that the reason for his success was that he could convey to everyone a feeling that he was singing just for them. Kirsty's voice at its most tender was the sound of a lover or a friend – or both – holding you and singing gently into your ear. At its most raucous, it was the sound of the same friend eagerly telling you a joke. Either way, always a friend. When you have a favorite singer, a new album from them is like checking in with a friend you haven't seen for a few years; having them tell you where they've been and what they've done and seen. I had expected, and hoped, to keep checking in with MacColl for decades. And the saddest thing for me is that I can't.

Ben Varkentine, USA

Not only was Kirsty a remarkable performer, she was also a remarkably generous and friendly human being. I discovered this when, after setting up one of the first Kirsty websites, I received an email from her saying hello and expressing surprise at having a fan down under. We began a brief but friendly correspondence. A couple of years later, I was visiting London and Kirsty sent me an email inviting me to meet her and hear some tracks she was working on (which would become Tropical Brainstorm*). Alas, she sent it to my work email address, and I didn't see it until after I'd returned.*

In 2000 I was back in the UK again, and hoped the opportunity would arise once more. I planned to go and see Kirsty in concert in Sheffield and London. In Sheffield, by the time I found the stage door, Kirsty and the band had already left. In London, I managed to finagle my way into the post-tour party in Camden Town, and finally got to meet Kirsty. She immediately knew who I was, and rushed to introduce me to James – she seemed very happy and proud to be with him. We didn't get much chance to talk. Kirsty suggested I email her and that we meet up in a pub somewhere the following week for a less frenzied chat. Alas, she got called away for PR in Italy and it never happened. Nonetheless, I remain grateful that I got to meet her at all, and astonished that she was happy to hook up with her fans so readily (especially given the lyrics of "Treachery", which she wrote after I'd first been in email contact with her – I have always hoped I wasn't part of the inspiration).

Favourite song: *"Still Life". My first exposure to Kirsty was via her* French and Saunders *appearances, and it was a source of frustration to me for years that I couldn't find a CD version of this beautiful and underrated ballad. It even inspired me to visit Milton Keynes to see if it deserved the trashing it gets in the song. Of course, it does, but it wasn't until I visited that I realized that the "sacred cows" line could be taken as a reference to the city's infamous concrete cows. I had thought it was simple Thatcher-bashing, which Kirsty also did very well!*

Angus Kidman, Australia

Appendix II

Bibliography

Balls, Richard: *Sex & Drugs & Rock 'n' Roll: The Life of Ian Dury* (Omnibus Press, 2000)

Broughton, Simon et al: *The Rough Guide To World Music* (Rough Guides, 1994)

Collins, Andrew: *Still Suitable for Miners: Billy Bragg – The Official Biography* (Virgin, 1998)

Elsom, John: *Post-War British Theatre* (Routledge and Kegan Paul, 1979)

Hinchcliffe, Arnold P: *British Theatre 1950-70* (Basil Blackwell, 1974)

Laban, Rudolf (revised by Ullmann, Lisa): *The Mastery of Movement* (MacDonald and Evans, 1980)

Leymarie, Isabelle: *Cuban Fire: The Story of Salsa and Latin Jazz* (Continuum, 2002)

Littlewood, Joan: *Joan's Book* (Minerva, 1995)

MacColl, Ewan: *Journeyman* (Sidgwick and Jackson, 1990)

Source articles and background research:

Magazines, newspapers, webzines, journals, TV and radio programmes used as source material or background reading included: *bbc.co.uk, Belfast Telegraph, Birmingham Post, Croydon Advertiser, Cuba Si, Daily Mail, Daily Telegraph, Debut, The Economist,* elviscostello.com, *Evening Standard, Folk Roots,* gold.ac.uk, *Goldmine, The Guardian, Hot Press,* kirsty-maccoll.com, *The Independent, Independent on Sunday, Interview, Irish Times, Los Angeles Times, Mail on Sunday, The Mirror, Mojo, Morning Star,* morrissey-solo.com, *Muse, New York Times, NME, The Observer,* papa-hogs.com, peggyseeger.com, *Q, Record Collector, Record Mirror, Rolling*

Stone, The Scotsman, Smash Hits, The *Spectator, Sunday Herald, Sunday Times, The Times, Washington Post,* wcml.org.uk, *Western Mail,* World Socialist Website.

Appendix III

Discography

Title THE DRUG ADDIX MAKE A RECORD
Release Date 1978
Catalogue No. Chiswick Records SW3947 (7'' single)
Tracks
1. Gay Boys In Bondage (Smith)
2. Addington Shuffle (Smith, Lloyd)
3. Special Clinic (Smith, Lloyd)
4. Glutton For Punishment (Smith)

Title THEY DON'T KNOW
Release Date June 1979
Catalogue No. Stiff BUY47 (7'' picture sleeve), P-BUY47 (7'' picture disk)
Tracks
1. They Don't Know (MacColl)
2. Turn My Motor On (MacColl)

Title YOU CAUGHT ME OUT
Release Date October 1979
Catalogue No. Stiff BUY57 (7'' single) unreleased
Tracks
1. You Caught Me Out (MacColl, Briquette, Crowe)
2. Boys (MacColl, Lloyd)

Title	KEEP YOUR HANDS OFF MY BABY
Release Date	February 1981
Catalogue No.	Polydor POSP225 (7'' single), 2059 316 (German release 7'' single)
Tracks	1. Keep Your Hands Off My Baby (Goffin & King)
	2. I Don't Need You (MacColl)

Title	THERE'S A GUY WORKS DOWN THE CHIP SHOP SWEARS HE'S ELVIS
Release Date	May 1981
Catalogue No.	Polydor POSP250 (7'' single)
Tracks	1. There's A Guy Works Down The Chip Shop Swears He's Elvis (MacColl, Rambow)
	2. Hard To Believe (MacColl)
	3. There's A Guy Works Down The Chip Shop Swears He's Elvis (country version) (MacColl, Rambow)

Title	DESPERATE CHARACTER
Release Date	June 1981
Catalogue No.	Polydor POLS1035 (LP), POLSC1035 (MC)
Tracks	1. Clock Goes Round (MacColl)
	2. See That Girl (MacColl)
	3. There's A Guy Works Down The Chip Shop Swears He's Elvis
	4. Teenager In Love (MacColl)
	5. Mexican Sofa (MacColl, Lu)
	6. Until The Night (MacColl, Johnstone)
	7. Falling For Faces (MacColl, Lu)
	8. Just One Look (Payne, Carroll)
	9. The Real Ripper (MacColl, Lu)
	10. Hard To Believe
	11. He Thinks I Still Care (Lipscombe, Duffy)
	12. There's A Guy Works Down The Chip Shop Swears He's Elvis (country version)

Title SEE THAT GIRL
Release Date September 1981
Catalogue No. Polydor POSP326 (7'' single)
Tracks 1. See That Girl
2. Over You (MacColl)

Title YOU STILL BELIEVE IN ME
Release Date November 1981
Catalogue No. Polydor POSP368 (7'' single)
Tracks 1. You Still Believe In Me (Wilson, Asher)
2. Queen Of The High Teas (MacColl)

Title I WANT OUT (Matchbox)
Release Date 1983
Catalogue No. Magnet 105.166 (7'' single)
Tracks 1. I Want Out (Hodgson, Peters, Colton)
2. Heaven Can Wait (Hodgson, Callan)

Title BERLIN
Release Date August 1983
Catalogue No. North of Watford Records, NOW100 (7'' single),
NOWX100 (12'' single)
Tracks 1. Berlin (MacColl)
2. Rhythm Of The Real Thing (MacColl)

Title TERRY
Release Date October 1983
Catalogue No. 7'' version (Stiff BUY190)
Tracks 1. Terry (MacColl, Povey)
2. Quietly Alone (MacColl)

Catalogue No. 12'' version (Stiff SBUY190)

Tracks   1. Terry (extended version)
               2. Quietly Alone

Title   A NEW ENGLAND
Release Date   December 1984
Catalogue No. Stiff BUY216 (7'' single), DBUY216 (UK shaped picture
                   disk), S107117 (reissued in 1985)
Tracks   1. A New England (Bragg)
                   2. Patrick (MacColl)

Catalogue No. Stiff BUYIT216 (12'' single), available in two versions with
                   reversed cover artwork
Tracks   1. A New England
                   2. Patrick
                   3. I'm Going Out With An 80-Year-Old Millionaire
                      (MacColl)

Title   KIRSTY MACCOLL
Release Date   March 1985
Catalogue No. Polydor SPELP95 (LP). US Release on Charisma 91232-1
Tracks   1. Clock Goes Round
                   2. See That Girl
                   3. There's A Guy Works Down The Chip Shop Swears
                      He's Elvis
                   4. Teenager In Love
                   5. Annie (MacColl)
                   6. Until The Night
                   7. Falling For Faces
                   8. Roman Gardens (H.MacColl, Povey)
                   9. The Real Ripper
                   10. Hard To Believe
                   11. He Thinks I Still Care
                   12. Berlin (MacColl)

Title	HE'S ON THE BEACH
Release Date	June 1985
Catalogue No.	Stiff BUY225 (7'' single), DBUY225 (picture disk shaped like an aeroplane)
Tracks	1. He's On The Beach (MacColl)
	2. Please, Go To Sleep (MacColl)

Catalogue No.	Stiff BUYIT225 (12'' single)
Tracks	1. He's On The Beach
	2. Please, Go To Sleep
	3. He's On The Beach (extended version)

Title	FAIRYTALE OF NEW YORK by the Pogues featuring Kirsty MacColl
Release Date	November 1987
Catalogue No.	Pogue Mahone YZ628BTG (12'' single), Stiff NYG7 (7'' gatefold single)
Tracks	1. Fairytale Of New York (MacGowan)
	2. A Pair Of Brown Eyes (by the Pogues)
	3. The Sick Bed Of Cuchulainn (by the Pogues)
	4. Maggie May: The Pogues (by the Pogues)

Title	FREE WORLD
Release Date	February 1989
Catalogue No.	Virgin KMA1 (7'' single), KMAC1 (cassette single)
Tracks	1. Free World (MacColl)
	2. Closer To God? (MacColl)

Catalogue No.	Virgin KMAN1 (10'' single)
Tracks	1. Free World
	2. Closer To God?
	3. The End Of A Perfect Day (original demo version) (MacColl, Marr)

Catalogue No.	Virgin KMAT1 (12'' single)
Tracks	1. Free World
	2. Closer To God?
	3. You Just Haven't Earned It Yet, Baby (Morrissey, Marr)

Catalogue No.	Virgin KMACD1 (CD single)
Tracks	1. Free World
	2. Closer To God?
	3. You Just Haven't Earned It Yet, Baby
	4. La Fôret de Mimosas (MacColl)

Title	KITE
Release Date	April 1989
Catalogue No.	Virgin KMLP1 (LP)
Tracks	1. Innocence (MacColl, Glenister)
	2. Free World
	3. Mother's Ruin (MacColl, Glenister)
	4. Days (Davies)
	5. No Victims (MacColl)
	6. Fifteen Minutes (MacColl)
	7. Don't Come The Cowboy With Me Sonny Jim! (MacColl)
	8. Tread Lightly (MacColl, Glenister)
	9. What Do Pretty Girls Do? (MacColl, Glenister)
	10. Dancing In Limbo (MacColl)
	11. The End Of A Perfect Day
	12. You And Me Baby (MacColl, Marr)

Catalogue No.	Virgin CDKM1 (CD)
Tracks	As above, plus:
	13. You Just Haven't Earned It Yet, Baby
	14. La Fôret de Mimosas
	15. Complainte Pour Ste Catherine (A. McGarrigle, Tatartcheff)

Title	DAYS
Release Date	June 1989
Catalogue No.	Virgin KMA2 (7" single), KMAC2 (cassette single)
Tracks	1. Days
	2. Happy (MacColl)

Catalogue No.	Virgin KMAN2 (10'' single)
Tracks	1. Days
	2. Still Life (MacColl)
	3. El Paso (Robbins)
	4. Happy
Catalogue No.	Virgin KMAT2 (12'' single)
Tracks	1. Days
	2. Still Life
	3. Happy
Catalogue No.	Virgin KMACD2 (CD single), KMACDX2 (CD single in Kite shaped box)
Tracks	1. Days
	2. Please Help Me, I'm Falling (Robertson, Blair)
	3. Still Life
	4. Happy

Title	INNOCENCE
Release Date	September 1989
Catalogue No.	Virgin KMA3 (7'' single), KMAC3 (cassette single)
Tracks	1. Innocence (remix)
	2. Clubland (MacColl)
Catalogue No.	Virgin KMAN3 (10'' single)
Tracks	1. Innocence (remix)
	2. Don't Run Away From Me Now (MacColl, Rambow)
	3. Innocence (The Guilt mix)
	4. Clubland
Catalogue No.	Virgin KMAT3 (12'' single), KMACD3 (CD single)
Tracks	1. Innocence (remix)
	2. No Victims (Guitar Heroes mix)
	3. Innocence (The Guilt mix)
	4. Clubland

Title	DON'T COME THE COWBOY WITH ME, SONNY JIM!
Release Date	March 1990

Catalogue No. Virgin KMA4 (7'' single), KMAC4 (cassette single)
Tracks
1. Don't Come The Cowboy With Me, Sonny Jim!
2. Other People's Hearts (MacColl, Povey)

Catalogue No. Virgin KMAT4 (12'' single)
Tracks
1. Don't Come The Cowboy With Me, Sonny Jim!
2. Other People's Hearts
3. Complainte Pour Ste Catherine

Catalogue No. Virgin KMACD4 (CD single)
Tracks
1. Don't Come The Cowboy With Me, Sonny Jim!
2. Other People's Hearts
3. Complainte Pour Ste Catherine
4. Am I Right? (MacColl)

Title MISS OTIS REGRETS by Kirsty MacColl with the Pogues
Release Date November 1990
Catalogue No. Chrysalis CHS123629 (12'' single)
Tracks 1. Miss Otis Regrets/Just One Of Those Things (Porter)

Title WALKING DOWN MADISON
Release Date May 1991
Catalogue No. Virgin VS1348 (7'' single), VSC1348 (cassette single)
Tracks
1. Walking Down Madison (MacColl, Marr)
2. One Good Thing (MacColl, Glenister)

Catalogue No. Virgin VST1348 (12'' single)
Tracks
1. Walking Down Madison
2. One Good Thing
3. Walking Down Madison (6am Ambient Mix)
4. Walking Down Madison (12'' Mix)

Catalogue No. Virgin VSCDT1348 (CD single 1)
Tracks
1. Walking Down Madison
2. One Good Thing
3. Walking Down Madison (6am Ambient Mix)
4. Walking Down Madison (Club Mix)

Catalogue No.   Virgin VSCDG1348 (CD single 2)
Tracks   1. Walking Down Madison (Urban mix)
                    2. Days
                    3. Darling, Let's Have Another Baby (Berk)
                    4. Walking Down Madison (LP Extended Mix)

Title   ELECTRIC LANDLADY
Release Date   June 1991

Catalogue No.   Virgin V2663 (LP), CDV2663 (CD), also CDVIP209 (???)
Tracks   1. Walking Down Madison
                    2. All I Ever Wanted (MacColl, Crenshaw)
                    3. Children Of The Revolution (MacColl, Marr)
                    4. Halloween (MacColl, Nevin)
                    5. My Affair (MacColl, Nevin)
                    6. Lying Down (MacColl, Glenister)
                    7. He Never Mentioned Love (MacColl, Finer)
                    8. We'll Never Pass This Way Again (MacColl)
                    9. The Hardest Word (MacColl, H. MacColl)
                    10. Maybe It's Imaginary (MacColl)
                    11. My Way Home (MacColl)
                    12. The One And Only (MacColl, Nevin)

Notes
Reissued in 2001 on Disky.
Released in the US on IRS 27896 (CD)

Title   MY AFFAIR
Release Date   July 1991
Catalogue No.   Virgin VS1354 (7'' single), VSC1354 (cassette single)
Tracks   1. My Affair
                    2. All The Tears That I Cried (MacColl)

Catalogue No.   Virgin VST1354 (12'' single)
Tracks   1. My Affair (Ladbroke Groove Mix)
                    2. My Affair (Bass Sexy Mix)
                    3. My Affair (Olive Groove Mix)

Catalogue No.   VSCDG1354 (CD single)
Tracks
1. My Affair
2. Don't Go Near The Water (Jardine, Love)
3. All The Tears That I Cried
4. My Affair (Olive Groove Mix)

Title   ALL I EVER WANTED
Release Date   October 1991
Catalogue No.   Virgin VS1373 (7'' single), VSC1373 (cassette single)
Tracks
1. All I Ever Wanted
2. There's A Guy Works Down The Chip Shop Swears He's Elvis (live version)

Catalogue No.   Virgin VST1373 (12'' single)
Tracks
1. All I Ever Wanted (MacColl, Crenshaw)
2. What Do Pretty girls Do?
3. Walk Right Back (live) (Curtis)
4. There's A Guy Works Down The Chip Shop Swears He's Elvis (live version)

Catalogue No.   Virgin VSCDT1373 (CD single 1)
Tracks
1. All I Ever Wanted
2. What Do Pretty Girls Do?
3. Walk Right Back (live)
4. There's A Guy Works Down The Chip Shop Swears He's Elvis (live version)

Catalogue No.   Virgin VSCDG1373 (CD single 2) gatefold sleeve
Tracks
1. All I Ever Wanted
2. There's A Guy Works Down The Chip Shop Swears He's Elvis (live version)
3. Walk Right Back (live)
4. A New England (live)

Title   THE ESSENTIAL COLLECTION
Release Date   1993
Catalogue No.   Stiff CD17 (CD). Possible reissue on Disky label in 2000.

Tracks
1. There's A Guy Works Down The Chip Shop Swears He's Elvis
2. A New England
3. Patrick
4. Eighty-Year-Old Millionaire
5. See That Girl
6. Until The Night
7. Just One Look
8. He Thinks I Still Care
9. They Don't Know
10. Turn My Motor On
11. Please, Go To Sleep
12. Terry
13. Quietly Alone
14. Teenager In Love
15. A New England (12'' version)
16. Terry (12'' version)
17. There's A Guy Works Down The Chip Shop Swears He's Elvis (country version)

Title	ANGEL
Release Date	December 1993
Catalogue No.	ZTT ZANG46 (7'' single), ZANG46C (cassette single)
Tracks	1. Angel (MacColl)
	2. Angel (Jay's edit)

Catalogue No.	ZTT ZANG46T (12'' single)
Tracks	1. Angel
	2. Angel (Apollo 440 Remix)
	3. Angel (Jay's edit)
	4. Angel (Stuart Crichton Remix)

Catalogue No.	ZTT ZANG46CD (CD single)
Tracks	1. Angel
	2. Angel (Apollo 440 Remix)
	3. Angel (Jay's edit)
	4. Angel (Stuart Crichton Remix)
	5. Angel (Into the Light Mix)

Catalogue No. Australian release on Liberation D11684 – it comes in a
cardboard slipcase

Tracks 1. Angel (Jay's edit)

2. Angel (Apollo 440 Edit)

3. Angel (Stuart Crichton Remix)

4. Angel (Into the Light Mix)

Title TITANIC DAYS

Release Date February 1994

Catalogue No. ZTT 450 994711-1 (LP), 450 994711-2 (CD)

Tracks 1. You Know It's You (MacColl, Nevin)

2. Soho Square (MacColl, Nevin)

3. Angel

4. Last Day Of Summer (MacColl, Nevin)

5. Bad (MacColl)

6. Can't Stop Killing You (MacColl, Marr)

7. Titanic Days (MacColl, Nevin)

8. Don't Go Home (MacColl, Nevin)

9. Big Boy On A Saturday Night (MacColl, Nevin)

10. Just Woke Up (MacColl, Ruffy)

11. Tomorrow Never Comes (MacColl, Nevin)

Notes

Released in the US on IRS 27214 (CD) in Oct/Nov 1993
Released in Australia on Liberation D31070 (CD) in 1993
Can't Stop Killing You/Touch Me/Fabulous Garden –
Australia.

Title TITANIC DAYS

Release Date 1994

Catalogue No. US release on IRS 581612 (CD single)

Tracks 1. Titanic Days

2. Angel (Piano Mix)

3. Free World (Live)

4. Miss Otis Regrets (Live)

5. Walking Down Madison

Title	CAROLINE
Release Date	February 1995
Catalogue No.	Virgin VS1517 (7'' single)
Tracks	1. Caroline (MacColl)
	2. Irish Cousin (MacColl, Nevin)

Catalogue No.	Virgin VSCDT1517 (CD single 1)
Tracks	1. Caroline (MacColl)
	2. Irish Cousin (MacColl, Nevin)
	3. A New England
	4. Butcher Boy (Trad., arranged MacColl)

Catalogue No.	Virgin VSCDX1517 (CD single 2)
Tracks	1. Caroline (MacColl)
	2. El Paso (Robbins)
	3. My Affair (Ladbroke Groove Mix)

Title	GALORE
Release Date	6 March 1995
Catalogue No.	Virgin CDV2763 (CD), TCV2763 (Cassette)
Tracks	1. They Don't Know
	2. A New England
	3. There's A Guy Works Down The Chip Shop Swears He's Elvis
	4. He's On The Beach
	5. Fairytale Of New York
	6. Miss Otis Regrets
	7. Free World
	8. Innocence
	9. You Just Haven't Earned It Yet, Baby
	10. Days
	11. Don't Come The Cowboy With Me, Sonny Jim!
	12. Walking Down Madison
	13. My Affair
	14. Angel
	15. Titanic Days
	16. Can't Stop Killing You
	17. Caroline
	18. Perfect Day (Lou Reed)

Notes
Released in the US on IRS 30257 (CD)
Released in Australia on RH Records 89451555 (CD)

Title	PERFECT DAY
Release Date	June 1995
Catalogue No.	Virgin VSCDT1552 (CD single)
Tracks	1. Perfect Day
	2. Tread Lightly
	3. He's On The Beach (Extended version)
	4. Terry

Title	DAYS
Release Date	July 1995
Catalogue No.	Virgin VSCDT1558 (CD single)
Tracks	1. Days
	2. Still Life
	3. Happy
	4. Walking Down Madison (Club Mix)

Title	AS LONG AS YOU HOLD ME
Release Date	1995
Tracks	1. As Long As You Hold Me (Bragg)

Title	WHAT DO PRETTY GIRLS DO?
Release Date	23 February 1998
Catalogue No.	Hux HUX001 (CD)
Tracks	1. Don't Come The Cowboy With Me, Sonny Jim!
	2. What Do Pretty Girls Do?
	3. Don't Run Away From Me Now
	4. Still Life
	5. There's A Guy Works Down The Chip Shop Swears He's Elvis

6. Walk Right Back
7. Darling Let's Have Another Baby
8. A New England
9. My Affair
10. Bad
11. Can't Stop Killing You
12. Caroline
13. Free World
14. He's On The beach
15. A New England

Notes

(1) BBC Radio sessions (2) US Releases: 30 July 1998
Cleopatra CLP0282 (CD), also Griffin GRF2747CD

Title	MAMBO DE LA LUNA
Release Date	8 November 1999
Catalogue No.	V2 VVR5010973 (CD single 1)
Tracks	1. Mambo de la Luna (Edit) (MacColl, Glenister, Ruffy)
	2. Golden Heart (MacColl, N. MacColl)
	3. Things Happen (MacColl, Gouldman)
Catalogue No.	V2 VVR5010978 (CD single 2)
Tracks	1. Mambo de la Luna
	2. Mambo de la Luna (Mint Royale Edit)
	3. Mambo de la Luna (Mint Royale Version)

Title	IN THESE SHOES?
Release Date	28 February 2000
Catalogue No.	V2 VVR5012183 (CD single 1)
Tracks	1. In These Shoes? (MacColl, Glenister)
	2. My Affair (live at the Jazz Cafe)
	3. Good For Me (MacColl, Knight)
Catalogue No.	V2 VVR5012188 (CD single 2)
Tracks	1. In These Shoes?
	2. In These Shoes? (Le Rosbifs Mix)
	3. In These Shoes? (P. Mix)

Catalogue No. V2 VVR5014183 (German CD single with "Adidas" sticker: *"In these shoes" aus der adidas Werbung*)

Tracks
1. In These Shoes?
2. In These Shoes? (UR Crazy Remix)
3. In These Shoes? (UR Crazy Edit)
4. In These Shoes? (P. Mix)
5. My Affair (live at the Jazz Cafe)

Title TROPICAL BRAINSTORM

Release Date 27 March 2000

Catalogue No. V2 VVR1009872 (CD), VVR1009874 (Cassette)

Tracks
1. Mambo de la Luna
2. In These Shoes?
3. Treachery (MacColl, Gouldman)
4. Here Comes That Man Again (MacColl, Glenister)
5. Autumngirlsoup (MacColl)
6. Celestine (MacColl)
7. England 2, Colombia 0 (MacColl)
8. Não Esperando (MacColl, Glenister)
9. Alegria (MacColl, Ruffy)
10. Us Amazonians (MacColl, Glenister)
11. Wrong Again (MacColl)
12. Designer Life (MacColl, Crouch)
13. Head (MacColl)

Catalogue No. US & Canada release on Instinct Records, INS557-2. Different sleeve artwork from UK release. (24 April 2001)

Tracks As above, plus:
14. Golden Heart
15. Things Happen
16. Good For Me
Bonus: Mambo de la Luna video track.

Title THE ONE AND ONLY

Release Date 6 August 2001

Catalogue No. Metro Square METROCD063

Tracks

1. A New England
2. They Don't Know
3. Terry
4. Libertango (Sharon Shannon feat. Kirsty MacColl)
5. Turn My Motor On
6. I'm Going Out With An 80-Year-Old Millionaire
7. Patrick
8. He's On The Beach
9. The Manchester Rambler (by Ewan MacColl featuring Kirsty MacColl) (trad.)
10. Quietly Alone
11. Please, Go To Sleep
12. Terry (12" mix)
13. Greetings To The New Brunette (by Billy Bragg with Kirsty MacColl and Johnny Marr) (Bragg)
14. A New England (12" mix)

Index